colorado *classique*

A COLLECTION OF FRESH RECIPES FROM THE ROCKIES

JUNIOR LEAGUE OF DENVER

Women building better communities®

JUNIOR LEAGUE OF DENVER
Women building better communities

colorado *classique*
A COLLECTION OF FRESH RECIPES FROM THE ROCKIES

Mission

The Junior League of Denver, Incorporated (founded in 1918), is an organization of women committed to promoting voluntarism, developing the potential of women, and improving communities through the effective action and leadership of trained volunteers. Its purpose is exclusively educational and charitable.

Vision

Recognized as Metro Denver's leading women's organization, the Junior League of Denver develops leaders who positively impact our community.

Focus

Improving the community through the health and education of women and children.

The proceeds from the sale of **colorado** *classique* support the mission of The Junior League of Denver, Inc.

Additional copies of **colorado** *classique* and other cookbooks published by The Junior League of Denver may be obtained

WIMMER
COOKBOOKS

A CONSOLIDATED GRAPHICS COMPANY

800.548.2537 wimmerco.com

FSC

10%

Mixed Sources
Product group from well-managed forests, controlled sources and recycled wood or fiber
www.fsc.org Cert no. SW-COC-001530
© 1996 Forest Stewardship Council

The Junior League of Denver has once again
brought to you another wonderful addition to our cookbook collection,
colorado *classique*

Whether it's macaroni and cheese for the family or gnocchi soufflé with truffles for a special occasion, cooking from scratch is a time-honored tradition that feeds the soul and satisfies the palate. colorado *classique* continues the Junior League of Denver's cookbook tradition of tried and true recipes that focus on cooking from scratch using fresh ingredients. colorado *classique* features more than 200 triple-tested recipes accompanied by wine and beer pairings along with chef's tips. Not only are traditional classics featured but also recipes from 25 of the area's renowned restaurants. colorado *classique's* recipes contain nutritional information to help you make healthy choices for your family's dietary needs. Recipes are also categorized by faire, so you can easily find a recipe for entertaining, quick preparation, vegetarian, family friendly, and gluten-free just to name a few. Throughout the side bars you will find culinary tips provided by local growers and retailers. colorado *classique* contains essential classics that you will turn to again and again, as well as surprising twists on tradition that will draw you into the kitchen to try something new.

A memorable meal is often one that is exciting to the eye as well as to the tongue. colorado *classique* will inspire you with over 70 mouthwatering images featuring some of our favorite recipes. Colorado is known for its visually stunning landscapes that range from high sandy desert plains to snow-capped Rocky Mountains. This visual tour of Colorado's natural wonders will be told with 16 breathtaking John Fielder photos.

colorado *classique* is truly a community cookbook. It was a collaborative effort that included the hands-on efforts of over two hundred Junior League of Denver members with recipe contributions from hundreds of home cooks and 25 of the finest restaurants and hotels in Colorado. We would like to extend special thanks to the businesses that have contributed their time and effort to bringing this cookbook to life. All of our sponsors are Colorado businesses and their participation has elevated our new cookbook to new heights.

The proceeds generated from colorado *classique* provide essential funding to support the Junior League's focus; women building better communities through the health and education of women and children.

Thank you to everyone that made this cookbook possible.

 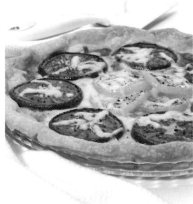  

colorado *classique*
table of contents

STATE OF COLORADO

OFFICE OF THE GOVERNOR

136 State Capitol Building
Denver, Colorado 80203
(303) 866 - 2471
(303) 866 - 2003 fax

Bill Ritter, Jr.
Governor

June 1, 2009

Greetings:

On behalf of the State of Colorado, it is my distinct pleasure to congratulate the Junior League of Denver on the release of its 5th cookbook, *Colorado Classique*.

The Junior League of Denver is a staple within our community, answering the call to serve people throughout our state for the past 90 years. The mission of this philanthropic organization has inspired thousands, and has made lasting contributions to enrich and strengthen our state. Our communities still continue to feel this resounding impact.

It is with a keen interest that we promote Colorado to others around the nation and globe, and the Junior League has helped facilitate this goal for decades. The *Colorado Classique* cookbook, the latest example of the organization's delicious exportation of Colorado's flavor, culture, and colorful lifestyle, is filled with new recipes that focus on fresh ingredients and healthy preparation techniques, and is complimented by the breathtaking photography of Colorado's own John Fielder. As always, the cookbook pays homage to the spirit of service that has come to define the Junior League for close to a century.

Junior League cookbooks are a favorite of both myself and First Lady Jeannie Ritter. *Colorado Classique* will certainly find a home in our kitchen. The unique scope of our famous homegrown cookbooks is something we take pride in as Coloradans.

Sincerely,

Bill Ritter, Jr.
Governor

colorado *classique*
committee members

COOKBOOK CHAIR	STEPHANIE DUNCAN
DESIGN & EDITING CHAIR	NADIA HELENA HARTMAN
MARKETING CHAIR	BECKY SEELY
RECIPE TESTING & COLLECTION CHAIRS	KRISTEN BUSANG
	BECKY HAFEMEISTER SCHAUB
SPONSORSHIP CHAIR	PATRICIA BAINTER
SUSTAINING ADVISORS	MELLY KINARD
	LAUREN EIGNER
	VICTORIA VERNON

RECIPE TESTING CHAIRS

APPETIZERS & BEVERAGES	KATIE MOORE
	HEATHER POLLOCK
BREAKFAST, BRUNCH & BREADS	JOYCE GRAVLEE
	MIMI NELSON
SOUPS & SANDWICHES	PAM WEBER
	JENNIFER KNOLLENBERG
SALADS	CISSIE MEGYESY
	JULIE RUMFELT
PASTA & GRAINS	CRYSTAL HODGE
	NICHOLE MONTOYA
POULTRY	MARCI BLOCK
MEATS	CATHY CARLOS HOLLIS
SEAFOOD	LEIGH-ANNE KENT
	LEIGH MCMAHON
VEGETARIAN & SIDES	ALEATHIA HOSTER
	ERIKA KESSENGER
DESSERTS	JENNIFER BICKNELL GREER
	KIMBERLY HARRINGTON

SPONSORSHIP & MARKETING COMMITTEE	CATHERINE BAYLESS BRUNKS
	KELLY HAPP
	LINDSAY KORSTANGE
	ASHLEY STEVENS
	EVA VASILAS-FRY
	MARGARET RHODES WYSOCKI

PROVISIONAL COMMITTEE

PROVISIONAL ADVISOR	JESSICA MORRISON
CHAIR	LAUREL WALK
	KRISTEN LEWIS ABEL
	CHERYL L. FITZGIBBON
	REBECCA GARSKE
	ASHLEY HODGKIN
	EMILY HOSKINS
	RENA MARSON
	JESSICA MORRISON
	MARY CATHERINE SEARS
	CHRISTINA SEPIC
	ANDREA SNYDER

acknowledgements

SCENIC PHOTOGRAPHY:
John Fielder

FOOD PHOTOGRAPHER:
Rick Souders, Souders Studios

FOOD STYLING:
Karen Kaehler and
Stephen Shern

PROPS:
Crate and Barrel

BOOK TITLE:
Jennifer Bicknell Greer

COVER DESIGN
AND LAYOUT:
Andrea Snyder

WINE CONSULTANT:
Rich Richter,
The Vineyard Wine Shop

BEER CONSULTANT:
Dan Weitz and Jeff Brown of the
Boulder Beer Company

CHEF TIPS:
Chef Jorge de la Torre,
Dean of Culinary Education at
Johnson & Wales University

GLUTEN FREE CONSULTANT:
Connie Logan RD, CDE

colorado *classique*
professional credits

Fresh Foods and the Natural World

JOHN FIELDER

It is my great pleasure to have been asked to contribute my nature photographs to *Colorado Classique* and to benefit one of Colorado's outstanding non-profit organizations, Junior League of Denver. The Junior League works to improve the health and welfare of families and children, not inconsistent with my personal goal to help people pursue healthier lifestyles by bringing them closer to nature. I believe that individuals who are connected to nature enjoy improved physical and psychological health. The recreation we enjoy in Colorado-hiking, climbing mountains, biking, skiing-makes our bodies stronger and gives us confidence and self-esteem. Furthermore, an appreciation for all things wild and natural allows us not only to be grateful for our own life, but also to have a respect for things bigger than us, like the miracle of four billion years of organic evolution on earth. This acknowledgement of things more permanent and grand begets humility, which makes it easier for us to get along with our fellow humans, and makes the planet a safer place.

When it comes to staying strong and sound, no amount of exerting ourselves in nature can substitute for a healthy diet. And Power Bars, as good as they are in a pinch, are not the ticket to longevity! Fresh foods as part of a balanced diet are the perfect compliment to our physical Colorado life. Fresh, if not organically produced, foods are not only good for our bodies, but also for our economy and ecology.

Rising energy and transportation costs demand that we buy more locally produced food. This food is fresher, more nutritious, and supports agriculture in America, thereby saving rural working landscapes. Protecting these bucolic landscapes means preserving the views of hay meadows, fields of corn, and verdant pastures that define Colorado and the West. This scenery attracts visitors from around the world to spend their money here as tourists-and perhaps to buy cookbooks from the Junior League of Denver as souvenirs to take back home! The circle is complete: physical fitness and wholesome eating encourage one to be an advocate for preserving natural and rural environments, which begets a planet that is not only healthier, but more economically viable and sustainable as well.

The photographs of Colorado inside *Colorado Classique* have been made over the past thirty years of my career as a nature photographer. I hope that they complement the remarkable recipes in this book, and that both forms of expression will make your life healthier and more rewarding.

John Fielder's thirty-ninth book, Ranches of Colorado, will be published in September, 2009. It is a photographic portrait of the landscapes of fifty working Colorado ranches; places that help define the heritage, economy, and ecology of the West. For more information about the book, as well as John Fielder's work, visit www.johnfielder.com.

Souders Studio

FOOD PHOTOGRAPHY

Souders Studios, under the direction of Photographer Rick Souders and his Studio Team, produced all of the beautiful Food Photography for the Cover as well as all interior food imagery for *Colorado Classique*. Rick Souders has been in the Food Photography Business for 23 years and is known as one of the best food photographers in America. Rick Souders has also been honored as the best beverage photographer in the World for two consecutive years at the World Food Media Awards in Australia. To see all of Rick's photography work and services, please visit www.SoudersStudios.com or contact Rick @ 1-800-990-3330. Also a special thanks to Paul Kooiman, Souders Studios Inc, Studio Manager and Shelly Ruybalid, extrodinary Baker who helped with this project.

DIGITAL IMAGING SERVICES
Square Pixels handled all of the color management, retouching and image manipulation for the Cover as well as all interior Food Photographs. John Wood, Photographer and Digital Imaging Specialist, has been in the business for 26 years and John does all of the retouching and image manipulation for Souders Studios as well as photography. You'll find a link to John's portfolio on the Souders Studios web site.

PROFESSIONAL FOOD STYLIST
Stephen began his career as a professional chef at the age of 20 working as a chef at the Sheraton Hotel in Boulder, Colorado. After years of success in and around Denver, Stephen set his sights on new challenges and took his talents to New York City where he worked closely with nationally recognized chefs Leslie Revsin and Michel Fitoussi contributing recipes for new menus. Over the next seven years, as a Consulting Chef he specialized in recipe development, menu and kitchen design, restaurant and cookbook reviews and private cooking lessons with celebrities. Fresh from being a chef, he had the artists' eye and creative touch to cultivate his food styling focus. Over 20 years later Food Styling is still his love and passion. He is widely known and looked up to as one of the best in the business today.

PROFESSIONAL CHEF AND STYLIST
Karen Kaehler spent her culinary career in South Florida, working for Royal Caribbean Cruises, Johnson & Wales University, and Chef Norman Van Aken, amongst others. She moved to Colorado in 2001 and currently works as a Research Chef, consultant, and food stylist. She would like to thank Rick, John, and Stephen for opening up the world of food styling to her-with great patience and humor.

Boulder Beer Company
Boulder Beer Company, Colorado's First Microbrewery, is pleased to be included in *Colorado Classique* and support the Junior League. In your hands you hold an example of the philosophy that homegrown creativity can enrich our lives every day. For 30 years, we at Boulder Beer have challenged ourselves to rise above the average with innovation and fun, and have fostered an atmosphere of creativity and beer education here in Colorado, a state that now has over 90 breweries and produces the most beer in the United States!

We also recognize that we wouldn't be here today without local support, and every year we return that support to our community. By striving to improve and educate ourselves, and by donating our time, hand-crafted beers and financial support to the worthy non-profits in our home state, we would like to think that the Junior League and Boulder Beer Co. complement each other as well as the food and beer pairings you'll find on these pages. Enjoy!

Johnson & Wales University
Johnson & Wales University, founded in 1914, is a nonprofit, private institution. A recognized leader in career education, the Denver Campus offers accredited degrees in business, hospitality, and culinary arts. JWU prepares students for personal and professional success by integrating rigorous academics and professional skills, community leadership opportunities and our unique career education model. The university is committed to urban revitalization and thoughtful historic renovation. Through active civic participation and by offering unique learning opportunities, JWU improves the quality of life throughout Denver and the State of Colorado through partnerships with community organizations like the Junior League of Denver. For more information, visit www.jwu.edu/denver.

The Vineyard Wine Shop
For nearly forty years The Vineyard Wine Shop has been Denver's favorite source for wine, wine gifts, and wine accessories. Founded in 1971 as the region's first wine-only store, The Vineyard has kept that focus through the years, with friendly staff who know their food and wine, a cellar stocked with tens of thousands of bottles, and great programs for wine lovers of all stripes, from neophytes to hardcore collectors. Our famous Wine-of-the-Month Club has introduced thousands of wine lovers to a vast array of different wines, ranging from everyday sippers to highly rated classics; and our wine tastings and events make learning about wine both fun and educational. We're proud to support the work of the Junior League of Denver and, as always, excited to encourage everyone to get more pleasure out of life with great cooking and great wine.

classique
appetizers & beverages

fire and ice watermelon salsa

Makes: *4 cups* Serves: *12 portions*

Prep: less than 30 minutes, plus 2 hours refrigeration

3 cups finely chopped watermelon

1 cup chopped green bell pepper

¼ cup chopped fresh cilantro

1 tablespoon chopped green onion

¼ cup lime juice

2-3 medium jalapeño peppers, seeded and chopped

1 teaspoon garlic salt

2 navel oranges, peeled and sliced into rounds

Combine all ingredients and mix well. Drain juices. Cover and refrigerate for 2 hours.

To serve, spoon over sliced oranges, or serve with tortilla chips.

NUTRITION INFORMATION: 28 calories, 0 g fat, 0 g saturated fat, 0 mg cholesterol, 81 mg sodium, 7 g carbohydrate, 5 g sugars, 1 g fiber, 1 g protein.

Beer Pairing: A sweet German-style Hefeweisen matches this refreshing salsa.

pineapple salsa

Serves: *6 portions*

Prep: less than 30 minutes

1 whole pineapple, peeled, cored, and finely chopped

½ medium-size red onion, finely chopped

1 tablespoon raspberry vinegar

1½ tablespoons chopped fresh basil

1½ tablespoons chopped fresh cilantro

1 jalapeño pepper, seeded and chopped

1 lime, cut into wedges

Combine pineapple, onion, vinegar, basil, cilantro, and jalapeño in a bowl and toss until thoroughly mixed. Squeeze juice from lime wedges over mixture. Cover and refrigerate at least 1 hour. Great with tortilla chips.

NUTRITION INFORMATION: 46 calories, 0 g fat, 0 g saturated fat, 0 mg cholesterol, 2 mg sodium, 12 g carbohydrate, 9 g sugars, 1 g fiber, 1 g protein.

jalapeño poppers

Serves: *24 portions*

Prep: 45 minutes | Bake: about 1 hour

---

12 medium fresh jalapeño peppers, halved lengthwise and seeded

8 ounces light cream cheese

1 8 ounce block Cheddar cheese

4 strips bacon, cooked crisp and crumbled

1 lemon, cut into wedges

Preheat oven to 300 degrees. Spread cream cheese in jalapeño halves. Place jalapeños on a baking sheet. Bake for about 45 minutes; the longer they bake, the less spicy the jalapeños will be.

While baking, cut Cheddar cheese into thin slices to be placed on each jalapeño. When baked, remove jalapeños from oven and top each with a cheese slice. Return to oven and bake until Cheddar cheese is melted. Sprinkle bacon over jalapeños and squeeze lemon juice on top. Serve hot.

NUTRITION INFORMATION: 68 calories, 5 g fat, 3 g saturated fat, 17 mg cholesterol, 126 mg sodium, 1 g carbohydrate, 1 g sugars, 0 g fiber, 3 g protein.

Beer Pairing: Bring out the heat of the jalapeños with a hopped-up Double IPA.

berry apple salsa

Serves: *16 portions*

Prep: less than 30 minutes

---

2 medium Granny Smith apples, peeled, cored, and cut into quarters

1½ cups sliced strawberries

1 kiwi, peeled and chopped

juice and zest of 1 small orange

2 tablespoons brown sugar

2 tablespoons apple jelly

Chop apple quarters with a food chopper. Combine apples, strawberries, and kiwi in a small bowl. Mix orange juice and zest, brown sugar, and apple jelly. Add to fruit mixture and mix gently. Spoon salsa into a chilled bowl. Serve with store-bought cinnamon pita chips.

NUTRITION INFORMATION: 31 calories, 0 g fat, 0 g saturated fat, 0 mg cholesterol, 1 mg sodium, 8 g carbohydrate, 6 g sugars, 1 g fiber, 0 g protein.

sweet and minty citrus salad

Serves: *4-6 portions*

Prep: less than 30 minutes

2	grapefruits	1	0 ounce package fresh cherries, pitted (if in season, otherwise use dried)
2	navel oranges		
8	small sprigs fresh mint	2	tablespoons honey

Remove skin and white pith from grapefruits and oranges; slice citrus into rounds. Stack ingredients in the following order: 1 slice grapefruit, 1 slice orange, 1 sprig mint, 1 cherry. Drizzle fruit stacks with honey. Place a toothpick through middle of stack for serving.

NUTRITION INFORMATION: 162 calories, 0 g fat, 0 g saturated fat, 0 mg cholesterol, 1 mg sodium, 42 g carbohydrate, 33 g sugars, 5 g fiber, 2 g protein.

Beer Pairing: A crisp craft-brewed Pilsener will balance the mint in this salad.

sun-dried tomato hummus

Serves: *12 portions*

Prep: less than 30 minutes

1½	ounces dry sun-dried tomatoes	2	tablespoons lemon juice
6	cloves garlic	¼	cup Parmesan cheese
1	15 ounce can garbanzo beans, drained	2	teaspoons dried basil
2	tablespoons extra virgin olive oil	1	teaspoon cayenne pepper
½	cup light mayonnaise	1	teaspoon salt

Blanch sun-dried tomatoes in boiling water for 4 minutes or until softened; drain. Chop garlic in a food processor with a metal blade until finely minced. Add rehydrated tomatoes and process until chopped into small pieces. Add garbanzo beans, olive oil, mayonnaise, lemon juice, Parmesan cheese, basil, cayenne pepper, and salt and process until smooth. Serve with crackers, toasted pita wedges, or raw vegetables.

NUTRITION INFORMATION: 103 calories, 7 g fat, 1 g saturated fat, 5 mg cholesterol, 390 mg sodium, 8 g carbohydrate, 2 g sugars, 2 g fiber, 3 g protein.

brie with figs and pecans

Serves: *8 portions*

Prep: less than 30 minutes | Bake: 30 minutes

1 sheet frozen puff pastry (half of a 17.3 ounce package)	½ cup chopped pecans
2 tablespoons butter, divided	1 8 ounce round Brie cheese
	½ cup fig jam

Preheat oven to 400 degrees. Unfold pastry sheet and lay out for 20 minutes to bring to room temperature. Meanwhile, melt 1 tablespoon butter in a saucepan over medium heat. Add pecans and sauté until golden brown. Place toasted pecans on top of cheese. Spread jam over pecans.

Melt remaining 1 tablespoon butter in microwave for 2 minutes. Brush both sides of pastry with melted butter. Center cheese round on top of pastry sheet. Bring all four corners of pastry together above Brie, twist slightly together at top, and secure with cooking string.

Place Brie-pastry on an ungreased baking sheet. Bake for 25 to 30 minutes. Serve with crackers or bread, or alone with green grapes, figs, and olives; also looks nice served with just green and red grapes.

NUTRITION INFORMATION: 398 calories, 28 g fat, 9 g saturated fat, 36 mg cholesterol, 282 mg sodium, 29 g carbohydrate, 10 g sugars, 1 g fiber, 9 g protein.

Chef Tip: Let puff pastry thaw before trying to unfold or it will easily break.

Beer Pairing: Raspberry Wheat or German Hefeweisens are excellent with soft-ripened cheese.

Wine Pairing: A Fino sherry with its dry nuttiness would marry well the sweetness of the figs and the pecans.

peanut dip with fruit

Serves: *6 portions*

Prep: less than 30 minutes

8 ounces light cream cheese	3 1¾ ounce packages salted peanuts, finely chopped in food processor
⅓ cup brown sugar	4 Granny Smith or Braeburn apples, cut into wedges
1 teaspoon vanilla extract	

Mix cream cheese, brown sugar, vanilla and peanuts and refrigerate until chilled. Serve chilled dip in a bowl surrounded by apple wedges.

Great for outdoor parties or kid parties. Other fresh fruit of choice can be substituted for apple wedges.

NUTRITION INFORMATION: 348 calories, 19 g fat, 5 g saturated fat, 24 mg cholesterol, 260 mg sodium, 36 g carbohydrate, 28 g sugars, 5 g fiber, 10 g protein.

tomato mozzarella tapenade stacks

Serves: *6 portions*

Prep: less than 30 minutes

5	Roma tomatoes, sliced	1	8 ounce ball fresh mozzarella

FRESH BASIL OLIVE TAPENADE

¾ cup pitted kalamata olives

¼ cup grated Romano or Pecorino cheese

10-12 leaves fresh basil, chopped, plus 6 leaves for garnish

1 tablespoon extra virgin olive oil

VINAIGRETTE

½ cup extra virgin olive oil

¼ cup red wine vinegar

1 teaspoon Dijon mustard

1 teaspoon sugar

pinch of dried oregano, rubbed between fingers to release flavors

sea salt to taste

cracked black pepper to taste

Reserve 12 tomato slices. Chop remaining tomato slices, ends, and pieces; set aside. Cut mozzarella into 6 slices.

Combine all tapenade ingredients in a food processor and process to make a paste.

To make vinaigrette, combine all ingredients in a small jar and shake until well blended.

To assemble, place a tomato slice on each of 6 individual serving plates. Spread with tapenade. Top with a slice of mozzarella and another tomato slice. Drizzle with vinaigrette and sprinkle with extra basil for garnish. Season with extra sea salt and cracked pepper and serve.

NUTRITION INFORMATION: 353 calories, 34 g fat, 9 g saturated fat, 32 mg cholesterol, 342 mg sodium, 4 g carbohydrate, 2 g sugars, 1 g fiber, 8 g protein.

blue cheese crumble

Serves: *8 portions*

Prep: less than 30 minutes

1	8 ounce package blue cheese, crumbled		juice of ½ lemon
2	cloves garlic, chopped	4	green onions, white and green parts, chopped
⅓	cup olive oil	½	cup chopped fresh parsley
2	tablespoons red wine		black pepper to taste

Place crumbled blue cheese in a serving dish. Combine garlic, olive oil, red wine, lemon juice, green onions, and parsley in a food processor and pulse until blended. Pour mixture over blue cheese and mix together.

Sprinkle some black pepper over top. Chill for 3 to 4 hours before serving. Serve with crackers or pita chips.

NUTRITION INFORMATION: 191 calories, 17 g fat, 7 g saturated fat, 21 mg cholesterol, 401 mg sodium, 2 g carbohydrate, 1 g sugars, 1 g fiber, 6 g protein.

Beer Pairing: The sweet, roasted flavors of a Brown Ale balance the dry saltiness in the blue cheese.

garlic grilled shrimp

Serves: *8 portions*

Prep: less than 30 minutes | Bake: 5 minutes

3	garlic cloves, minced	¼	teaspoon freshly ground black pepper
¼	cup minced fresh parsley	¼	cup olive oil
¼	cup fresh basil, minced		juice of 2 lemons
1	teaspoon dry mustard	2	pounds jumbo shrimp, peeled and deveined with tails intact
2	teaspoons Dijon mustard		
2	teaspoons kosher salt		

Combine garlic, parsley, basil, both mustards, salt, pepper, olive oil, and lemon juice. Add shrimp and toss to cover shrimp with marinade. Marinate for 1 to 2 hours at room temperature.

When ready to grill, preheat grill and brush with olive oil to prevent shrimp from sticking. Skewer 3 to 4 shrimp on each skewer; discard marinade. Grill for 2 minutes on each side.

NUTRITION INFORMATION: 92 calories, 3 g fat, 0 g saturated fat, 147 mg cholesterol, 649 mg sodium, 0 g carbohydrate, 0 g sugars, 0 g fiber, 16 g protein.

Wine Pairing: Sauvignon Blanc for its citrus flavors would enhance the flavors of the shrimp. France has Sancerre and Pouilly Fume but California and New Zealand make excellent wines as well.

baked gouda

Serves: *6 portions*

Prep: less than 30 minutes | Bake: 30 minutes

½	8 ounce can crescent roll dough (4 crescent rolls)	1	8 ounce round Gouda cheese, rind removed
		½	cup red pepper jelly

Preheat oven to 400 degrees. Press together perforations to seal crescent dough and roll out into a square. Place Gouda in the center of the square. Wrap dough around Gouda forming a secure seal all around the cheese. Flatten the excess dough on the top and pat down to form a well in center of excess dough that will eventually hold the jelly.

Place on a baking sheet. Bake for 20 minutes, being careful to NOT let crust get too done. Remove from oven and turn off the oven. Spoon pepper jelly into well on top. Return to oven (with heat off) for 10 minutes. Cool, cut into slices, and serve! Crackers are optional but not necessary because of the puff pastry.

NUTRITION INFORMATION: 275 calories, 14 g fat, 8 g saturated fat, 43 mg cholesterol, 505 mg sodium, 26 g carbohydrate, 20 g sugars, 0 g fiber, 11 g protein.

Beer Pairing: The coriander spices of a Belgian Witbier complement the nutty creaminess of baked Gouda.

Wine Pairing: A crisp, refreshing white would be delightful. Sauvignon Blanc makes the most sense.

spicy italian stuffed mushrooms

Serves: 30-36 portions

Prep: less than 30 minutes | Bake: 20 minutes

30-36 mini Portobello mushrooms, brushed clean

1 pound Canino's Hot Italian Sausage, casings removed

4 cloves garlic, chopped

½ teaspoon ground cayenne pepper

½ teaspoon black pepper

½ cup seasoned bread crumbs

½ cup cream cheese, softened

¼ cup Parmesan cheese

Preheat oven to 350 degrees. Remove mushroom stems and chop; set aside. Arrange mushroom caps, bottoms up, on a baking sheet. Brown sausage and drain.

In medium saucepan over medium heat, combine chopped mushrooms stems, browned sausage, garlic, cayenne pepper, black pepper, and bread crumbs. Slowly cook and stir for 5 to 7 minutes or until bread crumbs start to brown. Remove from heat and cool.

Mix cream cheese and Parmesan cheese into cooled bread crumb mixture. Stuff each mushroom cap with mixture. Bake for 20 minutes.

NUTRITION INFORMATION: 73 calories, 5 g fat, 2 g saturated fat, 12 mg cholesterol, 192 mg sodium, 4 g carbohydrate, 1 g sugars, 1 g fiber, 4 g protein.

confetti black bean salsa

Serves: 15 portions

Prep: less than 30 minutes, plus 2 hours or more marinating time

2 16 ounce cans black beans, rinsed and drained

1 18 ounce package frozen corn, thawed

2 large tomatoes, seeded and diced

1 red onion, finely diced

1 large avocado, diced

2 fresh jalapeños, seeded and chopped

½ cup fresh cilantro leaves, chopped

1½ tablespoons red wine vinegar

3 limes, cut into wedges

salt and pepper to taste

Mix all ingredients in large bowl, except lime wedges, salt and pepper. Squeeze lime wedges over mixture and stir together. Cover and chill at least 2 hours or overnight.

To serve, season with salt and pepper to taste. Serve with tortilla chips.

The longer the salsa stands, the better the flavor. This is also great with grilled chicken, tacos, etc.

NUTRITION INFORMATION: 122 calories, 3 g fat, 0 g saturated fat, 0 mg cholesterol, 191 mg sodium, 20 g carbohydrate, 3 g sugars, 6 g fiber, 5 g protein.

Chef Tip: Open the can from the bottom, so that the tough to get beans come out first and easily.

cilantro chicken skewers

Serves: *6 portions*

Prep: 1 hour, 15 minutes | Bake: 7 minutes

2	cups loosely packed cilantro with stems	¼	teaspoon ground black pepper
½	cup loosely packed Italian parsley with stems	¼	cup extra virgin olive oil
2	tablespoons chopped walnuts	2	pounds chicken tenders
2	medium cloves garlic	3	limes, cut into wedges
1	teaspoon kosher salt		

Combine cilantro, parsley, walnuts, garlic, salt, and pepper in a food processor until finely chopped. While the blade is running, slowly add olive oil to create a smooth sauce. Transfer marinade to a gallon zip-top bag. Add chicken tenders to bag and seal. Shake to coat chicken thoroughly. Refrigerate 3 to 4 hours, or overnight for best results.

When ready to cook, bring chicken to room temperature and preheat broiler. Thread chicken tenders onto 20 to 24 skewers and place on a broiling pan. Broil for 7 to 10 minutes or until chicken is firm. Squeeze some lime wedges over chicken; serve remaining lime wedges on the side.

NUTRITION INFORMATION: 272 calories, 13 g fat, 2 g saturated fat, 88 mg cholesterol, 424 mg sodium, 3 g carbohydrate, 1 g sugars, 1 g fiber, 36 g protein.

Wine Pairing: The lime flavors would do well with a Gavi from the Piedmont region of Italy. The citrus notes of the wine with its medium-body and acidity would be a great way to start off the evening.

fast and fresh guacamole

Makes: *1-2 cups,* Serves: *6 portions*

Prep: less than 30 minutes

2	ripe avocados	½	teaspoon kosher salt, or to taste
½	tomato, diced	1	tablespoon lime juice
¼	medium red onion, finely diced	½	tablespoon finely chopped fresh cilantro
1	clove garlic, crushed or very finely chopped	2-6	dashes Tabasco sauce, depending on taste
1	tablespoon cumin		

To easily remove the avocado flesh from the peel and pit, hold the avocado gently in one hand. Carefully cut the avocado lengthwise around the seed with a sharp knife. Open the 2 halves to expose the pit. Remove the pit with your fingers, or if necessary, pry it out with a spoon. Spoon the avocado flesh into a medium bowl; it should be easily removed from the peel. Using a hand-held potato masher or a fork, mash the avocado flesh to desired texture.

Mix avocado with all remaining ingredients and stir to combine. Guacamole will turn slightly brown as it ages, so it's best to prepare only an hour or so in advance. Serve with your favorite chips and enjoy.

NUTRITION INFORMATION: 116 calories, 10 g fat, 1 g saturated fat, 0 mg cholesterol, 168 mg sodium, 7 g carbohydrate, 1 g sugars, 5 g fiber, 2 g protein.

asparagus spears with prosciutto

Serves: *25-30 (2 piece) portions*

Prep: 45 minutes | Bake: 15 minutes

2   bunches asparagus

3   4 ounce packages thinly sliced prosciutto

2-3   tablespoons balsamic vinegar

3   tablespoons freshly grated Parmigiano-Reggiano cheese

Preheat oven to 350 degrees. Wash asparagus and cut off 2 to 3 inches from the stem end. While asparagus is drying, use kitchen scissors to cut the prosciutto into thirds, resulting in about 1-inch wide strips. Once asparagus is completely dry, wrap a strip of prosciutto around 1 piece of asparagus, barber-pole style; leave the tip of the asparagus showing.

Place asparagus on 1 to 2 cookie sheets and bake for 12 to 15 minutes. Remove from oven and use spatula to transfer to serving dish. Drizzle balsamic vinegar and sprinkle Parmesan cheese over asparagus. Can be enjoyed as finger food or served with tongs.

NUTRITION INFORMATION: 45 calories, 2 g fat, 1 g saturated fat, 12 mg cholesterol, 253 mg sodium, 2 g carbohydrate, 2 g sugars, 1 g fiber, 4 g protein.

Chef Tip: Look for asparagus with tight tips, an indicator of freshness.

Beer Pairing: This rich appetizer is perfectly balanced with light Kolsh or Pilsener.

Wine Pairing: Chenin Blanc has the soft pear-like fruit to handle the asparagus. If it is off-dry it will work even better with the saltiness of the prosciutto.

smoked salmon with fresh dill

Serves: *6 portions*

Prep: less than 30 minutes

¼   cup honey Dijon mustard

¼   cup light mayonnaise

4   4 ounce filet-style packages smoked salmon, chopped into ¼-inch cubes

¼   cup chopped red onion (chopped in food processor for finer consistency)

¼   cup chopped fresh dill

2   tablespoons drained capers

2   tablespoons fresh lime juice

2   tablespoons minced shallot

2   teaspoons olive oil

½   teaspoon kosher salt

½   teaspoon black pepper

Mix mustard and mayonnaise in a small bowl until blended. Combine salmon, onion, dill, capers, lime juice, shallot, olive oil, salt, and pepper in a medium bowl. Add mustard mixture and blend well. Serve with slices of plain or toasted French baguette or crackers.

NUTRITION INFORMATION: 230 calories, 10 g fat, 2 g saturated fat, 74 mg cholesterol, 786 mg sodium, 7 g carbohydrate, 0 g sugars, 0 g fiber, 27 g protein.

citrus shrimp and avocado

Serves: *6 portions*

Prep: less than 30 minutes | Bake: 8-10 minutes on grill

1	cup orange juice		1	small red onion, thinly sliced (about 1¾ cups)
1	cup fresh lime juice		1	jalapeño, seeded and diced (for extra heat, do not seed)
¾	cup ketchup		1	cup finely chopped fresh cilantro
⅓	cup vodka		1	avocado, diced
¼	teaspoon Tabasco sauce			
¼	cup olive oil			
1½	pounds peeled and deveined jumbo shrimp			

Combine juices, ketchup, vodka, and Tabasco sauce in a large bowl. Whisk in oil. Sauté or grill shrimp; grilling is preferable for better flavor. Add shrimp, onion, jalapeños, and cilantro to ketchup mixture and mix well. Cover and refrigerate at least 3 hours or up to 6 hours.

To serve, drain excess juice. Serve over diced avocado in a dish or martini glass.

NUTRITION INFORMATION: 158 calories, 6 g fat, 1 g saturated fat, 168 mg cholesterol, 309 mg sodium, 7 g carbohydrate, 4 g sugars, 3 g fiber, 19 g protein.

Chef Tip: Do not marinate over 6 hours or the acids in citrus will start to break apart shrimp, making it mushy.

Wine Pairing: A Semillon with its melon flavors has enough acidity to offset the citrus flavors. Australia and the Pacific Northwest make some very good ones. It also can be blended with Sauvignon Blanc.

spiced pecans

Serves: *16 (¼-cup) portions*

Prep: less than 30 minutes | Bake: 10 minutes

4	tablespoons unsalted butter		½	teaspoon cinnamon
½	cup brown sugar		1	teaspoon black pepper
¼	cup water		1	teaspoon cayenne pepper
1	teaspoon salt		4	cups pecans
2	teaspoons Chinese five-spice powder			

Preheat oven to 350 degrees. Melt butter in large skillet over medium heat. Add brown sugar, water, salt, five-spice powder, cinnamon, black pepper, and cayenne pepper. Stir until sugar dissolves.

Add pecans to mixture and cook, stirring often, for 5 minutes or until syrup thickly coats nuts. Transfer nuts to a greased baking sheet. Bake 10 minutes or until golden; cool.

NUTRITION INFORMATION: 259 calories, 24 g fat, 4 g saturated fat, 8 mg cholesterol, 148 mg sodium, 11 g carbohydrate, 8 g sugars, 3 g fiber, 3 g protein.

baked oysters on the half shell

Serves: *12 portions*

Prep: 45 minutes | Bake: 5-7 minutes

1	clove garlic	2	tablespoons Pernod or Herbsaint
2	cups fresh spinach	1-2	teaspoons Tabasco sauce
1	bunch watercress, stems trimmed		Coarse sea salt and pepper to taste
½	cup chopped green onions	16	ounces rock salt
¾	cup unsalted butter, softened	24	fresh oysters, shucked with shells reserved
½	cup panko bread crumbs	½	cup Parmigiano-Reggiano cheese

Move the oven rack to the highest level. Preheat broiler. Chop garlic in a food processor. Add spinach, watercress, and green onions and process until finely chopped. Transfer to another bowl.

Add butter, bread crumbs, Pernod, and Tabasco to the food processor bowl (don't bother rinsing) and process until blended. Add spinach mixture to the bread mixture and season with sea salt and pepper. Spread rock salt over a rimmed baking sheet. Position oyster shells in salt and place oysters in shells. Divide spinach mixture evenly across tops of oysters. Sprinkle with cheese. Broil for 5-7 minutes.

Call local grocer a day or two before preparing recipe to be sure they have fresh pre-shucked oysters on hand.

NUTRITION INFORMATION: 155 calories, 13 g fat, 8 g saturated fat, 48 mg cholesterol, 126 mg sodium, 5 g carbohydrate, 1 g sugars, 0 g fiber, 4 g protein.

Beer Pairing: A classic oak-aged stout goes perfectly with oysters!

Wine Pairing: A crisp, dry white is the perfect companion to the baked oysters. Muscadet from the Loire with citrus notes and brisk acidity is delightful with any clams or oysters.

fourteener beef jerky

Serves: *10 servings*

Prep: less than 30 minutes | Bake: 10-12 hours

1	pound flank steak	¼	teaspoon garlic salt
½	cup soy sauce	¼	teaspoon lemon pepper

Preheat oven to 175 degrees or lowest temperature possible. Cut flank steak lengthwise with the grain into desired size pieces, about ¼-inch thick. Combine soy sauce, garlic salt, and lemon pepper. Dip meat slices in seasoning mixture for a few minutes, then place on a baking sheet. Bake for 10 to 12 hours.

The meat is easier to cut if slightly frozen.

NUTRITION INFORMATION: 68 calories, 3 g fat, 1 g saturated fat, 19 mg cholesterol, 409 mg sodium, 0 g carbohydrate, 0 g sugars, 0 g fiber, 10 g protein.

raspberry kicker

Serves: *1 portion*

Prep: less than 30 minutes

---

2 shots raspberry vodka

4 shots cran-raspberry juice

Chambord

fresh raspberries

Fill a shaker halfway with ice. Add vodka and juice, cover, and shake. Drizzle Chambord on the inside of a chilled martini glass. Place a few raspberries in the bottom of the glass. Pour vodka mixture into glass and serve.

cranberry sparkler

Serves: *3 portions*

Prep: less than 30 minutes

---

1 12 ounce can frozen cranberry juice cocktail concentrate; slightly thawed

1 8 ounce can crushed pineapple packed in juice, undrained

1¼ cups sparkling water

1 orange, sliced

1 kiwi, sliced

½ cup freshly sliced pineapple

10 fresh cherries, pitted (or jarred if not in season)

1 lemon, cut into wedges

Combine cranberry juice and pineapple with juice in a blender and mix for 20 seconds. Add sparkling water and blend another 5 seconds.

Add orange, kiwi, and pineapple slices to mixture along with cherries. Refrigerate several hours. Serve over ice and garnish with lemon wedges.

champagne mojitos

Serves: *24 portions*

Prep: less than 30 minutes

---

2 handfuls fresh mint (about 1 cup)

1 12 ounce can diet lemonade concentrate

1 12 ounce can diet limeade concentrate

1 2 liter bottle diet Sprite

2 750 ml bottles champagne

3 limes, each cut into 8-9 wedges

In a large punch bowl or spigot jar, muddle three-fourths of the mint with a wooden spoon to bring out the juices from the mint. Add lemonade and limeade concentrates. Pour Sprite slowly over concentrates and mint and mix thoroughly. Finally, add champagne and stir a little more. Set aside until ready to serve.

To serve, squeeze juice of 2 lime wedges into punch. Serve over ice and garish with remaining lime wedges and mint. Punch gets better as it stands; making it at least an hour or more before serving is best.

Chef Tip: Basil and mint are from the same family, so try basil in your next mojito and mint in your next pesto.

sparkling sangría

Serves: *6-8 portions*

Prep: less than 30 minutes

1   750 ml bottle Pinot Grigio wine

¼   cup white rum

24 ounces diet lemon-lime soda

2   limes, sliced into ¼-inch thick rounds

1   orange, sliced into ¼-inch thick rounds

1   pint fresh strawberries, halved, or quartered if large

2   peaches, sliced

2-3 baby Key limes, sliced into rounds

Fill a large pitcher half way with ice. Add wine, rum, soda, and lime and orange slices; stir. Pour mixture into glasses and garnish with strawberries, peaches, and baby Key limes.

the tea spot's
boulder blues tea sparkler

Serves: *6 (6 ounce) portions*

1   bottle champagne or sparkling apple cider

3   tablespoons Boulder Blues tea leaves

6   strawberries

1. Bring 1 liter water to a boil and then let cool for 3 minutes, to about 175 degrees. Place tea leaves in a pitcher. Pour hot water over tea and steep for 2 to 3 minutes. Strain tea leaves, reserving leaves to re-steep. Chill tea for 4 hours.

2. To serve, pour 3 ounces Boulder Blues tea and 3 ounces champagne (or sparkling cider) in a flute. Garnish each serving with a strawberry.

Tea Facts and Tips

Brought to you by:

The Tea Spot

"Modern brewing, Conscious living."

DID YOU KNOW...Loose leaf tea is more flavorful, healthful, and economical than bagged tea?

All tea comes from the same plant, Camellia sinensis.

There are 4 types of tea, each has a different amount of caffeine: white (10-15 mg), green (20-25 mg), oolong (30-50 mg), and black (40-70 mg).

Tips to Steep the Perfect Cup of Tea:

1. Pick good quality tea

2. Use fresh, filtered water

3. Heat water to appropriate temperature

   White: about 165 degrees (boil and cool for 4 minutes)

   Green: about 175 degrees (boil and cool for 3 minutes)

   Oolong: about 185 degrees (boil and cool for 2 minutes)

   Black: about boiling (212 degrees)

   Herbal: about boiling (212 degrees)

4. Steep tea to appropriate time

   White: about 3-6 minutes

   Green: about 2-3 minutes

   Oolong: about 2-3 minutes

   Black: about 4-5 minutes

   Herbal: about 6+ minutes

www.theteaspot.com

holiday spiced punch

Serves: *8-10 portions*

Prep: less than 30 minutes | Cook: 30 minutes

1	gallon jug apple cider	6	whole cinnamon sticks
1	cup pineapple juice	1	cup mulling spices
2	oranges	8	ounces spiced rum
20	whole cloves		

Combine apple cider and pineapple juice in large saucepan. Peel oranges and poke cloves into the oranges; add to saucepan along with cinnamon sticks. Place mulling spices in a spice ball and add to punch. Cook over low heat until warm. Add rum and cook for 5 minutes longer over low heat.

traditional sangría

Serves: *6-8 portions*

Prep: less than 30 minutes

2	oranges	½	cup sugar
3	limes	16	ounces club soda
3	lemons	1	750 ml bottle red wine (Cabernet or Shiraz)
2	red apples		
½	cup brandy	10	cherries
½	cup Triple Sec	10	raspberries

Slice oranges, limes, lemons, and apples; set aside, saving some slices for garnish.

Mix brandy, Triple Sec, sugar, club soda, and wine together. Add the fruit slices, cherries, and raspberries and mix. Refrigerate overnight. Serve over ice garnished with reserved fruit.

pomegranate margarita

Serves: *2-4 portions*

Prep: less than 30 minutes

1½	cups Jose Cuervo Gold tequila	3	cups Jose Cuervo margarita mix
1½	cups Pama pomegranate liquor		fresh pomegranate seeds

Combine all ingredients except pomegranate seeds in a blender. Add a tall glass of ice and blend lightly. Pour mixture into glasses with lightly salted or sugared rims. Float pomegranate seeds on top and serve.

limoncello spritzer

Serves: *4 portions*

Prep: less than 30 minutes

½	pint lemon sorbet	1	750 ml bottle Prosecco
2	shots citron vodka		juice of 2 lemons
2	shots limoncello	1	lemon, cut into wedges

In a blender, combine lemon sorbet, vodka, and limoncello. Add Prosecco to mixture and stir. Add lemon juice and refrigerate for 1 hour.

Serve over ice and garnished with lemon wedges.

Chef Tip: Save the peels! Soak citrus peels, with all the white pith cut away, in vodka for 2 weeks. Then add simple syrup to taste...homemade limoncello at half the price of store bought.

peach fuzz

Serves: *6-8 portions*

Prep: less than 30 minutes

1	12 ounce can lemonade concentrate	4	ounces Triple Sec
1	6 ounce can limeade concentrate	12	ice cubes
1	12 ounce lemonade can vodka		mint and fresh peach slices for garnish
4	peaches, unpeeled		

Process all ingredients except garnish together in a blender. Pour into wine glasses or over crushed ice in highball glasses. Garnish with mint and fresh peach slices.

If in Colorado, use Palisade Peaches, which are at their peak ripeness in August.

sweet almond tea

Serves: *6 portions*

Prep: less than 30 minutes

4	ginger green tea bags	½	cup sugar
7¼	cups water	4	teaspoons almond extract
1	6 ounce can frozen lemonade concentrate	2	lemons, cut into wedges

Brew tea. Mix all ingredients except lemon wedges together. Refrigerate with tea bags overnight. Remove tea bags and serve cold over ice. Garnish with lemon wedges.

classique
salads

grilled vegetable salad

Serves: *6 portions*

Prep: 1 hour | Grill: 20 minutes

¾	cup olive oil, plus extra for bread		1	French baguette, cut into ¼- to ½-inch thick slices
⅓	cup balsamic vinegar		10-12	cups mixed baby greens
1	large red onion, cut into ¾-inch rounds		5	large tomatoes, sliced
10	baby beets, stems trimmed to 1-inch, peeled and halved lengthwise		¼	cup chopped fresh basil
3-4	small zucchini, each cut lengthwise into 4 slices		3	tablespoons chopped fresh chives or green onions
1	eggplant, peeled and cut into 2-inch wide bite-size strips		1½	tablespoons fresh marjoram
2	medium-size red bell peppers, cut into 2-inch wide strips		¾-1	cup chilled fresh mild goat cheese, crumbled
	salt and pepper to taste		⅔	cup freshly grated Pecorino Romano
			¾	cup kalamata olives

Preheat grill to medium-high heat. Whisk ¾ cup olive oil and vinegar in a medium bowl to blend. Place onions, beets, zucchini, eggplant, and red bell peppers on a baking sheet. Brush both sides with some of the vinaigrette and sprinkle with salt and pepper. Grill vegetables until just cooked through; 10 minutes per side for beets, 6 minutes per side for onions, and 4 minutes per side for zucchini, eggplant, and peppers. Vegetables can be grilled up to 1 hour ahead of time and left at room temperature until serving.

Brush baguette slices with extra olive oil and sprinkle with pepper. Grill bread 2 minutes on each side or until beginning to brown. Arrange mixed greens on a large platter. Overlap tomatoes atop greens in the center of the platter. Sprinkle tomatoes with salt and pepper. Arrange grilled vegetables atop greens around the edge of the platter. Drizzle remaining vinaigrette over tomatoes and grilled vegetables. Sprinkle tomatoes and vegetables with basil, chives, and marjoram. Sprinkle tomatoes with goat cheese and sprinkle Romano cheese over all. Garnish with olives. Serve with grilled bread.

NUTRITION INFORMATION: 592 calories, 38 g fat, 8 g saturated fat, 11 mg cholesterol, 765 mg sodium, 53 g carbohydrate, 19 g sugars, 11 g fiber, 15 g protein.

Beer Pairing: This salad would go together well with a Golden Ale or Robust Pilsener.

Wine Paring: The grilled aspect would warrant a wine with more body. Chardonnay would be the choice, especially one that is more fruit driven.

confetti salad with mint

Serves: *6 portions*

Prep: less than 30 minutes | Cook: less than 30 minutes

2 large English cucumbers	3 large tomatoes, seeded and coarsely chopped
⅓ cup red wine vinegar	⅓ cup chopped red onion
1 tablespoon sugar	⅓ cup chopped fresh mint
1 teaspoon salt	3 tablespoons olive oil
4-5 ears sweet corn	salt and pepper to taste

Cut cucumbers in half lengthwise and scrape out seeds. Cut halves diagonally into ½-inch-wide slices. Place cucumber slices in a large bowl. Add vinegar, sugar, and salt and let stand at room temperature for about 1 hour, stirring occasionally.

Meanwhile, cook corn in boiling water and for 3 to 5 minutes. Cool corn and then cut from cob to yield about 2 cups. Add corn along with tomatoes, onion, mint, and olive oil to cucumbers and toss to blend. Season salad with salt and pepper.

NUTRITION INFORMATION: 155 calories, 8 g fat, 1 g saturated fat, 0 mg cholesterol, 406 mg sodium, 21 g carbohydrate, 8 g sugars, 4 g fiber, 4 g protein.

corn and avocado salad

Serves: *12 portions*

Prep: less than 30 minutes | Cook: 5 minutes

4 large ears corn	2 tablespoons olive oil
2 avocados, pitted, peeled, and chopped	1 tablespoon lime juice
½ red onion, chopped	½ teaspoon grated lime zest
1 carton cherry tomatoes, halved	¼ teaspoon salt
¼ cup chopped cilantro	¼ teaspoon pepper

Cook corn in boiling water and for 3 to 5 minutes. Cool corn, then cut from cob to yield about 3 cups. Combine corn in a bowl with avocados, onions, tomatoes, and cilantro. Add olive oil, lime juice, and lime zest and season with salt and pepper. Stir and serve.

NUTRITION INFORMATION: 125 calories, 8 g fat, 1 g saturated fat, 0 mg cholesterol, 64 mg sodium, 14 g carbohydrate, 4 g sugars, 4 g fiber, 3 g protein.

Wine Pairing: Sauvignon Blanc is a great accompaniment to the corn flavors and avocado because it has the crispness to address the avocado and enough fruit for the corn.

summer spinach salad

Serves: *6-8 portions*

Prep: less than 30 minutes

DRESSING

¼	cup sugar		1	teaspoon minced onion, fresh or dried
2	tablespoons apple cider vinegar		⅛	teaspoon paprika
½	teaspoon poppy seeds		¼	cup olive oil

SALAD

1	cup sliced almonds		1	bunch spinach
1	teaspoon sesame seeds		1	pint fresh strawberries, sliced
1	tablespoon butter			

Mix all dressing ingredients in a jar, adding olive oil last.

For the salad, toast almonds and sesame seeds in butter. Combine spinach, strawberries, almonds, and sesame seeds in a bowl. Add dressing to taste and toss to mix.

NUTRITION INFORMATION: 258 calories, 19 g fat, 3 g saturated fat, 5 mg cholesterol, 52 mg sodium, 19 g carbohydrate, 13 g sugars, 5 g fiber, 5 g protein.

Beer Pairing: A floral Blonde Ale complements this summer salad.

rocky mountain beef salad

Serves: *4 portions*

Prep: less than 30 minutes | Cook: 15 minutes

1	1 pound cut good-quality of beef		¼	cup balsamic vinegar
	salt and pepper to taste		1	tablespoon Dijon mustard
1	clove garlic, minced		¾	cup chopped fresh herbs, such us basil, cilantro, or mint
1	tablespoon olive oil		2	cups chopped arugula or spinach leaves
8	ounces dry penne pasta		1-2	cups cherry tomatoes, halved
½	cup olive oil			

Season beef with salt and pepper and garlic. In a skillet, heat 1 tablespoon olive oil over medium heat. Add beef and cook 7 minutes per side. Remove from heat and let rest. Cut beef into slices and set aside.

Cook pasta in a large pot of boiling water for 10 minutes or until al dente. Drain pasta, reserving ¼ cup pasta water. In a small bowl, whisk ½ cup olive oil, balsamic vinegar, and mustard. Season with salt and pepper to taste and fresh herbs. In large bowl toss the pasta with half of the dressing and ¼ cup pasta water. Add arugula, tomatoes, beef, and more dressing to taste. Toss and serve.

NUTRITION INFORMATION: 660 calories, 36 g fat, 6 g saturated fat, 46 mg cholesterol, 144 mg sodium, 50 g carbohydrate, 7 g sugars, 2 g fiber, 33 g protein.

sophisticated salad

Serves: *8 portions*

Prep: 45 minutes | Cook: 10 minutes

DRESSING

½	cup dried tart cherries	⅓	cup olive oil
⅔	cup port wine	⅓	cup red wine vinegar
10-12	ounces thinly sliced bacon	1	tablespoon sugar
3	shallots, finely chopped (about ½ cup)		salt and freshly ground pepper to taste
3	cloves garlic, minced		

SALAD

1	head red leaf lettuce	1	cup toasted pine nuts
1	head Bibb or Boston lettuce	8	ounces blue cheese, crumbled

Combine cherries and wine in small heavy saucepan and bring to a boil over medium heat. Remove from heat and let stand 15 minutes or until cherries swell; do not drain. Cook bacon in a large heavy skillet over medium heat until crisp. Remove bacon from skillet, crumble, and chill until serving time. Drain off all but 1 tablespoon of bacon drippings from skillet. Cook shallots and garlic in drippings for 2 to 3 minutes or until tender. Carefully add olive oil, vinegar, and sugar. Cook and stir mixture until sugar dissolves. Remove from heat and stir in undrained cherries. Season dressing with salt and pepper. Dressing can be made ahead and refrigerated until serving time, bring to room temp before serving.

When ready to serve, tear salad greens into bite-size pieces and place in a large bowl. Add pine nuts. Pour dressing over greens and toss to blend. Top salad with blue cheese and bacon.

NUTRITION INFORMATION: 415 calories, 31 g fat, 10 g saturated fat, 36 mg cholesterol, 682 mg sodium, 16 g carbohydrate, 9 g sugars, 2 g fiber, 15 g protein.

grilled pear salad with blue cheese dressing

Serves: *4 portions*

Prep: less than 30 minutes | Grill: 15 minutes

DRESSING

2	cloves garlic, peeled
⅓	cup fresh parsley leaves, stems removed
¼	small onion, peeled and quartered
1	cup mayonnaise (prefer Hellmann's, avoid brands that are too "sugary")
½	cup sour cream

1	tablespoon lemon juice
1	tablespoon tarragon vinegar
2	tablespoons Worcestershire sauce
	freshly ground black pepper to taste
	Tabasco sauce to taste
1¼	cups crumbled blue cheese, or to taste

SAUTÉED OR GRILLED PEARS

3	pears, each peeled and cut lengthwise into 8 slices
	fresh lemon juice
3	tablespoons butter
1	tablespoon flavorless salad oil (lite olive, canola or soy)

	pinch of salt
	pinch of freshly ground black pepper
	freshly ground nutmeg to taste
4-8	cups mixed greens
¼	cup toasted walnuts

Mince garlic in a food processor. Add parsley leaves and pulse until finely minced. Add onion quarters and pulse until finely chopped. Add mayonnaise, sour cream, lemon juice, vinegar, and Worcestershire sauce. Process until smooth and well blended. Season to taste with pepper and Tabasco sauce. Add blue cheese and pulse to desired texture.

To prepare pears, toss pears carefully in a bit of fresh lemon juice; set aside. If sautéing, melt butter with oil in a skillet until hot. When the sizzling has subsided, carefully sauté pear slices, turning, until they are golden on both sides. To grill pears, heat a narrow-ridged grill pan, brushing grids with the mixture of butter and oil. Grill pears until nicely marked on both sides. Season finished pears with light sprinklings of salt, pepper, and fresh nutmeg. Divide mixed greens among 4 individual plates. Top greens equally with pear slices. Serve salad with dressing and top with toasted walnuts.

Keep in mind that some blue cheeses are stronger in flavor than others; adjust amount added as needed.

NUTRITION INFORMATION: 858 calories, 78 g fat, 23 g saturated fat, 94 mg cholesterol, 1061 mg sodium, 29 g carbohydrate, 16 g sugars, 6 g fiber, 13 g protein.

Chef Tip: Buy bleu cheese in a block and crumble. You will get better flavor and it is usually less expensive than the already crumbled cheese.

Wine Pairing: An unoaked Chardonnay would match the pear flavors and have the body to hold up to the blue cheese.

savory fruit salad

Serves: *4-6 portions*
Prep: 45 minutes

2	cups diced fresh pineapple		1	tablespoon thinly sliced fresh cilantro or mint
1	cup diced honeydew melon		1	tablespoon finely minced crystallized ginger
1	cup diced mango			
2	tablespoons thinly sliced fresh basil		1	tablespoon minced red bell pepper
2	tablespoons fresh lime juice		1	tablespoon sesame seeds
2	tablespoons honey			

Mix all ingredients except sesame seeds in a large bowl; let stand 10 minutes to allow flavors to blend. Serve in wine glasses with sesame seeds sprinkled on top.

NUTRITION INFORMATION: 143 calories, 2 g fat, 0 g saturated fat, 0 mg cholesterol, 11 mg sodium, 34 g carbohydrate, 27 g sugars, 3 g fiber, 1 g protein.

Sunflower Farmers Markets Today

Sunflower Farmers Markets is a rapidly growing chain of full service grocery stores offering consumers the highest quality natural and organic products at the lowest possible price. The company, founded in 2002, is a pioneer in developing the emerging value segment of the natural and organic foods retailing industry. The company has 20 stores located in Colorado, Arizona, New Mexico, Nevada, Utah, and Texas.

Candied Pecans

3 tablespoons light corn syrup

1½ tablespoons sugar

¾ teaspoon salt

¼ teaspoon freshly ground black pepper, or to taste

⅛ teaspoon cayenne pepper

1½ cups pecan pieces

Preheat oven to 325 degrees. Combine corn syrup, sugar, salt, black pepper, and cayenne in large bowl and stir until blended. Stir in pecans to coat. Spread pecans on a greased baking sheet.

Bake for 5 minutes. Using a fork, stir pecans to recoat with sugar mixture. Bake for 10 minutes longer or until pecans are golden and coating bubbles. Transfer to foil. Working quickly, separate nuts with fork; cool. Pecans can be made ahead; store in an airtight container at room temperature.

pear and cheese salad

Serves: *4 portions*

Prep: less than 30 minutes

DRESSING

3	tablespoons white wine vinegar		1	tablespoon chopped fresh rosemary
⅛-¼	teaspoon salt		6	tablespoons olive oil
¼	cup honey			

SALAD

1	16 ounce bag lettuce		½	cup shredded white Cheddar cheese
1	pear, julienned		¼	cup Candied Pecans (see recipe in sidebar)

Mix all dressing ingredients.

Combine all salad ingredients in a bowl. Just before serving, stir in dressing to taste.

NUTRITION INFORMATION: 405 calories, 30 g fat, 6 g saturated fat, 15 mg cholesterol, 249 mg sodium, 33 g carbohydrate, 26 g sugars, 4 g fiber, 5 g protein.

granny smith apple and blue cheese salad

Serves: *8 portions*

Prep: less than 30 minutes

POPPY SEED DRESSING

½	cup sugar		1½	teaspoons minced fresh onion
¼	cup cider vinegar		¼	teaspoon Worcestershire sauce
½	cup vegetable oil		¼	teaspoon paprika
1	tablespoon poppy seeds			

SALAD

1	head green leaf lettuce, torn into bite-size pieces (1½-2 bags pre-cut)		2	cups sliced grilled chicken breast
3	Granny Smith apples, peeled and chopped		½	6 ounce bag sea salt or garlic bagel chips, broken into pieces
4	ounces blue cheese, crumbled			

Whisk together all dressing ingredients or shake in a cruet or narrow jar.

Place lettuce in a large serving bowl. Add apples, then cheese and chicken. Just before serving, add the bagel chip pieces to the top. Apply dressing and toss, or serve dressing alongside.

NUTRITION INFORMATION: 367 calories, 22 g fat, 5 g saturated fat, 40 mg cholesterol, 353 mg sodium, 26 g carbohydrate, 18 g sugars, 1 g fiber, 16 g protein.

Wine Pairing: Riesling is something that has the acidity to match the apple and the fruit to handle the salt of this delicious strong cheese. It can be dry riesling or even one with some sweetness.

the ultimate salad

Serves: *8 portions or more*
Prep: 45 minutes | Bake: 30-40 minutes

VINAIGRETTE

⅔	cup sugar	3	tablespoons apple cider vinegar
1	teaspoon dry mustard	4½	teaspoons onion juice
1	teaspoon salt	2	tablespoons Worcestershire sauce
⅔	cup distilled white vinegar	1	cup vegetable oil

SALAD

4	cups mixed field greens	1	Granny Smith apple, chopped
2	green onions, chopped	¼	cup coarsely chopped Spicy Pecans (see recipe in sidebar)
4	ounces blue cheese, crumbled		

Combine sugar, mustard, salt, and vinegars and stir until sugar is dissolved. Whisk in onion juice and Worcestershire sauce. Add oil slowly, whisking continuously until blended.

Combine all salad ingredients in a salad bowl. Add desired amount of vinaigrette, tossing to coat. Salad should be "wilted" upon serving.

NUTRITION INFORMATION (includes half of vinaigrette recipe): 263 calories, 21 g fat, 4 g saturated fat, 12 mg cholesterol, 400 mg sodium, 15 g carbohydrate, 13 g sugars, 2 g fiber, 4 g protein.

Spicy Pecans

- 2 egg whites
- 1½ teaspoons salt
- ¾ cup sugar
- 2 teaspoons Worcestershire sauce
- 2 tablespoons Hungarian paprika
- 1½ teaspoons cayenne pepper
- 4½ cups pecan halves
- 6 tablespoons unsalted butter, melted and cooled

Preheat oven to 325 degrees. Beat egg whites with salt until foamy. Add sugar, Worcestershire sauce, paprika, and cayenne. Fold in pecans and melted butter. Spread pecans evenly on a baking sheet. Bake for 25 to 30 minutes, stirring every 10 minutes; cool. Store in an airtight container. Pecans will keep for quite a while; use a little every time you make this salad.

mile high salad

Serves: *8 portions*
Prep: less than 30 minutes

DRESSING

¼	cup olive oil	¼	cup honey
2	tablespoons finely chopped green onions	2-3	teaspoons Tabasco sauce
2	tablespoons white wine vinegar		

SALAD

10	ounces mixed salad greens	4	ounces dried cranberries
4	ounces feta, goat, or blue cheese	½	cup toasted walnuts
4	ounces chopped pecans		

Mix all dressing ingredients together; shake well.

Combine all salad ingredients in a bowl. Toss salad with desired amount of dressing.

NUTRITION INFORMATION: 329 calories, 25 g fat, 4 g saturated fat, 13 mg cholesterol, 176 mg sodium, 25 g carbohydrate, 21 g sugars, 3 g fiber, 5 g protein.

baby lettuce salad with maple tangerine vinaigrette

Serves: *4 portions*

Prep: 1 hour

VINAIGRETTE

¼ cup fresh tangerine juice

2 tablespoons pure dark amber Maple syrup

1 tablespoon sherry vinegar

1 tablespoon finely chopped shallots

1 teaspoon fresh lime juice

1½ teaspoons chopped chipotle chiles in adobo

½ teaspoon tangerine zest

2 tablespoons extra virgin olive oil

salt and freshly ground pepper to taste

SALAD

3 tangerines or clementines

4-5 cups baby lettuces, such as winter density, jem, butter, romaine

1 cup frisee

1 cup baby arugula

2 tablespoons snipped fresh chives

½ cup chopped roasted and lighted salted pistachios

French feta cheese, preferably made with goat milk, shaved into curls

Whisk together tangerine juice, syrup, vinegar, shallots, lime juice, chiles, and tangerine zest. Slowly whisk in olive oil. Season vinaigrette with salt and pepper.

Peel tangerines, removing as much of the white pith as possible. Cut oranges crosswise into ¼-inch thick slices, then divide slices into thirds, or just peel and separate into sections. Just before serving combine lettuces and toss with some of the vinaigrette. Divide salad between 4 plates. Top with chives, pistachios, tangerines, and feta and drizzle with a little extra vinaigrette.

Freeze remaining chipotle chiles in a zip-top bag for later use.

A bag or box of mixed greens can be used.

French feta cheese is less salty than Greek feta. Chill the cheese first to make it easier to chop or slice.

NUTRITION INFORMATION: 232 calories, 15 g fat, 2 g saturated fat, 0 mg cholesterol, 151 mg sodium, 24 g carbohydrate, 16 g sugars, 5 g fiber, 4 g protein.

Beer Pairing: A British-style Pale Ale or E.S.B. sets off the sweetness of the maple tangerine flavors.

summer time orzo

Serves: *6 portions*

Prep: less than 30 minutes | Cook: 10 minutes

1	pound dry orzo pasta	½	cup toasted pine nuts
½	cup olive oil	3	tablespoons lemon juice
2	cups fresh spinach, torn into pieces	1½	teaspoons salt
4	ounces crumbled feta cheese	1	teaspoon freshly ground black pepper
½	cup dried cranberries	1	carton cherry tomatoes, halved
8	fresh basil leaves, torn		

Cook orzo in a large pot of boiling salted water, stirring occasionally, for 8 to 10 minutes or until tender but still firm to the bite. Drain pasta and spread on a large baking sheet to cool. Transfer cooled orzo to a large serving bowl. Add all remaining ingredients and toss gently to combine. Serve chilled.

NUTRITION INFORMATION: 611 calories, 29 g fat, 6 g saturated fat, 17 mg cholesterol, 820 mg sodium, 75 g carbohydrate, 17 g sugars, 5 g fiber, 16 g protein.

Chef Tip: Buy a block of feta and crumble it yourself. It is usually less expensive and if in brine, it will taste fresher.

Wine Pairing: Rosé from Europe with dry flavors of berry and cherry would be a great summer evening under the stars with this tasty salad.

curry chicken salad

Serves: *2 portions*

Prep: less than 30 minutes | Cook: 5 minutes

2	cups chopped chicken breast (rotisserie chicken works well)	¼	cup mayonnaise
1¼	cups halved seedless red grapes	1	teaspoon honey
½	cup thinly sliced green onions	½	teaspoon freshly squeezed lemon juice
1	tablespoon dried currants or cranberries	⅛	teaspoon salt
2	teaspoons curry powder (use red curry for extra spice)	⅛	teaspoon black pepper
		⅓	cup sliced almonds

Combine chicken, grapes, onions, and currants in a large bowl. Stir curry powder in a small skillet over medium heat for 30 seconds or until fragrant. In a separate bowl, whisk curry powder with mayonnaise, honey, lemon juice, salt, and pepper. Pour mayonnaise mixture over chicken mixture and toss gently to coat. Cover and chill. Toast almonds in a skillet for 3 to 5 minutes or until lightly brown; cool. Stir almonds into salad just before serving.

Light mayonnaise can be substituted for a low-fat version.

NUTRITION INFORMATION: 629 calories, 35 g fat, 5 g saturated fat, 129 mg cholesterol, 413 mg sodium, 31 g carbohydrate, 23 g sugars, 5 g fiber, 48 g protein.

Wine Pairing: The mayonnaise would require a white wine with more acidity and one that has some fruitiness to go with the curry. A white wine from the Trebbiano grape in Italy would serve quite nicely.

vegetable couscous with herb vinaigrette

Serves: *8 portions*

Prep: 45 minutes

DRESSING

1	teaspoon minced fresh chives	1	tablespoon lemon juice
1	teaspoon minced fresh parsley	1	tablespoon Dijon mustard
½	teaspoon chopped fresh thyme	2	tablespoons champagne vinegar
2	large shallots, minced	½	cup extra virgin olive oil
2	cloves garlic, minced		salt and pepper to taste
1	teaspoon lemon zest		

SALAD

1½	cups chicken broth	¼	cup chopped kalamata olives
1	cup dry couscous	¼	cup chopped artichoke hearts (not marinated)
2	cups chopped red bell pepper		
2	cups chopped tomatoes	¼	cup chopped fresh parsley
½	cup crumbled feta cheese	¼	cup chopped fresh basil or cilantro
½	cup finely chopped green onions	½	cup toasted pine nuts

Combine chives, parsley, thyme, shallots, and garlic in a small food processor and pulse; transfer to a mixing bowl. Add lemon zest, lemon juice, mustard, and vinegar and whisk together. Slowly whisk in olive oil. Season with salt and pepper. Chill dressing for about 6 hours, remove from refrigerator 10 minutes before serving.

To make salad, bring chicken broth to a boil in a medium saucepan. Gradually stir in couscous and remove from heat. Cover and let stand 5 minutes. Fluff couscous with a fork and transfer to a large bowl. Add bell peppers, tomatoes, feta, green onions, olives, artichokes, parsley, basil and pine nuts. Add dressing and toss salad gently to coat.

This salad can be served with marinated chicken.

NUTRITION INFORMATION: 312 calories, 21 g fat, 4 g saturated fat, 9 mg cholesterol, 423 mg sodium, 25 g carbohydrate, 5 g sugars, 3 g fiber, 7 g protein.

Marinated Chicken

1 tablespoon fresh lemon juice

½ teaspoon salt

½ teaspoon freshly ground black pepper

1 tablespoon sugar

2 cups nonfat plain yogurt

1 tablespoon olive oil

1 teaspoon chopped fresh mint

1-2 pounds chicken breast

In a small mixing bowl, whisk together lemon juice, salt, pepper, and sugar. Whisk in yogurt and olive oil, then stir in mint. Marinade can be made in advance and stored in the refrigerator for several days. In a resealable bag or shallow container, combine chicken breast with marinade. Marinate in refrigerator for 15 minutes or overnight. Grill the chicken over medium heat for 6 minutes on each side or until cooked through. Transfer chicken to a cutting board and slice into thin strips when cool enough to handle. Add to salad after chicken and couscous are cool.

chicken couscous salad

Serves: *4 portions*

Prep: less than 30 minutes | Cook: 30 minutes

DRESSING/MARINADE

1	tablespoon fresh lemon juice		2	cups plain nonfat yogurt
½	teaspoon salt		1	tablespoon olive oil
	freshly ground black pepper		1	teaspoon chopped fresh mint
1	tablespoon sugar			

SALAD

4	4 to 6 ounce boneless, skinless chicken breasts		1	cup dry instant couscous
1	cup cherry or grape tomatoes, halved		¼	cup halved black olives
1	medium cucumber, peeled, halved lengthwise, seeded, and sliced		½	cup crumbled feta cheese
½	cup chopped green onions			fresh mint sprigs for garnish

Whisk lemon juice, salt, pepper, and sugar together in a small bowl. Whisk in yogurt and olive oil. Stir in mint. The dressing can be made in advance and stored in the refrigerator for several days.

To prepare salad, marinate chicken in 1 cup of the dressing in a zip-top bag or a shallow container. Refrigerate for 15 minutes or overnight. In a large mixing bowl, combine tomatoes, cucumbers, green onions, and the remaining dressing. Cover and refrigerate for 15 minutes or overnight.

When ready to cook, preheat a well-greased grill to medium. Grill chicken for about 6 minutes on each side or until cooked through. Transfer chicken to a cutting board. When cool enough to handle, slice chicken into thin strips; cool completely. Toss cooled chicken with vegetable mixture and refrigerate. Bring 1½ cups water to a boil. Stir in couscous and a pinch of salt. Cover, remove from heat, and let stand for 5 minutes. Fluff couscous with a fork and transfer to a large serving bowl; cool completely. Stir couscous into salad and season with salt and pepper. The salad can be made in advance and stored in the refrigerator for up to 2 days. Serve chilled or at room temperature, garnished with olives, feta cheese, and mint sprigs.

NUTRITION INFORMATION: 426 calories, 9 g fat, 4 g saturated fat, 84 mg cholesterol, 652 mg sodium, 46 g carbohydrate, 10 g sugars, 4 g fiber, 39 g protein.

Chef Tip: In a hurry? Use the roasted chicken at the store for your next chicken salad recipe.

Wine Tip: Albarino from Spain has intense flavors of stone fruit. This would be a great match to the subtle texture of the meal and the mint.

spinach salad with grilled prawns

Serves: *4 portions*

Prep: 1 hour | Cook: 15 minutes

1-1¼ pounds colossal (10/15 count) or extra-colossal (8/10 count) prawns	1 teaspoon soy sauce
¼ cup dry sherry	1 teaspoon finely shredded orange zest, optional
¼ cup rice wine vinegar	2 mangoes, peeled and sliced
1 tablespoon sesame oil	10 ounces spinach leaves, rinsed and torn into bite-size pieces
1 tablespoon olive oil	1 large red bell pepper, cut into thin slivers
1 tablespoon minced fresh ginger	salt and pepper to taste

Peel prawns and devein. Butterfly cleaned prawns by cutting down back of each prawn about three-fourths of the way through and spread flat; rinse and pat dry. Mix sherry, vinegar, sesame and olive oils, ginger, soy sauce, and orange zest. Combine 2 tablespoons of sherry mixture with shrimp; cover and chill 30 to 60 minutes. Reserve remainder of sherry mixture for later. In a large bowl, combine mango slices, spinach, and bell pepper. Cover and chill about an hour.

Preheat grill over high heat. Grill prawns, turning once, for 1½ minutes on each side or until opaque in the thickest part; do not overcook. Add prawns and reserved dressing to spinach mixture and toss lightly. Season with salt and pepper.

NUTRITION INFORMATION: 243 calories, 8 g fat, 1 g saturated fat, 147 mg cholesterol, 306 mg sodium, 23 g carbohydrate, 17 g sugars, 4 g fiber, 19 g protein.

Wine Pairing: Viognier with its dried peach and apricot flavors would play off the spinach and the grilled aspect of this shellfish dish.

sesame shrimp salad

Serves: *6 portions*

Prep: 1 hour | Grill: 35 minutes

DRESSING

¼ cup seasoned rice vinegar	1 teaspoon sesame oil
½ teaspoon sugar	freshly ground black pepper to taste
5 tablespoons corn or vegetable oil	

SALAD

2 cups shredded iceberg lettuce	1 pound medium to large shrimp, grilled
2 cups shredded red cabbage	⅔ cup slivered almonds, toasted
3 green onions, white and green parts julienned and cut in 1 to 1½-inch lengths	⅓ cup drained and sliced pickled ginger
½ cup chopped fresh cilantro leaves	1 teaspoon roasted sesame seed
	handful of chow mein noodles (optional)

Combine vinegar and sugar. Slowly whisk in corn oil, then sesame oil. Grind in pepper; adjust seasoning as needed.

Combine all salad ingredients. Just before serving, toss with dressing, being careful not to overdress the salad. Sprinkle chow mein noodles on top. This salad can also be made with chicken for a different flavor.

NUTRITION INFORMATION: 281 calories, 19 g fat, 2 g saturated fat, 112 mg cholesterol, 426 mg sodium, 12 g carbohydrate, 6 g sugars, 3 g fiber, 15 g protein.

Chef Tip: This recipe is also amazing with chicken.

Wine Pairing: A white that has some fruit character to handle the ginger and enough body to go with the shrimp. A Torrontés from Argentina would be a delight with this delicious salad.

italian chopped salad

Serves: *6 portions*

Prep: less than 30 minutes | Cook: 15 minutes

BALSAMIC DRESSING

2	tablespoons balsamic vinegar
½	heaping teaspoon Dijon mustard
½	teaspoon kosher salt
¼	teaspoon freshly ground pepper
¼	cup olive oil

SALAD

¼	cup pine nuts
1-2	red bell peppers
1	pound finely julienned romaine lettuce and field greens
½	cup crumbled Gorgonzola cheese
1	cup red grape tomatoes, halved
½	cup pitted kalamata olives, halved
1	tablespoon capers, drained
10	thin slices Soppressata hard salami, sliced in strips
10	thin slices prosciutto ham, sliced in strips

In a blender or food processor, blend vinegar, mustard, salt, and pepper until smooth. With the motor running, slowly add oil and blend until smooth. Set dressing aside.

To prepare the salad, toast pine nuts in a pan until lightly browned; cool. Char bell peppers over an open flame or under a broiler until blackened on all sides. Transfer peppers to large bowl, cover tightly with plastic wrap, and let stand 15 minutes. Peel and seed peppers and cut into strips to yield ½ cup.

Just before serving, toss pine nuts and roasted peppers with lettuce, cheese, tomatoes, olives, capers, salami, and ham in a large bowl. Add dressing and toss to coat.

NUTRITION INFORMATION: 276 calories, 23 g fat, 5 g saturated fat, 30 mg cholesterol, 985 mg sodium, 9 g carbohydrate, 5 g sugars, 3 g fiber, 11 g protein.

Chef Tip: Kosher salt or table salt? Kosher salt can be used for everything. Kosher is flakier and will not wilt a salad as quickly as crystal salt. Table salt can be used to salt water for cooking pastas and vegetables, and for making brines.

Wine Paring: A dry, light, refreshing white would do nicely with this salad. The meats have some saltiness that would require a little more fruitiness. This would be ideal for a Soave from Italy.

classique
soups & sandwiches

denver chowder

Serves: *6 portions*

Prep: 45 minutes | Cook: 30 minutes or less

2	tablespoons butter, softened		4	cups chicken broth
2	tablespoons flour		1	cup heavy cream
2	tablespoons butter		2	teaspoons sugar
1	medium onion, finely chopped		½	teaspoon cayenne pepper
4	stalks celery, finely chopped		1	pound raw shrimp, peeled and deveined, chopped
2	large poblano or pasilla chiles, seeded and chopped		¼	cup chopped fresh cilantro
2	15 ounce cans cream-style corn			salt and pepper to taste
1	16 ounce package frozen corn, or 2 cups fresh		2	tablespoons chopped fresh cilantro for garnish

Mix 2 tablespoons softened butter with flour in a small bowl to blend; set aside. Melt 2 tablespoons butter in a large pot over medium-high heat. Add onion, celery, and chiles and sauté 6 minutes or until softened. Add cream-style corn, frozen corn, broth, cream, sugar, and cayenne. Bring to a boil and reduce heat. Whisk in flour mixture and simmer 15 minutes. Add shrimp and ¼ cup cilantro. Simmer 5 minutes or until shrimp are cooked through. Season with salt and pepper. Ladle into soup bowls and garnish with remaining cilantro.

NUTRITION INFORMATION: 476 calories, 25 g fat, 14 g saturated fat, 172 mg cholesterol, 946 mg sodium, 51 g carbohydrate, 12 g sugars, 7 g fiber, 18 g protein.

Wine Pairing: Chardonnay would be great for the fullness of its flavors. A Central Coast wine would be better with its tropical notes to go with the spice of the peppers.

roasted corn and sweet potato soup

Serves: *8 portions*

Prep: 45 minutes | Cook: 1 hour

5	ears corn, husks left on		½	stalk celery, chopped
1	large red bell pepper		3	quarts vegetable stock
1	small yellow bell pepper		½	tablespoon minced fresh thyme
1	small green bell pepper		½	tablespoon minced fresh basil
4-5	sweet potatoes (about 1½ pounds), cut into 2-inch chunks		1	bay leaf
¼	cup olive oil		½	tablespoon minced fresh chives
½	onion, chopped		2	quarts heavy cream
5	large cloves garlic, minced			salt and freshly ground pepper to taste
¼	cup sliced leeks		½	tablespoon minced fresh parsley for garnish

Preheat oven to 350 degrees. Place corn and all bell peppers on baking sheets. Roast the peppers for 20 minutes and the corn for 30 minutes. Place bell peppers in a paper or plastic bag to steam. When cool, peel, seed, and dice peppers and set aside. Shuck roasted corn and cut the kernels from the cobs with a sharp knife, cutting downwards along the cob, behind the kernels; set kernels aside. Cut cobs into 2-inch pieces and set aside.

Meanwhile, cook sweet potatoes in boiling water for 20 minutes or until softened. Drain and cool, then peel and dice into the same size as the bell peppers; set aside. Heat olive oil in a large saucepan or stockpot. Sauté onions, garlic, leeks, celery, and corn cobs over medium heat for 5 minutes or until vegetables are translucent and lightly caramelized. Add stock, thyme, basil, bay leaf, and chives and bring to a boil. Reduce heat and simmer, uncovered, until the liquid is reduced to about 1 quart. Add cream and simmer 30 minutes over low heat to reduce the liquid; do not boil after cream is added. Strain through a fine sieve into a clean pan. Return chowder to heat and simmer, watching closely, for 5 to 10 minutes or until it thickens and reaches the desired consistency. Season with salt and pepper.

When ready to serve, add sweet potato, corn, and bell peppers, and warm through. Ladle chowder into serving bowls. Garnish with the chopped parsley.

NUTRITION INFORMATION: 1045 calories, 96 g fat, 56 g saturated fat, 326 mg cholesterol, 221 mg sodium, 41 g carbohydrate, 8 g sugars, 5 g fiber, 12 g protein.

Wine Pairing: Torrontés from Argentina will have the fruit character to match the roasted corn quite nicely.

Denver Books And Gifts

20568 E. Hamilton Circle
Aurora, CO 80013

Packing Slip

Order Date: 11/21/2009	denverbooksandgifts@comcast.net
Order Number: 102-7826644-5209064	**Customer Contact:** Nancy Brenner

If you wish to contact us regarding this order, please email us at
denverbooksandgifts@comcast.net .

Thank you for your purchase!

leek and mushroom soup

Serves: *6 portions*

Prep: less than 30 minutes | Cook: 20 minutes

4	tablespoons unsalted butter
4	large leeks, white and pale green parts only, thinly sliced to yield 3½ cups
8	ounces shiitake mushrooms, stemmed and sliced
10	ounces crimini mushrooms, sliced
2	tablespoons all-purpose flour
4	cups chicken stock or canned low-salt chicken broth
1	cup heavy cream
2	tablespoons dry sherry
	salt and pepper to taste
5	green onions, sliced, or to taste
12	¼-inch thick slices French or sourdough baguette
⅔	pound Brie cheese, rind removed, cut into ¼-inch thick slices (keep very cold until ready to use)
3	tablespoons chopped fresh chives

Melt butter in large stock pot over medium-high heat. Add leeks and all mushrooms and sauté 8 minutes. Add flour and cook and stir for 1 minute. Gradually mix in stock. Bring to a boil, stirring frequently. Reduce heat and simmer 10 minutes. Add cream and sherry and simmer 5 minutes. Season to taste with salt and pepper. Stir in green onions. Soup can be made 1 day ahead up to this point; cool slightly, refrigerate uncovered until cold, then cover and keep refrigerated until ready to serve.

Preheat oven to 350 degrees. Place bread slices on a baking sheet. Bake 10 minutes or until light golden; cool. Top croutons with cheese slices. Preheat broiler. Place 6 ovenproof bowls or souffle dishes on a baking sheet. Bring soup to a simmer. Ladle soup into bowls. Top each with about 2 croutons. Broil for 2 minutes or until cheese is completely melted. Sprinkle with chives and serve.

NUTRITION INFORMATION: 541 calories, 37 g fat, 23 g saturated fat, 125 mg cholesterol, 578 mg sodium, 33 g carbohydrate, 6 g sugars, 3 g fiber, 19 g protein.

Chef Tip: To make this soup vegetarian, make a stock from mirepoix, and mushroom stems and peelings. Mirepoix is a mixture of chopped or finely diced sautéed carrots, onions, celery, and herbs. Finely diced mirepoix is used to season sauces, soups, and stews.

Wine Pairing: Sauvignon Blanc is a suitable match. New Zealand produces some with good zingy citrus flavors.

cauliflower and brie soup

Serves: *4 portions*

Prep: less than 30 minutes | Cook: 1 hour, 15 minutes

1	head cauliflower		1	pint chicken stock
1	onion, chopped		1	pint heavy cream
4	stalks celery, chopped			salt and pepper to taste
1	tablespoon olive oil		4	ounces Brie cheese
1	teaspoon ground coriander			

Remove leaves from cauliflower and separate florets from stalk. Place cauliflower florets, onions, celery, olive oil, and coriander in a stockpot over medium-high heat. Cook until onions are translucent and cauliflower is soft. Add chicken stock and bring to a boil. Boil for 2 minutes, then reduce heat to medium. Simmer for 1 hour or until cauliflower is completely cooked; cool.

Purée cooled soup until smooth using a blender or food processor. Return soup to the pot and reheat. Whisk in cream and season with salt and pepper. Add cheese just before serving.

NUTRITION INFORMATION: 595 calories, 56 g fat, 33 g saturated fat, 191 mg cholesterol, 330 mg sodium, 15 g carbohydrate, 7 g sugars, 5 g fiber, 13 g protein.

roasted red pepper soup

Serves: *4-6 portions*

Prep: more than 2 hours | Cook: 45 minutes

1½	cups chopped onions		1	teaspoon salt
3	tablespoons olive oil		3	cups roasted and peeled red peppers (recipe below), cut into 1-inch pieces
2-3	cloves garlic, minced			
2	cups chicken broth		1	tablespoon lemon juice
2	cups water		8-10	leaves basil, chopped and divided
2	shakes cayenne pepper		¼-½	cup heavy cream, whipped, optional garnish

In a soup pot, sauté onions in olive oil for 3 to 5 minutes or until softened. Add garlic and sauté 2 to 3 minutes longer. Add chicken broth, water, cayenne, and salt and bring to a boil. Reduce heat and simmer, partially covered, for 20 minutes. Add roasted peppers and continue to simmer, partially covered, for 10 minutes longer. Pour mixture into a blender and purée until creamy. Return to soup pot. Add lemon juice and half of chopped basil and cook 3 minutes longer. Top each serving with 1 to 2 tablespoons whipped cream and a sprinkle of chopped basil.

To make roasted peppers: Cut about 7 red bell peppers (about 2½ pounds) in half lengthwise and remove seeds and ribs. Place peppers on a sprayed baking sheet, cut-side down, and broil for 15 to 25 minutes or until the skins blister and darken. Remove baking sheet from the oven and cover immediately with foil for 15 to 25 minutes. Peel off skins.

To make this recipe vegetarian, substitute vegetable broth for chicken broth.

NUTRITION INFORMATION: 259 calories, 17 g fat, 5 g satura dted fat, 20 mg cholesterol, 850 mg sodium, 24 g carbohydrate, 14 g sugars, 7 g fiber, 4 g protein.

curried butternut squash soup

Serves: *6-8 portions*

Prep: 45 minutes | Cook: 30 minutes

2½	pounds butternut squash, cooked until tender		1	tablespoon curry powder
4	tablespoons butter		4	cups chicken broth
4	large shallots, coarsely chopped			plain yogurt and fresh mint for garnish
2	cloves garlic, coarsely chopped			

Cook squash in oven or boiling water until tender; set aside until cool enough to handle. Alternatively, cook in microwave, cut side down, on a plate for 8 to 10 minutes or until tender. Meanwhile, melt butter in a stockpot. Add shallots, garlic, and curry and sauté for 5 minutes. Scoop out pulp of cooled squash and add to pot. Add broth and bring to a simmer. Cook for 30 minutes. Purée soup in a blender and season to taste. Garnish with plain yogurt and fresh mint.

To make this recipe vegetarian, substitute vegetable broth for chicken broth.

NUTRITION INFORMATION: 153 calories, 8 g fat, 5 g saturated fat, 20 mg cholesterol, 389 mg sodium, 21 g carbohydrate, 4 g sugars, 4 g fiber, 3 g protein.

chilean seafood stew

Serves: *4-6 portions*

Prep: less than 30 minutes | Cook: 45-60 minutes

3	tablespoons olive oil		1	cup dry white wine
1	large onion, thinly sliced		1	bay leaf
2	cloves garlic, minced		¼	cup lemon juice
½	tablespoon sweet paprika		4	sprigs parsley
¼	red bell pepper, thinly sliced			salt and pepper to taste
6	small potatoes, thinly sliced		1	pound (2-inch thick) firm white fish, cut into 1-inch cubes
2	carrots, thinly sliced		1	pound clams in the shell, or mussels
6	cups fish stock or clam juice		½	cup minced fresh parsley for garnish

Heat oil in a large saucepan over medium heat. Add onions and sauté 4 minutes or until softened but not browned. Add garlic, paprika, bell peppers, potatoes, and carrots. Cook, stirring occasionally, for about 2 minutes. Add stock, wine, bay leaf, lemon juice, parsley sprigs, and salt and pepper. Bring to a boil. Reduce heat and simmer for 15 to 20 minutes. Add fish and clams. Simmer over low to medium heat for 10 to 15 minutes until fish turns opaque and clams open. Remove bay leaf and parsley sprigs. Serve with crusty bread and garnish with minced parsley.

NUTRITION INFORMATION: 424 calories, 15 g fat, 2 g saturated fat, 56 mg cholesterol, 133 mg sodium, 28 g carbohydrate, 6 g sugars, 5 g fiber, 34 g protein.

Wine Pairing: A dry Riesling would be perfect. It has the acidity to handle the texture of the soup and the fruitiness to match the spices.

butternut squash and apple soup

Serves: *6 portions*

Prep: less than 30 minutes | Cook: 45 minutes

2	onions, chopped
3	tablespoons butter
2½	cups diced butternut squash
1	Granny Smith apple, peeled and chopped
3	tablespoons all-purpose flour
1½	teaspoons curry powder
	pinch of grated nutmeg
3	cups chicken broth

1	cup milk
½	cup half-and-half, or heavy cream for a richer result
	zest and juice of 1 orange
	salt and pepper to taste
½	teaspoon sugar, or to taste
	whipped cream or sour cream and chopped parsley for garnish

In a ½- to 3-quart saucepan, sauté onions in butter for about 5 minutes or until soft. Add squash and apples and sauté about 3 minutes, stirring occasionally. Add flour, curry powder, and nutmeg. Cook for 2 minutes. Add chicken broth, milk, half-and-half, and orange zest and juice. Simmer slowly, uncovered, for 15 to 20 minutes or until the vegetables are tender.

Purée the soup in a blender or food processor. Season with salt and pepper and sugar. Serve hot, topped with a dollop of cream and a sprinkling of parsley.

This soup improves with time. Prepare a day or two in advance, if time allows; keep refrigerated.

NUTRITION INFORMATION: 178 calories, 10 g fat, 6 g saturated fat, 27 mg cholesterol, 315 mg sodium, 22 g carbohydrate, 10 g sugars, 3 g fiber, 4 g protein.

Chef Tip: Why are Granny Smith apples used in so many recipes? They are slightly tart, giving good balance to recipes and do not have that grainy texture from other types of apples.

Beer Pairing: A malty Scottish Ale rinses the creamy butternut texture of this soup, while accenting its flavor.

Wine Pairing: Chenin Blanc has softer, fruitier flavors that would do well with the tartness of the apples and the sweetness of the broth. South Africa, France, and California.

chicken tortilla soup

Serves: *8 portions*

Prep: 45 minutes | Cook: 30 minutes

1   tablespoon vegetable oil

1   large onion, chopped

1   green bell pepper, chopped

1   red bell pepper, chopped

1   yellow bell pepper, chopped

4   carrots, chopped

1   4 ounce can chopped green chiles

1   teaspoon chili powder

1   teaspoon ground cumin

1   teaspoon minced garlic

1   teaspoon dried crushed oregano

¼   teaspoon cayenne pepper

6   cups chicken broth

1   16 ounce can diced tomatoes, with liquid

12   ounces boneless, skinless chicken breast, cut into thin strips

2   cups fresh or frozen corn kernels

     salt and pepper to taste

⅓   cup chopped fresh cilantro

⅓   cup fresh lime juice

     tortilla chips, or corn tortillas browned in canola oil

6   ounces Monterey Jack cheese, shredded

     diced tomato, diced avocado, and cilantro for garnish, optional

In a large stockpot, heat oil. Add onions, all bell peppers, and carrots and sauté over medium heat for 10 minutes or until onion is translucent. Add green chiles, chili powder, cumin, garlic, oregano, and cayenne. Cook, stirring constantly, for 1 minute. Stir in chicken broth and undrained tomatoes and bring to a boil. Reduce heat and add chicken. Simmer for 15 to 20 minutes. Add corn and simmer for 1 minute. Season with salt and pepper. Stir in cilantro and lime juice.

To serve, place a few tortilla chips in the bottom of soup bowls. Ladle soup into bowls and top with cheese. For a colorful presentation, also top with tomato, avocado, and cilantro.

NUTRITION INFORMATION: 228 calories, 9 g fat, 4 g saturated fat, 44 mg cholesterol, 701 mg sodium, 21 g carbohydrate, 8 g sugars, 5 g fiber, 18 g protein.

Chef Tip: Simmer soup uncovered to concentrate the flavor.

Wine Pairing: Riesling that has a touch of sweetness and more peach tones would be a treat. Colorado produces some wonderful examples.

chilled strawberry soup

Serves: *30 portions*

Prep: less than 30 minutes | Cook: 30 minutes

9	cups water	6	quarts strawberries, stemmed and puréed, or frozen, thawed and puréed
4½	cups light red wine	3½	cups heavy cream, whipped
3	cups sugar	1½	cups sour cream
¾	cup fresh lemon juice		
4	sticks cinnamon		

Combine water, wine, sugar, lemon juice, and cinnamon sticks in large pot. Boil, uncovered, for 15 minutes, stirring occasionally. Add strawberry purée. Boil, stirring frequently, for 10 minutes. Discard cinnamon sticks. Chill strawberry mixture.

Combine whipped cream with sour cream and fold into strawberry mixture. Serve slightly chilled.

NUTRITION INFORMATION: 248 calories, 13 g fat, 8 g saturated fat, 46 mg cholesterol, 19 mg sodium, 31 g carbohydrate, 26 g sugars, 2 g fiber, 2 g protein.

thai chicken and coconut soup

Serves: *6 portions*

Prep: less than 30 minutes | Cook: 30 minutes

5	cups chicken broth	3	tablespoons brown sugar
¼	teaspoon hot chile flakes, optional	1	13½ ounce can regular coconut milk
⅓	cup fresh lime juice	1	13½ ounce can reduced fat coconut milk
¼	cup thinly sliced ginger	4	cups bite-size chopped cooked chicken
2	cloves garlic, thinly sliced	1	fresh jalapeño pepper, sliced
2	tablespoons soy sauce	3	cups cooked rice
1	tablespoon Thai fish sauce	¼-½	cup slivered fresh basil, optional

In a large pot, combine chicken broth, chile flakes, lime juice, ginger, garlic, soy sauce, fish sauce, and brown sugar. Bring to a boil, then reduce heat. Cover and simmer for 20 minutes. Remove garlic and ginger with a slotted spoon. Add all coconut milk, chicken, and jalapeños. Stir over medium heat just until hot; do not boil. Divide rice among soup bowls and spoon soup over top. Garnish with basil.

NUTRITION INFORMATION: 489 calories, 24 g fat, 16 g saturated fat, 84 mg cholesterol, 1055 mg sodium, 36 g carbohydrate, 9 g sugars, 1 g fiber, 31 g protein.

grand junction gazpacho

Serves: *12 portions*

Prep: 45 minutes

1	46 ounce can spicy hot tomato juice	2	tablespoons chopped fresh basil
1	28 ounce can Italian-style tomatoes	2	tablespoons chopped fresh oregano
1	10½ ounce can condensed beef broth	2	cloves garlic, minced
2	yellow tomatoes, chopped	2	tablespoons white vinegar
3	red tomatoes, chopped	1	tablespoon Worcestershire sauce
1	large cucumber, seeded and chopped	½	teaspoon salt
1	green bell pepper, chopped	1	teaspoon black pepper
1	bunch green onions, chopped		avocado slices for garnish

Combine all ingredients except avocado in a food processor and pulse. Cover and refrigerate 2 hours or overnight. Serve chilled. Top with avocado slices.

To make this recipe vegetarian, substitute vegetable broth for the beef broth.

NUTRITION INFORMATION: 64 calories, 0 g fat, 0 g saturated fat, 0 mg cholesterol, 747 mg sodium, 12 g carbohydrate, 8 g sugars, 3 g fiber, 3 g protein.

supper soup (italian stew)

Serves: *6-8 portions*

Prep: less than 30 minutes | Cook: 45 minutes

2	tablespoons olive oil	½	cup red wine
1	medium onion, chopped	2	14 ounce cans chicken or beef broth
1	pound ground turkey or lean ground beef	1	teaspoon salt
1	medium eggplant, diced	1	teaspoon sugar
1	large clove garlic, minced	½	teaspoon black pepper
½	cup chopped carrot	½	cup dry macaroni pasta, or pasta of choice
½	cup chopped celery	2	tablespoons chopped Italian parsley
1	28 ounce can Italian-style tomatoes, chopped, with liquid		Parmesan cheese for garnish

Heat olive oil in a 5-quart kettle over medium heat. Add onions and cook, stirring, until softened. Crumble meat into kettle and cook, stirring to break up, until browned. Add eggplant, garlic, carrots, celery, tomatoes with liquid, wine, broth, salt, sugar, and pepper. Bring to a boil. Cover, reduce heat, and simmer for about 30 minutes. Add pasta and parsley and cover. Simmer 10 minutes or until macaroni is tender. Sprinkle individual servings with Parmesan cheese.

NUTRITION INFORMATION: 248 calories, 10 g fat, 2 g saturated fat, 43 mg cholesterol, 1310 mg sodium, 20 g carbohydrate, 8 g sugars, 5 g fiber, 19 g protein.

southwestern crab chowder

Serves: *6 portions*

Prep: less than 30 minutes | Cook: about 40 minutes

5	ounces slab bacon	¼	cup dry orzo pasta
3	tablespoons butter	1	14 ounce can corn, drained, or 1¾ cups frozen
2	medium onions, finely minced	2	6 ounce cans lump crabmeat, or ½ pound fresh, picked over
1	large red bell pepper, finely diced	3	tablespoons minced fresh cilantro
2	teaspoons seeded and finely minced jalapeño peppers	1-3	teaspoons Creole or Old Bay seasoning, or a little of both per taste, optional
1	4 ounce can roasted diced green chiles		salt and freshly ground pepper to taste
2	tablespoons all-purpose flour		
2	cups low-sodium chicken broth		
2	cups half-and-half		

Place enough water in a pot to cover bacon. Bring water to a boil and blanch bacon for 2 to 3 minutes or until the bacon begins to cook; this will help reduce the saltiness of the bacon, but leave the great smoky flavor. Drain off water and dry bacon with a kitchen or paper towel. (Make sure not to leave any paper on bacon.) Dice bacon into small cubes.

Melt butter in a 3½-quart soup pot over medium heat. Add bacon and cook until lightly browned. Add onions and both peppers. Cook for 5 minutes or until onions start to become translucent. Add chiles and cook and stir 1 minute to warm. Stir in flour and cook for 1 minute. Whisk in broth and half-and-half and simmer, partially covered, for 15 minutes. Add orzo and cook for 5 to 7 minutes or until tender. Add corn and crabmeat and heat through. Add cilantro and season to taste with Creole seasoning and salt and pepper.

In the summer, substitute fresh corn, cut from the cob and add with liquids to cook. You can also lighten up in the summer with 4 cups broth and 1 cup cream.

For a more Mediterranean flair, omit green chiles, cilantro, and Creole or Old Bay seasoning and substitute 1 14-ounce can diced tomatoes, drained, basil, and fines herbes or Italian seasoning.

NUTRITION INFORMATION: 458 calories, 30 g fat, 15 g saturated fat, 111 mg cholesterol, 701 mg sodium, 25 g carbohydrate, 8 g sugars, 3 g fiber, 20 g protein.

kielbasa black bean chili

Serves: *8 portions*

Prep: 45 minutes | Cook: 1-2 hours

---

2 tablespoons olive oil, or more if needed

1½ pounds turkey or beef kielbasa or Canino's Bratwurst, quartered lengthwise, then cut into ½-inch pieces

2 cups chopped onions

1 red bell pepper, coarsely chopped

1 green bell pepper, coarsely chopped

4 large cloves garlic, chopped

4 15 ounce cans black beans, drained and rinsed

1 32 ounce box organic chicken broth

1 28 ounce can diced tomatoes in juice

3-4 tablespoons chili powder, depending on desired spiciness

2 tablespoons sugar

2½ tablespoons red wine vinegar

3 small bay leaves

1½ tablespoons dried oregano

2½ teaspoons ground cumin

1½ tablespoons salt, or more to taste

sour cream and chopped green onions for topping

Heat 2 tablespoons olive oil in heavy large pot over medium-high heat. Add kielbasa or bratwurst and sauté 12 minutes or until beginning to brown. Using a slotted spoon, transfer kielbasa or bratwurst to a bowl. If necessary, add more olive oil to drippings in pot to measure 2 tablespoons, or discard all but 2 tablespoons of drippings. Add onions, both bell peppers, and garlic. Sauté 10 minutes or until beginning to brown. Add beans, broth, tomatoes with juice, chili powder, sugar, vinegar, bay leaves, oregano, and cumin. Bring to a boil, stirring occasionally. Reduce heat to medium, cover, and simmer 30 minutes. Return kielbasa or bratwurst to pot. Reduce heat to low. Simmer, uncovered, for 30 minutes or until chili is thick, stirring occasionally. Season with salt and pepper.

Chili can be made a day ahead. Cool slightly; cover, and chill. Rewarm before serving.

NUTRITION INFORMATION: 388 calories, 8 g fat, 1 g saturated fat, 30 mg cholesterol, 3035 mg sodium, 53 g carbohydrate, 14 g sugars, 16 g fiber, 24 g protein.

Chef Tip: Try to make all soups, stews, and chilis at least a day ahead so that the flavors mesh and develop.

Beer Pairing: Cleanse your palate for the next bite of this rich chili with a mildly hoppy British Pale Ale.

sweet chicken salad sandwich

Serves: *8-10 portions*

Prep: less than 30 minutes

4	cups chopped cooked chicken	⅓	cup orange blossom or plain honey
3	stalks celery, chopped	¼	teaspoon salt
1	cup dried sweetened cranberries	¼	teaspoon black pepper
½	cup pecans, toasted	8-10	small croissants
1½	cups light mayonnaise		

Combine chicken, celery, cranberries, and pecans in a bowl. In a separate bowl, whisk together mayonnaise, honey, salt, and pepper. Combine dressing with chicken mixture. Serve on croissants or bread of choice.

NUTRITION INFORMATION: 597 calories, 34 g fat, 10 g saturated fat, 106 mg cholesterol, 801 mg sodium, 48 g carbohydrate, 28 g sugars, 3 g fiber, 24 g protein.

not-your-ordinary reuben sandwich

Serves: *12 portions*

Prep: less than 30 minutes | Cook: 5 minutes

1	loaf light or dark rye bread		8	ounces cream cheese
	mustard to taste		1	pound corn beef, sliced deli thin
1	16 ounce can sauerkraut, drained		1	pound Swiss cheese, thinly sliced

Preheat broiler. Spread one side of bread slices with mustard. Combine sauerkraut and cream cheese with a mixer. Put corn beef on a bread slice and add cream cheese mixture on top of corn beef. Place a slice of cheese on top. Repeat for each sandwich. Broil until cheese bubbles.

NUTRITION INFORMATION: 368 calories, 21 g fat, 12 g saturated fat, 82 mg cholesterol, 1150 mg sodium, 23 g carbohydrate, 3 g sugars, 3 g fiber, 23 g protein.

Chef Tip: Why is it called corned beef? The size of salt that used to be used to cure the beef is corn kernel size.

cuban sandwich

Serves: *4 portions*

Prep: less than 30 minutes | Bake: 20 to 30 minutes in oven, not including cooking time for pork

CUBAN PORK

3	heads garlic		⅓	cup lime juice
2	teaspoons salt		1	cup minced onion
1	teaspoon black peppercorns		2	teaspoons oregano
¾	cup orange juice		1	cup olive oil
⅓	cup lemon juice		3-4	pounds pork roast

SANDWICH

1	French baguette bread		4	deli slices Black Forest ham
2	tablespoons butter		4	deli slices Swiss cheese
2	cups shredded Cuban Pork		4-6	dill pickle slices

Combine all pork ingredients and marinate overnight. Drain pork, reserving marinade. Brown pork in a skillet for 2 to 3 minutes on each side to seal in juices. Place browned pork and ¾ cup reserved marinade in a greased crock pot. Cook for 8 to 10 hours. Shred pork.

To make sandwich, preheat oven to 350 degrees. Cut bread in half lengthwise. Butter inside of both halves. Layer pork, ham, cheese, and pickle one side of bread. Place top of bread on sandwich and press down. Wrap in foil and bake for 20 to 30 minutes, or grill with butter in a skillet or pressed in a sandwich press. Sandwich should be served hot with cheese melted so flavors can combine.

NUTRITION INFORMATION: 476 calories, 22 g fat, 11 g saturated fat, 108 mg cholesterol, 1091 mg sodium, 34 g carbohydrate, 2 g sugars, 1 g fiber, 35 g protein.

Beer Pairing: Try this with a sweet Pumpkin beer or Raspberry Wheat.

Wine Pairing: This is a sandwich that would need a full-flavored white that is more fruit driven. Chardonnay would be delicious, just try one with less oak.

mountain muffulettas

Serves: *8 portions*

Prep: less than 30 minutes | Cook: 8 hours with refrigeration

2 cups Olive Salad (recipe below)

1 French, Italian, or Sourdough bread bowl, halved horizontally

½ pound sliced salami

½ pound sliced ham

8 slices provolone cheese

Spread half of Olive Salad evenly over bottom half of bread. Layer salami, ham, and cheese on top and spread with remaining Olive Salad. Cover with top half of bread. Refrigerate 4 hours.

NUTRITION INFORMATION: 685 calories, 44 g fat, 7 g saturated fat, 56 mg cholesterol, 2343 mg sodium, 46 g carbohydrate, 2 g sugars, 3 g fiber, 26 g protein.

OLIVE SALAD

1 1 quart jar hot giardiana pickled vegetables

1 red onion, diced

1 16 ounce jar pitted green olives, drained

2 2¼ ounce cans chopped ripe olives, drained

¼ cup chopped pepperoncini peppers

5 cloves garlic, minced

½ cup olive oil

1 teaspoon dried parsley

1 teaspoon dried oregano

1 teaspoon dried basil

½ teaspoon black pepper

½ teaspoon salt

For Olive Salad: Drain pickled vegetables, reserving ¼ cup liquid. Combine pickled vegetables with all other ingredients in a food processor and pulse until coarsely chopped. Stir in reserved vegetable liquid. Cover and refrigerate 8 hours.

Wine Pairing: A soft, fruity Merlot with lots of red fruits would be the perfect accompaniment to the olives and spices for this delightful sandwich.

grilled apple sandwich

Serves: *1 portion*

Prep: 10 minutes | Cook: 5 minutes

2   slices whole wheat bread

1½   teaspoons olive oil

½   Granny Smith apple, peeled and thinly sliced (use a mandolin or food processor for best results)

⅓   cup shredded Swiss cheese, or baby Brie cut into small cubes, rind removed

Preheat a skillet over medium heat. Lightly brush 1 side of each slice of bread with olive oil. Place 1 slice of bread, olive oil-side down, into skillet. Arrange apple slices evenly over bread. Sprinkle with cheese and top with remaining slice of bread, olive oil-side up. Cook until bread is golden brown, then turn sandwich and cook 1 to 2 minutes longer or until the other side is golden brown and the cheese has melted.

NUTRITION INFORMATION: 368 calories, 19 g fat, 8 g saturated fat, 34 mg cholesterol, 335 mg sodium, 33 g carbohydrate, 10 g sugars, 5 g fiber, 17 g protein.

green chile and chicken sandwich

Serves: *4 portions*

Prep: less than 30 minutes | Bake: 15-20 minutes

softened butter

4   hoagie rolls, split

1   pound cooked chicken strips, from leftover chicken or frozen packaged strips, thawed

¼   teaspoon salt

¼   teaspoon black pepper

¼   teaspoon ground cumin

¼   teaspoon cayenne pepper

½   teaspoon garlic powder

2   green onions, chopped

4   roasted green chiles, peeled and seeded, or 1 4-ounce can whole green chiles

6   ounces Pepper Jack cheese, shredded

Preheat oven to 400 degrees . Spread butter on inside of rolls. Place bottom of rolls on a baking sheet. Heat a medium skillet coated with cooking spray over medium heat. Add chicken and stir for 3 to 4 minutes or until chicken is warm. Add salt, black pepper, cumin, cayenne, garlic powder, and green onions and toss to combine. Divide chicken mixture among bottom halves of rolls. Top each with a green chile and one-fourth of cheese. Replace top halves of rolls. Bake for 5 to 10 minutes or until cheese melts. Serve hot.

NUTRITION INFORMATION: 564 calories, 23 g fat, 12 g saturated fat, 134 mg cholesterol, 941 mg sodium, 35 g carbohydrate, 4 g sugars, 4 g fiber, 51 g protein.

Chef Tip: If you have a gas range, roast your own directly over the fire. Use tongs to turn the peppers. Then rinse off charred skin with water. It makes the house smell great.

Beer Pairing: Chili plus chicken equals a great chance to enjoy an aggressive yet balanced India Pale Ale.

classique
vegetarian & sides

city style stuffed portabella mushrooms

Serves: *4 portions*

Prep: less than 30 minutes | Grill: 4 minutes

---

4   whole portabella mushrooms, washed and
        patted dry, stems removed

     olive oil for basting

2   cups fresh grape tomatoes, halved

     fresh basil, chiffonade

     sea salt and cracked black pepper to taste

4   ounces goat cheese

     pepperoncini peppers, chopped

Preheat grill over medium heat. Brush mushrooms lightly with olive oil. Grill mushrooms for 5 minutes, top-side down.

Meanwhile, combine tomatoes, basil, and salt and pepper in a glass bowl. Let stand 10 minutes to allow the juices to come out.

Stuff mushrooms with tomato mixture. Top with goat cheese and sprinkle with a few pepperoncini peppers. Grill 5 minutes longer. Serve immediately.

Pairs well with hummus and toasted pitas to complete the meal.

NUTRITION INFORMATION: 124 calories, 8 g fat, 4 g saturated fat, 13 mg cholesterol, 117 mg sodium, 8 g carbohydrate, 4 g sugars, 2 g fiber, 7 g protein.

garlic squash ribbons

Serves: *4-6 portions*

Prep: less than 30 minutes | Cook: 20-25 minutes including slicing time

---

2   large zucchini

2   large yellow squash

2   tablespoons extra virgin olive oil

1   clove garlic, minced

1   tablespoon chopped fresh oregano

3   tablespoons chopped fresh basil

     salt and pepper to taste

     shaved fresh Parmesan cheese

Slice zucchini and yellow squash lengthwise into long ribbons with a vegetable peeler. In a large skillet, heat olive oil over medium heat. Add garlic and cook 30 seconds, stirring constantly. Add zucchini and yellow squash ribbons and oregano and toss to coat with oil. Sauté, stirring frequently, for 3 to 5 minutes or until just tender; do not overcook. Add basil and season with salt and pepper. Top with Parmesan cheese. Serve immediately.

NUTRITION INFORMATION: 108 calories, 7 g fat, 1 g saturated fat, 0 mg cholesterol, 16 mg sodium, 10 g carbohydrate, 6 g sugars, 3 g fiber, 4 g protein.

grilled eggplant parmesan

Serves: *6 portions*

Prep: less than 30 minutes | Grill: 30-35 minutes

2 cups chopped tomatoes

¼ cup extra virgin olive oil

1 tablespoon butter

1 bay leaf

salt and freshly ground black pepper to taste

3 white eggplants or small purple eggplants, halved lengthwise

2 tablespoons olive oil

6 tablespoons Parmesan cheese

Combine tomatoes, ¼ cup olive oil, butter, and bay leaf in a small, nonreactive pot. Simmer over medium heat, stirring occasionally, for 15 to 20 minutes or until tomatoes break down and become saucy. Remove from heat and season with salt and pepper; discard bay leaf.

Preheat grill over medium-high heat. Brush eggplants with 2 tablespoons olive oil and season generously with salt and pepper. Set the eggplants, skin-side down, on grill. Cover and grill 25 to 30 minutes or until the eggplant skin chars, the juices boil up through the flesh, and the flesh is tender. Use tongs to move the eggplants around on grill so they cook evenly. Holding an eggplant half with tongs, make an indentation in the flesh with the back of a spoon. Spoon 1 generous tablespoon of puréed tomatoes into the indentation. Repeat for all eggplant halves. If there is extra sauce, use a fork to push down the soft flesh of the eggplant and spoon remaining sauce into the indentation. Grill, covered, for 2 minutes longer or until the sauce is hot. Sprinkle each eggplant with 1 tablespoon Parmesan and cook, covered, for 2 to 3 minutes or just until cheese begins to melt.

NUTRITION INFORMATION: 223 calories, 17 g fat, 4 g saturated fat, 9 mg cholesterol, 98 mg sodium, 16 g carbohydrate, 7 g sugars, 8 g fiber, 5 g protein.

parmesan potatoes

Serves: *12 portions*

Prep: 45 minutes | Cook: 3 minutes

12	small round red potatoes (about 1 pound)	⅛	teaspoon freshly ground black pepper
2	teaspoons olive oil	3	cloves garlic, minced
¾	cup minced red onion	½	cup freshly grated Parmesan cheese
¼	cup raw diced bacon (about 2 slices)	1	teaspoon rubbed sage

Cook potatoes in boiling water for 15 minutes or until tender; drain. Heat olive oil in a nonstick skillet over medium-high heat. Add onion, bacon, pepper, and garlic and sauté for 5 minutes or until tender.

Preheat broiler. Cut potatoes in half. Carefully scoop out pulp with a melon baller or spoon, leaving a ¼-inch shell. Mash potato pulp in a bowl with a fork. Stir in cheese and sage. Mix potato with onion mixture, stirring well. Spoon about 1 tablespoon of potato mixture into each potato shell. Arrange stuffed potatoes on a baking sheet. Broil 3 to 4 inches from heat for 3 minutes or until lightly browned. Serve warm.

NUTRITION INFORMATION: 77 calories, 4 g fat, 2 g saturated fat, 5 mg cholesterol, 80 mg sodium, 8 g carbohydrate, 1 g sugars, 1 g fiber, 3 g protein.

mustard roasted potatoes

Serves: *4-6 portions*

Prep: less than 30 minutes | Bake: 35-40 minutes

3	tablespoons Dijon mustard		freshly ground black pepper to taste
2	tablespoons olive oil	3	medium potatoes, peeled and 1½-inch cubed
2	tablespoons freshly grated Parmesan cheese		

Preheat oven to 425 degrees. Combine mustard, olive oil, cheese, and pepper in a large bowl and whisk to blend. Add potatoes and toss to coat well. Spread potatoes on a lightly greased baking sheet. Bake for 35 to 40 minutes or until browned and tender.

NUTRITION INFORMATION: 212 calories, 8 g fat, 1 g saturated fat, 2 mg cholesterol, 277 mg sodium, 31 g carbohydrate, 2 g sugars, 3 g fiber, 5 g protein.

Potato Tips

Brought to you by:

Colorado Potato Administrative Committee
"Quality at its Peak"

DID YOU KNOW...the San Luis Valley in Colorado is the largest and highest alpine valley in the world capable of producing controlled crops? Elevation in the Valley ranges from 7,400 to 8,000 feet above sea level.

Colorado potatoes are grown in the San Luis Valley, unique in world topography. The Valley is a large, flat intermountain valley that varies from 20 to 50 miles in width and is about 100 miles north to south. There are 56,000 acres of potatoes planted here! The Valley's spring and summer are filled with warm, sunny days and cool nights, the combination for a perfect growing season. The cool weather also contributes to the smoothness of the skin and reduces second-growth roughness. This isolated alpine desert with its cold winters helps eliminate or reduce pest and disease problems, reducing our need for many pesticides. Because the Valley receives less than seven inches of rain a year, it qualifies as a desert and must be irrigated. A natural underground water aquifer, recharged from runoff from heavy snowfall in the nearby mountains, offers a plentiful irrigation source.

Quick Tip

Fill your crock pot with as many washed and foil-wrapped potatoes as will fit. Cook on low for 8 hours or high for 4 hours to have perfectly-baked potatoes when you come home from work. You will also have potatoes ready for frying, soup, baked wedges, twice bakes, etc. for several meals in the future.

www.coloradopotato.org

oven roasted root vegetables

Serves: *4-6 portions*

Prep: 45 minutes | Bake: 60 minutes

3-4 yams, sweet potatoes, or kumara, peeled

1-2 large parsnips, peeled

4-8 baby turnips, peeled

1 bunch medium beets, peeled

4-6 slender carrots, peeled

1 medium onion

1 whole head garlic, separated into cloves, peeled

2 sprigs fresh rosemary

sea salt and freshly ground black pepper to taste

extra virgin olive oil

Preheat oven to 400 degrees. Cut all vegetables, on the diagonal, into 1½-inch chunks. Spread all cut vegetables, garlic, and rosemary sprigs in a single layer in a large baking dish or on a couple of baking sheets. Season with sea salt and freshly ground pepper. Drizzle with olive oil and toss with hands to coat the vegetables evenly. Roast, stirring occasionally, for 1 hour or until the vegetables are tender and golden brown.

NUTRITION INFORMATION: 263 calories, 4 g fat, 1 g saturated fat, 0 mg cholesterol, 246 mg sodium, 54 g carbohydrate, 22 g sugars, 12 g fiber, 6 g protein.

ratatouille salad with roasted yellow tomato sauce

Serves: *6 portions*

Prep: less than 30 minutes | Bake: 30 minutes

ROASTED YELLOW TOMATO SAUCE

2   6-inch branches fresh rosemary, stems removed and leaves finely chopped (2 teaspoons)

1   bunch fresh thyme, leaves only (1 teaspoon)

2   pounds yellow tomatoes (8 small), halved

2   tablespoons basil oil

    flaky sea salt

2   pinches saffron threads

1   tablespoon basil oil

    Freshly ground white pepper

RATATOUILLE SALAD

2   red bell peppers, cored and seeded, cut into 2-inch long julienne

1   yellow bell pepper, cored and seeded, cut into 2-inch long julienne

1   orange bell pepper, cored and seeded, cut into 2-inch long julienne

1   large zucchini, 2-inch julienne

2   tablespoons extra virgin olive oil

6   cloves garlic, poached until soft, then minced

24 oil-cured kalamata olives, finely chopped

8   large basil leaves, julienned

2   tablespoons basil oil

    sea salt flakes and freshly ground white pepper

1   6 ounce peppercorn goat cheese log, cut into ¼-inch disks

    basil florets for garnish

Preheat oven on convection setting of 450 degrees. If using a standard oven, increase temperature to 475 degrees. In a 1-gallon zip-top bag, combine rosemary, thyme, tomatoes, 2 tablespoons basil oil, and a large pinch of sea salt and toss until tomatoes are evenly coated. Place tomatoes with juice in a shallow casserole dish. Roast on top rack of oven for 20 minutes or until golden brown around the edges; cool. Transfer tomatoes to a blender and purée until smooth. Pass sauce through a sieve to remove skin and seeds. Transfer to saucepan. Crumble in saffron threads. Add 1 tablespoon basil oil and simmer 10 minutes or until reduced by half. Season with another large pinch of sea salt and white pepper to taste.

To make salad, combine all bell peppers, zucchini, olive oil, garlic, and olives in a 1-gallon zip-top bag. Microwave in bag for 2 to 3 minutes or until just hot and al dente; or sauté mixture over high heat for 2 to 3 minutes or until al dente. Transfer to a bowl and toss with fresh basil and basil oil. Season with sea salt and white pepper to taste.

To serve, ladle sauce onto a plate. Top with a mound of salad. Arrange goat cheese around salad and garnish with a basil floret.

Use Maldon brand sea salt flakes.

NUTRITION INFORMATION: 317 calories, 27 g fat, 7 g saturated fat, 13 mg cholesterol, 392 mg sodium, 13 g carbohydrate, 4 g sugars, 3 g fiber, 8 g protein.

garlic roasted tomatoes

Serves: *4 portions*

Prep: less than 30 minutes | Bake: 50 minutes

8	Roma tomatoes, halved length-wise	½	teaspoon dried thyme and/or basil
1	tablespoon olive oil	½	teaspoon black pepper
½	teaspoon salt	4	cloves garlic, minced

Preheat oven to 350 degrees. Place tomatoes, cut-side up, on a greased foil-lined baking sheet. Combine olive oil, salt, herbs, pepper, and garlic. Drizzle oil mixture over tomatoes. Bake for about 50 minutes.

NUTRITION INFORMATION: 58 calories, 4 g fat, 1 g saturated fat, 0 mg cholesterol, 298 mg sodium, 6 g carbohydrate, 3 g sugars, 2 g fiber, 1 g protein.

sesame asparagus

Serves: *4 portions*

Prep: 30 minutes | Cook: 15 minutes

1	pound asparagus, tough ends trimmed, sliced diagonally into 4-inch pieces	1	tablespoon rice wine vinegar
	Salt, optional	¼	teaspoon black pepper
2	tablespoons olive oil	¼	teaspoon dried red pepper flakes
6	green onions, thinly sliced diagonally	2	tablespoons sesame seeds, toasted
		1	teaspoon toasted sesame oil

Bring 2-3 inches of salted water to a rapid boil in a 2-quart saucepan. Meanwhile, prepare a large bowl of ice water. Add asparagus to boiling water and blanch for 2 to 3 minutes. Remove asparagus from water with tongs and place in ice water until cooled. Remove asparagus with tongs and let rest on a platter. Heat olive oil over medium heat in a skillet. Add asparagus, green onions, and vinegar and sauté 2 minutes. Season with black pepper and red pepper flakes. Add sesame seeds and sesame oil and turn gently to coat. Transfer with tongs to a serving dish. Serve hot.

NUTRITION INFORMATION: 135 calories, 11 g fat, 2 g saturated fat, 0 mg cholesterol, 10 mg sodium, 8 g carbohydrate, 4 g sugars, 4 g fiber, 3 g protein.

Chef Tip: For proper sautéing, make sure the oil is very hot. Listen to your food; if it does not sizzle when you add it to the pan, remove immediately and wait for the oil to heat. Otherwise you will have oily food.

mustard seed roasted corn

Serves: *6 portions*

Prep: less than 30 minutes | Cook: 10 minutes

6-8 ears corn, or 4 cups frozen, thawed

3 tablespoons olive oil

½ teaspoon brown mustard seed

1-2 serrano chiles, seeds and ribs removed, minced

¼ teaspoon turmeric

  salt to taste

1 tablespoon minced cilantro

Slice kernels off ears of fresh corn. Heat olive oil in a wok or skillet over medium-high heat. Add mustard seeds and cover. When seeds stop popping, reduce heat to medium and add chiles. Cook and stir for 30 seconds. Stir in turmeric. Add corn, season with salt, and toss to mix. Reduce heat to low, cover, and cook 5 minutes for fresh or 1 minute for frozen or until corn is tender. Serve warm.

NUTRITION INFORMATION: 139 calories, 8 g fat, 1 g saturated fat, 0 mg cholesterol, 14 mg sodium, 17 g carbohydrate, 3 g sugars, 3 g fiber, 3 g protein.

grape tomatoes with three vinegar dressing

Serves: *4-6 portions*

Prep: less than 30 minutes

2 cups grape tomatoes, halved

1 large clove garlic, minced

1 teaspoon champagne vinegar

1 teaspoon red wine vinegar

1 teaspoon sherry vinegar

1 tablespoon extra virgin olive oil

1 medium shallot, finely chopped

1 tablespoon finely chopped fresh basil, cilantro, and/or tarragon

Combine all ingredients. Marinate for at least 1 hour at room temperature, stirring occasionally, or prepare up to 6 hours in advance and refrigerate.

NUTRITION INFORMATION: 58 calories, 4 g fat, 1 g saturated fat, 0 mg cholesterol, 11 mg sodium, 6 g carbohydrate, 3 g sugars, 1 g fiber, 1 g protein.

mediterranean green beans

Serves: *4 portions*

Prep: less than 30 minutes | Cook: 15 minutes

⅓ cup pine nuts

1½ pounds fresh green beans, cut into ½-inch pieces

1½ teaspoons finely grated lemon zest

2 tablespoons chopped fresh flat-leaf parsley

4 teaspoons olive oil

salt and pepper to taste

Toast pine nuts in a hot skillet. Cook beans in salted boiling water for 7 minutes or until just tender; drain. Toss hot beans in a bowl with lemon zest, parsley, olive oil, and toasted pine nuts. Season with salt and pepper.

NUTRITION INFORMATION: 145 calories, 10 g fat, 1 g saturated fat, 0 mg cholesterol, 12 mg sodium, 14 g carbohydrate, 3 g sugars, 6 g fiber, 6 g protein.

rice and parmesan stuffed zucchini

Serves: *4 portions*

Prep: less than 30 minutes | Bake: 40 minutes

4 medium zucchini, ends trimmed, halved lengthwise

1 tablespoon butter

2 large shallots, finely chopped

½ teaspoon salt

¼ teaspoon freshly ground black pepper

2 sprigs fresh thyme

1 cup cooked brown rice

¼ cup Parmesan cheese

¼ cup shredded Monterey Jack cheese

1 egg

1 tablespoon butter, melted

¼ cup seasoned bread crumbs

Preheat oven to 400 degrees. Scoop out centers of zucchini halves, leaving a ¼-inch thick shell. Finely chop zucchini centers. Melt 1 tablespoon butter in a skillet over medium-high heat. Add chopped zucchini, shallots, salt, and pepper. Cook 8 to 10 minutes or until zucchini is lightly browned, stirring often. Add sprigs of thyme during final 4 minutes of cooking. Transfer to a bowl and mix with rice and both cheeses; remove thyme sprigs. Stir in egg. Stuff mixture into zucchini shells. Arrange shells in a single layer in a shallow casserole dish. Bake for 20 minutes or until shells are tender when pierced. Mix melted butter with bread crumbs and sprinkle over stuffed zucchini. Broil 1 to 2 minutes or until crumbs are browned.

NUTRITION INFORMATION: 235 calories, 12 g fat, 6 g saturated fat, 79 mg cholesterol, 627 mg sodium, 25 g carbohydrate, 4 g sugars, 3 g fiber, 10 g protein.

spicy zucchini couscous

Serves: *6-8 portions*

Prep: 45 minutes | Cook: 20 minutes

1 cup reduced-sodium chicken broth	½ teaspoon salt
¼ teaspoon salt	1½ teaspoons ground coriander
¾ cup dry plain couscous	¾ teaspoon chili powder
2 tablespoons extra virgin olive oil	½ teaspoon ground cumin
1 medium onion, chopped	¼ teaspoon cayenne pepper, or to taste
¼ teaspoon salt	¼ teaspoon black pepper
1 garlic clove, minced	¼ cup chopped fresh mint
1 pound zucchini, ½-inch cubed	1 tablespoon fresh lime juice

Bring broth with ¼ teaspoon salt to a boil in a small saucepan. Pour broth over couscous in a bowl, cover, and let stand 5 minutes. Fluff with a fork and set aside until ready to use.

Meanwhile, heat olive oil in a 10-inch skillet over medium-high heat until hot but not smoking. Add onions with ¼ teaspoon salt and sauté, stirring occasionally, for 6 minutes or until soft. Add garlic and sauté, stirring, for 1 minute or until fragrant. Add zucchini and ½ teaspoon salt and sauté, stirring occasionally, for 5 minutes or until just tender. Reduce heat to medium-low. Stir in coriander, chili powder, cumin, cayenne pepper, and black pepper and cook, stirring frequently, for 2 minutes. Gently stir zucchini mixture into couscous and cool to warm or room temperature. Just before serving, stir in mint and lime juice.

NUTRITION INFORMATION: 150 calories, 5 g fat, 1 g saturated fat, 0 mg cholesterol, 469 mg sodium, 23 g carbohydrate, 3 g sugars, 3 g fiber, 5 g protein.

corn and potato gratin with rosemary

Serves: *10 portions*

Prep: less than 30 minutes | Bake: 15 minutes on stove top, 1 hour in oven

1½ tablespoons vegetable oil	2 tablespoons finely chopped fresh rosemary
1½ tablespoons butter	¾ teaspoon salt
2 cups fresh corn kernels (3 to 4 ears) or frozen, thawed	⅛ teaspoon cayenne pepper
3 tablespoons vegetable oil	2 cups half-and-half
2 cups ½-inch diced red skin potatoes, not peeled (about ⅔ pound)	4 eggs
1 cup chopped onions	1½ cups Gruyère cheese, grated and divided
	rosemary sprigs for garnish

Preheat oven to 350 degrees. Heat 1½ tablespoons oil and butter in a large heavy skillet over medium heat until hot. Add corn and sauté 6 minutes or until golden brown. Remove corn and set aside. Return skillet to medium heat and add 3 tablespoons oil. When oil is hot, add potatoes and onions. Sauté, stirring constantly, for about 8 minutes. Remove from heat and stir in corn, rosemary, salt, and cayenne.

In a large bowl, whisk together half-and-half and eggs. Add corn mixture and half of the cheese. Stir well and transfer to a greased shallow 2-quart baking dish. Bake on center rack for 25 minutes. Sprinkle top with remaining cheese and bake 20 minutes longer. Garnish with rosemary sprigs before serving.

Gratin can be made a day ahead, covered, and refrigerated. Reheat at 300 degrees for 30 minutes.

NUTRITION INFORMATION: 285 calories, 21 g fat, 9 g saturated fat, 125 mg cholesterol, 296 mg sodium, 15 g carbohydrate, 2 g sugars, 2 g fiber, 11 g protein.

Beer Pairing: A ruby-red winter warmer is the perfect companion for these corn and potatoes.

orzo with roasted vegetables

Serves: *6 generous portions*

Prep: less than 30 minutes | Bake: 45 minutes

1	small eggplant, peeled and ¾-inch diced
1	red bell pepper, 1-inch diced
1	yellow bell pepper, 1-inch diced
1	small zucchini, 1-inch diced
1	red onion, 1-inch diced
2	cloves garlic, minced
¼	cup extra virgin olive oil
1½	teaspoons kosher salt

½	teaspoon freshly ground pepper
8	ounces dry orzo pasta, regular or whole wheat
4	green onions, white and green parts, thinly sliced
⅓	cup pine nuts, toasted
1	cup crumbled feta cheese
15	large fresh basil leaves, cut into chiffonade

DRESSING

⅓	cup freshly squeezed lemon juice
⅓	cup extra virgin cold pressed olive oil

1	teaspoon sea salt
½	teaspoon freshly ground black pepper

Preheat oven to 425 degrees. Toss eggplant, bell peppers, zucchini, onions, and garlic with the olive oil, salt, and pepper on a large baking sheet. Roast for 40 minutes or until browned, turning once with a spatula.

Meanwhile, cook orzo in boiling salted water for 7 to 10 minutes or until tender; do not overcook. Drain and transfer to a large serving bowl.

Combine all dressing ingredients and pour over orzo. Add roasted vegetables, scraping all the liquid and seasonings from the baking sheet into the pasta bowl. Cool to room temperature. Add green onions, pine nuts, feta, and basil. Adjust seasonings to taste. Serve at room temperature.

This dish is even better made ahead. Add green onions, pine nuts, feta, and basil leaves and adjust seasoning just before serving.

NUTRITION INFORMATION: 476 calories, 31 g fat, 7 g saturated fat, 22 mg cholesterol, 1159 mg sodium, 42 g carbohydrate, 9 g sugars, 6 g fiber, 12 g protein.

cornbread apricot dressing

Serves: *12 portions*

Prep: 45 minutes | Bake: 75 minutes

1	6 ounce package cornbread mix		1	cup diced dried apricots
4	tablespoons unsalted butter		1	cup water
1	yellow onion, chopped		¼	cup minced flat leaf parsley
1	tablespoon minced rosemary			salt and pepper to taste
1	tablespoon minced sage		2	cups reduced-sodium chicken or vegetable broth, warmed

Prepare cornbread according to package instructions. Cool cornbread, then crumble into a large bowl to yield 8 cups; set aside. Bread can be covered at this point and stored overnight, if necessary.

Preheat oven to 325 degrees. Melt butter in a small saucepan over high heat. Add onions and sauté, stirring occasionally, for 5 minutes or until onions are tender and translucent. Add rosemary and sage and sauté, stirring, for 1 to 2 minutes or until fragrant. Add apricots and water. Bring to a simmer and cook 4 to 5 minutes or until liquid has nearly evaporated. Add onion mixture and parsley to cornbread in large bowl. Season with salt and pepper and toss gently. Add warmed broth and stir to blend. Transfer to a greased shallow baking dish. Bake for 35 minutes or until top is browned.

Fresh herbs are best in this recipe. If necessary to substitute dried herbs, use smaller amounts.

NUTRITION INFORMATION: 244 calories, 10 g fat, 4 g saturated fat, 36 mg cholesterol, 430 mg sodium, 35 g carbohydrate, 11 g sugars, 3 g fiber, 6 g protein.

italian rice salad

Serves: *4-6 portions*

Prep: less than 30 minutes | Cook: 20 minutes

2	cups reduced-sodium chicken broth		¼	cup olive oil
1	cup dry rice		¼	cup red wine vinegar, or more to taste
1	bunch asparagus, cut into 1 inch pieces			Cavender's Greek Seasoning to taste
⅔	package grape tomatoes, halved		½	cup shredded Parmesan cheese

Bring broth to a boil. Add rice, reduce heat, and simmer for 20 minutes. In a separate shallow pan, bring about 2 inches of water to a boil. Add asparagus and blanch for 3 to 5 minutes. Drain asparagus and rinse with cold water. Refrigerate asparagus to further chill. Spread cooked rice into a thin layer on a greased baking sheet with a rim. Place rice in freezer for 10 minutes to thoroughly cool. When cool, combine rice, asparagus, and halved tomatoes in a large bowl. Whisk together olive oil, vinegar, and Cavender's Greek seasoning and pour over rice mixture. Sprinkle with Parmesan cheese and toss well.

NUTRITION INFORMATION: 376 calories, 17 g fat, 4 g saturated fat, 7 mg cholesterol, 376 mg sodium, 47 g carbohydrate, 6 g sugars, 4 g fiber, 12 g protein.

Canino's Sausage

"Since 1925."

DID YOU KNOW...Sausage's history is as colorful as the Italian enclave that flourished north of downtown Denver in an area called "Little Italy." Little Italy wrapped around Our Lady of Mount Carmel, a Roman Catholic church built for Italian immigrants.

In 1897, 9-month old Lena Pagliano came to America. She wed Joseph J. Canino the day after Christmas, 1917. Eight years later, the couple established the Navajo Meat Market on the corner of 35th and Navajo. The site is now a Denver landmark.

The Caninos, and their hand-crafted sausage, remain integral to Little Italy's history.

CANINO'S SAUSAGE SOUP

2 pounds Canino's Italian Sausage Link (bite size)

1 onion, chopped

1 clove garlic, chopped

1 potato, diced

1 2½-pound can tomatoes

2 cups beef consommé

2 cans water

1 package frozen chopped spinach

1 can white beans

2 zucchini, sliced, optional

In a large pot, brown sausage. Transfer to a colander to drain off grease. In same pan, over medium heat, sweat onion and garlic for 5 minutes or until lightly browned. Return the drained sausage with all other ingredients to the pan. Simmer for at least 30 to 45 minutes. Serve with hard Italian roll.

www.caninosausage.com

apres ski baked beans

Serves: *10 portions*

Prep: less than 30 minutes | Bake: 2 hours

½	pound bacon		2	teaspoons dry mustard
2	large onions, minced		1	teaspoon garlic powder
1	pound Canino's Hot Italian Sausage, casings removed		2	teaspoons salt, optional
1	cup brown sugar		2	15 ounce cans kidney beans, drained
1	cup ketchup		2	15 ounce cans butter beans, drained
⅓	cup vinegar		2	15 ounce cans pork 'n beans
			1	15 ounce can lima beans, drained

Brown bacon in a skillet. Remove bacon and drain off excess fat. In same skillet, fry onions in remaining bacon fat until softened; set aside. Add sausage to pan and cook until browned. Mix in brown sugar, ketchup, vinegar, mustard, garlic powder, and salt. Simmer for 30 minutes.

Preheat oven to 325 degrees. Combine sausage mixture with crumbled bacon, onions, and all canned beans. Transfer to a large baking dish. Bake for 2 hours.

Beans can be cooked in a crock pot instead of baking.

NUTRITION INFORMATION: 481 calories, 9 g fat, 3 g saturated fat, 34 mg cholesterol, 1359 mg sodium, 78 g carbohydrate, 36 g sugars, 14 g fiber, 27 g protein.

black beans and quinoa

Serves: *6 portions*

Prep: less than 30 minutes | Cook: 30 minutes

1	teaspoon olive oil		¼	teaspoon cayenne pepper
1	onion, chopped			salt and pepper to taste
3	cloves garlic, chopped		1	cup fresh or frozen corn kernels
¾	cup dry quinoa		2	15 ounce cans black beans, rinsed and drained
1½	cups vegetable broth		½	cup chopped fresh cilantro
1	teaspoon ground cumin		1	tomato, chopped

Heat oil in a medium saucepan over medium heat. Add onion and sauté until translucent. Add garlic and sauté for 30 seconds or until fragrant. Mix in quinoa and cover with vegetable broth. Season with cumin, cayenne pepper, and salt and pepper. Bring to a boil. Cover, reduce heat, and simmer for 20 minutes. Stir corn into saucepan and continue to simmer for 5 minutes or until heated through. Mix in beans and cilantro. Top with tomatoes before serving.

NUTRITION INFORMATION: 245 calories, 4 g fat, 0 g saturated fat, 0 mg cholesterol, 679 mg sodium, 41 g carbohydrate, 3 g sugars, 11 g fiber, 12 g protein.

classique
pastas & grains

zucchini and basil lasagna

Serves: *8 portions*

Prep: less than 30 minutes | Bake: 1 hour

2	cups low-fat cottage cheese	1	clove garlic, chopped
1	cup chopped fresh basil	1	26 ounce jar spicy tomato pasta sauce
1	egg	9	oven-ready (no-boil) lasagna noodles
3	medium zucchini, chopped	2	cups shredded mozzarella cheese
¼	cup chopped onion		

Preheat oven to 350 degrees. Combine cottage cheese, basil, and egg in a food processor; process until smooth. Heat a large nonstick skillet coated with cooking spray over medium-high heat. Add zucchini, onion, and garlic and sauté 5 minutes or until tender. Stir in pasta sauce and remove from heat. Spread ¼ cup zucchini mixture in the bottom of a greased 13x9x2-inch baking dish. Arrange a layer of 3 noodles over zucchini mixture. Top with one-third of cottage cheese mixture, one-third of zucchini mixture, and one-third of mozzarella. Repeat layers twice with the remaining noodles, cottage cheese mixture, zucchini mixture, and mozzarella. Bake, covered, for 45 minutes. Uncover and bake for 15 minutes longer or until lasagna is thoroughly heated.

NUTRITION INFORMATION: 271 calories, 8 g fat, 4 g saturated fat, 47 mg cholesterol, 726 mg sodium, 30 g carbohydrate, 10 g sugars, 3 g fiber, 20 g protein.

Wine Pairing: This dish would be fun with a lighter Italian red Valipolicella with its cherry fruit flavors; would liven up the herbs and the spiciness of the sauce.

spicy chicken pesto bowties

Serves: *8 portions*

Prep: less than 30 minutes | Cook: less than 30 minutes

4	ounces fresh basil	1	cup chicken broth
2-3	serrano peppers, seeded	1	cup white wine
½	cup walnut pieces	1	pound dry bowtie pasta
3	cloves garlic	1	grilled or rotisserie chicken, seasoned with salt and pepper before grilling
½	teaspoon salt		
1	cup olive oil	1	cup freshly grated Parmesan cheese

Process basil with serrano peppers, walnuts, garlic, salt, olive oil, broth, and wine in a blender to create the sauce. Warm sauce over low heat, bringing to a low boil and cooking for 5 minutes to reduce. Meanwhile, cook pasta in boiling water for 10 to 12 minutes; drain. Chop grilled chicken into bite-size pieces, or shred rotisserie chicken. Mix drained pasta, sauce, chicken, and Parmesan cheese.

NUTRITION INFORMATION: 700 calories, 39 g fat, 7 g saturated fat, 85 mg cholesterol, 514 mg sodium, 45 g carbohydrate, 2 g sugars, 2 g fiber, 36 g protein.

Beer Pairing: Pesto is complemented perfectly with a lightly hopped Pale Ale.

smoked gouda macaroni and cheese

Serves: *4 portions*

Prep: less than 30 minutes | Bake: 15-20 minutes

2 cups dry elbow macaroni	½ cup shredded fontina cheese
1 tablespoon butter	⅓ cup freshly grated Parmesan cheese
2 cloves garlic, minced	5 cups coarsely chopped fresh spinach
2 tablespoons all-purpose flour	¼ cup shredded smoked Gouda cheese
2 cups whole milk	2 strips bacon, cooked and crumbled
½ teaspoon salt	2 teaspoons extra virgin olive oil
¼ teaspoon black pepper	¼ cup panko bread crumbs

Preheat oven to 350 degrees. Cook macaroni in boiling salted water; drain, reserving 1 cup pasta water. Meanwhile, melt butter in a large saucepan over medium heat. Add garlic and cook for 1 minute. Add flour and cook for 1 minute, stirring constantly. Gradually whisk in milk, salt, and pepper until blended. Bring to a boil. Cook for 2 minutes or until thickened. Stir in fontina and Parmesan cheeses until melted. Add spinach and drained macaroni to cheese sauce and stir until well blended. Spoon mixture into a greased 2-quart baking dish. If mixture seems too dry, add up to 1 cup of reserved pasta cooking water until moist. Sprinkle with Gouda cheese and bacon. Mix olive oil with bread crumbs and sprinkle on top. Bake for 15 minutes or until bubbly.

NUTRITION INFORMATION: 475 calories, 19 g fat, 10 g saturated fat, 53 mg cholesterol, 740 mg sodium, 53 g carbohydrate, 8 g sugars, 3 g fiber, 22 g protein.

Chef Tip: What is panko? Japanese bread crumbs where the crust is cut so only the white is used.

Wine Pairing: All the different cheeses would warrant a wine with some acidity. A crisp, clean Pinot Grigio from Italy would do the trick, just make sure it is dry enough.

pasta puttanesca

Serves: *6 portions*

Prep: 45 minutes | Cook: 30-45 minutes

5 cloves garlic, chopped	1 pound mushrooms, sliced
1 tablespoon olive oil	1 tablespoon olive oil
1 bunch green onions, white parts only, chopped	2 tablespoons butter
15 kalamata olives, pitted and chopped	1 14½ ounce can chopped tomatoes with juice
1 8 ounce bottle capers with juice	½ cup white wine
1 8 ounce jar chopped sun-dried tomatoes with 1 tablespoon juice	1 pound dry pasta of choice, cooked and drained
1-2 inches imported Italian anchovy paste in a tube, optional for vegetarian preference	shaved Parmesan cheese

In a heavy cast iron pot, slowly sauté garlic in 1 tablespoon olive oil; do not overcook. Add chopped green onions and sauté until onions are clear. Add chopped olives, capers with juice, sun-dried tomatoes, and anchovy paste and simmer for 10 minutes. Sauté mushrooms in 1 tablespoon olive oil and butter; drain and add to olive mixture. Stir in canned tomatoes with juice and simmer for 10 minutes longer. Cool and refrigerate overnight. Add wine to sauce and simmer for 5 minutes. Serve on cooked pasta and top with shaved Parmesan cheese.

NUTRITION INFORMATION: 522 calories, 18 g fat, 4 g saturated fat, 11 mg cholesterol, 1310 mg sodium, 75 g carbohydrate, 7 g sugars, 7 g fiber, 17 g protein.

spinach and prosciutto lasagna

Serves: *9-12 portions*

Prep: 45 minutes | Bake: 35 minutes

8	ounces dry lasagna noodles		1	pound fontina cheese, shredded
4	tablespoons butter			salt to taste
1	medium onion, finely chopped (about 1 cup)		2	14 ounce cans artichoke bottoms, drained
½	cup all-purpose flour		2	10 ounce packages frozen chopped spinach, thawed
½	tablespoon white pepper		8	ounces prosciutto; thinly sliced
¼	teaspoon grated fresh or ground nutmeg		6	tablespoons shredded Parmesan cheese
1	quart milk			

Preheat oven to 375 degrees. Bring 3 quarts of water to a boil in a 5- to 6-quart saucepan over high heat. Add lasagna and cook 10 minutes or until barely tender to bite, stirring occasionally to separate noodles. Drain pasta, immerse in cold water until cool, and drain again; cover loosely so pasta stays moist. In same pan over medium-high heat, melt butter. Add onion and cook, stirring often, for 5 to 7 minutes or until translucent. Blend in flour, white pepper, and nutmeg and stir for 2 to 3 minutes or until smooth. Remove from heat and whisk in milk. Return to heat and simmer, stirring often, for 5 minutes. Remove from heat and add two-thirds of fontina cheese, whisking until cheese is melted and sauce is smooth. Season with salt. Rinse and drain artichoke bottoms and cut crosswise into ⅛-inch thick slices. Squeeze as much liquid as possible from spinach.

To assemble, layer one-third of noodles in a 13x9x2-inch baking dish or casserole dish at least 2 inches deep. Scatter half of artichokes over noodles. Layer half of prosciutto slices on top. Add half of spinach. Spoon one-third of cheese sauce over spinach and sprinkle with 2 tablespoons Parmesan cheese. Repeat layers of noodles, artichokes, prosciutto, spinach, cheese sauce, and Parmesan cheese. Cover with remaining noodles, then remaining sauce, remaining shredded fontina cheese, and remaining Parmesan cheese. Bake, uncovered, for 30 to 35 minutes or until hot in the center and lightly browned on top. Let stand for 10 minutes before serving.

NUTRITION INFORMATION: 546 calories, 30 g fat, 17 g saturated fat, 107 mg cholesterol, 1196 mg sodium, 40 g carbohydrate, 10 g sugars, 4 g fiber, 32 g protein.

Beer Pairing: A full-flavored Pilsener Lager won't weigh you down during this rich meal.

chicken pesto lasagna

Serves: *12 portions*

Prep: 45 minutes | Bake: 40-45 minutes

8 ounces lasagna noodles (do not use no-boil type) (8-10 noodles)	4-8 ounces boneless cooked chicken breast, rotisserie chicken works best, chopped
2½ cups ricotta cheese	⅔ 14 ounce can medium artichoke hearts, drained and chopped
1 egg	1¾ cups homemade or prepared refrigerated pesto sauce (see recipe below)
1 teaspoon garlic salt	12 ounces mozzarella cheese, sliced
1 teaspoon parsley flakes	½ cup shredded Parmesan cheese
dash of salt and pepper	

Preheat oven to 350 degrees. Cook noodles according to package directions; drain. Meanwhile, combine ricotta cheese, egg, garlic salt, parsley flakes, and salt and pepper in a medium bowl. Toss chicken and artichokes with 1½ cups pesto sauce until evenly coated with sauce. Spread half of chicken mixture in a 13x9x2-inch baking dish. Layer half of the lasagna noodles on top. Next layer half of mozzarella on noodles and spread half of ricotta mixture over mozzarella. Repeat all layers ending with ricotta cheese. Drizzle remaining ¼ cup pesto sauce over ricotta and sprinkle with Parmesan cheese.

Bake for 40 to 45 minutes or until bubbly along edges and hot in the middle when tested with a knife. For final 10 to 15 minutes of baking time, remove foil to brown and crisp the top.

FRESH PESTO (OPTIONAL)

3-4 cloves garlic	½ teaspoon black pepper
½ cup pine nuts	6 tablespoons Parmesan cheese
½ cup walnuts	6 tablespoons grated Asiago cheese
3 cups loosely packed fresh basil	1 cup olive oil
1 teaspoon salt	

Mince garlic in a food processor. Add pine nuts, walnuts, basil, salt, and pepper and process until well mixed. Add both cheeses and process until smooth. With food processor running, slowly add olive oil and process until smooth.

NUTRITION INFORMATION: 512 calories, 38 g fat, 12 g saturated fat, 72 mg cholesterol, 709 mg sodium, 20 g carbohydrate, 4 g sugars, 2 g fiber, 24 g protein.

crab and shrimp lasagna

Serves: *8 portions*

Prep: 45 minutes | Bake: 40 minutes

1	tablespoon olive oil		4	ounces crumbled goat or feta cheese
1	pound chopped mushrooms		1	cup reduced-fat cottage cheese
1	cup chopped onions		¼	cup chopped fresh basil
2	tablespoons chopped fresh thyme		1	tablespoon fresh lemon juice
2	cloves garlic, minced		1	clove garlic, minced
¼	cup white wine		¼	cup flour
2	6½ ounce cans lump crabmeat		1	cup 2% milk
1	pound raw large shrimp		¼	cup Parmesan cheese
2	cups water		1	8 ounce package no-boil lasagna noodles
1½	teaspoons celery salt		2	cups shredded mozzarella
1	teaspoon fennel seeds		¼	cup chopped Italian parsley

Preheat oven to 375 degrees. Heat oil in a large nonstick skillet over medium heat. Add mushrooms, onions, and thyme and cook until onions are translucent and mushrooms are soft. Add 2 cloves garlic and cook for 1 minute. Add wine and bring to a boil. Cook for 1½ minutes or until liquid is almost evaporated. Stir in crabmeat; set aside. Peel and devein shrimp, reserving shells. Cut each shrimp in half lengthwise, cover, and refrigerate. Combine reserved shrimp shells, water, celery salt, and fennel seeds in a small saucepan. Bring to a boil and cook 15 minutes or until reduced to 1½ cups. Strain shrimp stock through a sieve and set aside. Combine goat or feta cheese, cottage cheese, basil, lemon juice, and 1 garlic clove; set aside. Place flour in a small saucepan. Gradually whisk in milk. Stir in shrimp stock and bring to a boil. Reduce heat and simmer until thickened. Remove from heat and stir in Parmesan cheese. Spread ½ cup sauce in the bottom of a 13x9x2-inch baking dish coated with cooking spray. Arrange 4 noodles over sauce. Top with one-third goat cheese mixture, one-third crabmeat mixture, one-third of shrimp, ⅔ cup sauce, and ⅔ cup mozzarella. Repeat layers twice, ending with mozzarella. Bake for 40 minutes or until golden. Let stand 15 minutes and sprinkle with parsley.

NUTRITION INFORMATION: 405 calories, 13 g fat, 6 g saturated fat, 145 mg cholesterol, 825 mg sodium, 32 g carbohydrate, 5 g sugars, 2 g fiber, 39 g protein.

Wine Pairing: The lush ripe pear and apple flavors of Chardonnay would be well-suited to the fullness of the crab and shrimp. It would be better to have one with a little more acidity, but any Chardonnay would be delightful.

hearty bolognese sauce

Serves: *10 portions*

Prep: 45 minutes | Cook: 45 minutes

⅔	pound Maverick Ranch™ Certified Organic Ground Beef
3-4	slices pancetta or bacon, diced
1	stalk celery, diced
1	carrot, diced
½	onion, diced
1	28 ounce can stewed tomatoes
1	teaspoon dried parsley, or 1 tablespoon fresh
1	teaspoon dried marjoram, or 1 tablespoon fresh
1	teaspoon dried oregano; or 1 tablespoon fresh
½	bay leaf
½	teaspoon sugar
1	teaspoon garlic powder
1	6 ounce can tomato paste
2	ounces sweet vermouth
¾	cup beef stock

In a large pan, brown sirloin over medium-high heat; remove with a slotted spoon and set aside. Add pancetta or bacon to same pan and brown over medium-high heat. Add celery, carrots, and onions and sauté, then remove and combine with beef. In same pan, add tomatoes, a small amount at a time, crushing with a fork as added. Sauté tomatoes for 5 to 6 minutes. Add parsley, marjoram, oregano, bay leaf, sugar, garlic powder, and tomato paste. Cook 5 to 6 minutes. Return meat and vegetables mixture to pan. Mix in sweet vermouth and simmer for 15 minutes. Add beef stock and simmer for 10 to 15 minutes. Serve with your favorite pasta.

NUTRITION INFORMATION: 102 calories, 2 g fat, 1 g saturated fat, 19 mg cholesterol, 366 mg sodium, 10 g carbohydrate, 7 g sugars, 2 g fiber, 9 g protein.

Beer Pairing: Try this with an Octoberfest or a Marzen, a great match for rich, spicy foods.

sun-dried tomato and date marinara sauce

Serves: *2-4 portions*

Prep: *less than 30 minutes*

- 2½ cups chopped tomatoes
- 15 sun-dried tomatoes
- 3 dates, pitted
- ¼ cup olive oil
- 2 cloves garlic, peeled
- 2 tablespoons dried or fresh parsley
- 1 teaspoon sea salt
- ⅛ teaspoon cayenne pepper

Combine all ingredients in a food processor and blend to desired consistency. Pour sauce over cooked pasta or sliced vegetables, or use as a sauce for lasagna.

NUTRITION INFORMATION:
368 calories, 31 g fat, 4 g saturated fat, 0 mg cholesterol, 1237 mg sodium, 25 g carbohydrate, 14 g sugars, 5 g fiber, 4 g protein.

baked rigatoni

Serves: *12-15 portions*

Prep: less than 30 minutes | Bake: 1 hour 20 minutes

1½	pounds rigatoni pasta	3	tablespoons chopped fresh basil, or 2 teaspoons dried
1	tablespoon olive oil	1	tablespoon chopped fresh oregano, or 1 teaspoon dried
¼	cup diced onions		
2	pounds Canino's Hot and Mild Italian Sausages, casings removed (or bulk)	1	tablespoon chopped garlic
		1	tablespoon Italian seasoning
2	30 ounce cans Italian crushed tomatoes in purée	1	tablespoon chopped fresh parsley
		1	pound mozzarella cheese, shredded
2	cups water	1½	cups Parmesan cheese

In a large pot of boiling salted water, cook rigatoni for 10 to 12 minutes or until tender but still firm. Drain and rinse pasta under cool water; drain again well.

Meanwhile, in a large saucepan, heat olive oil over medium heat. Add onion and cook 3 to 4 minutes, or until soft. Add sausage and cook 6 to 8 minutes or until lightly browned, breaking up lumps of meat; pour off excess fat. Add tomatoes with purée, water, basil, oregano, garlic, Italian seasoning, and parsley to pan. Bring to a boil over medium heat. Reduce heat to low and cook, partially covered, for 25 minutes. Uncover, increase heat to medium, and cook, stirring occasionally, for 6 to 8 minutes or until sauce thickens.

Preheat oven to 350 degrees. In a large bowl, toss pasta with two-thirds of the sauce. Stir in mozzarella cheese and 1 cup Parmesan cheese. Pour pasta into a 13x9x2-inch baking dish. Cover with remaining sauce and Parmesan cheese. Cover with foil and bake 25 minutes. Uncover and bake 10 minutes longer or until bubbly and lightly browned on top.

NUTRITION INFORMATION: 550 calories, 21 g fat, 10 g saturated fat, 55 mg cholesterol, 1301 mg sodium, 57 g carbohydrate, 9 g sugars, 3 g fiber, 30 g protein.

Beer Pairing: An assertive Winter Warmer or Dopplebock are classic combinations with baked Italian dishes.

Wine Pairing: Is there anything better with an Italian meal than a Chianti? It has the red cherry fruit character and a hint of spice that goes so well with tomato sauce and pasta.

Canino's Today

Canino's Sausage Company produces nearly 5000 pounds daily of the highest quality sausage available. Our products are free of gluten, soy, dairy, wheat, MSG, preservatives, and nitrates. Our products are made with all natural ingredients, and approved by the Celiac Sprue Association. ColoradoBiz Magazine has rated Canino's 64th of the top 100 women-owned companies, and 196 in the Top Private Companies for 2008.

chicken linguine with sweet cherry tomatoes

Serves: *4 portions*

Prep: less than 30 minutes | Cook: 30 minutes

¼	cup pine nuts	½	pound dry linguine
	salt to taste	1	9 ounce bag fresh spinach
3	tablespoons olive oil	4	ounces soft goat cheese, crumbled
1	pound boneless, skinless chicken breasts, cubed	¾	pound cherry tomatoes
1	tablespoon minced garlic	1	tablespoon olive oil
¼	cup dry sherry	¼	cup sugar
½	cup chicken broth	¼	cup red wine vinegar

Bring a large pot of salted water to a boil for the linguine and spinach. Meanwhile, toast the pine nuts in a large saucepan over medium heat for 3 minutes or until golden, tossing often. Transfer pine nuts to a plate and season with salt. Return pan to medium-high heat. Add 3 tablespoons olive oil to pan. Add chicken and sauté for 5 minutes or until brown. Add garlic and cook 30 seconds. Deglaze pan with sherry, then add broth. Boil for 1 minute. Remove from heat, cover, and set aside.

Cook linguine according to package directions. Just before draining, add spinach and cook 30 seconds. Drain, reserving ½ cup of pasta water. Toss pasta and spinach with goat cheese and chicken mixture in a large bowl; thin with pasta water, if needed. Cover pasta and keep warm. In same pan used to cook chicken, sauté tomatoes in 1 tablespoon olive oil for 2 minutes over medium-high heat. Add sugar and vinegar and simmer 2 to 3 minutes or until syrupy. Season with salt. Garnish pasta with tomatoes and pine nuts.

NUTRITION INFORMATION: 667 calories, 26 g fat, 7 g saturated fat, 79 mg cholesterol, 367 mg sodium, 64 g carbohydrate, 18 g sugars, 4 g fiber, 43 g protein.

Wine Pairing: The touch of sweetness of the dish requires a wine with a lot of fruit, Primitivo from Italy has just that. Zinfandel from California that is not real full-bodied would also work.

creamy fiesta chicken fettuccini

Serves: *6 portions*

Prep: 45 minutes | Cook: 15 minutes

1 pound dry spinach fettuccini pasta

⅓ cup chopped fresh cilantro

2 tablespoons minced fresh garlic

1 jalapeño pepper, seeded and minced

1 serrano pepper, seeded and minced

2 tablespoons unsalted butter

½ cup chicken stock (preferably homemade)

2 tablespoons gold tequila

2 tablespoons freshly squeezed lime juice

3 tablespoons soy sauce

1¼ pounds seasoned chicken breast, baked and diced into ¾-inch pieces (can substitute rotisserie chicken)

½ large red onion, thinly sliced

½ medium-size red bell pepper, thinly sliced

½ medium-size yellow bell pepper, thinly sliced

½ medium-size orange bell pepper, thinly sliced

1 tablespoon unsalted butter

1½ cups heavy cream

2 tablespoons chopped fresh cilantro for garnish

Cook pasta in rapidly boiling, salted water for 8 to 10 minutes or until al dente; if pasta is fresh, cook about 3 minutes. (Pasta may be cooked slightly ahead of time, rinsed, and oiled, then "flashed" (reheated) in boiling water.)

Sauté ⅓ cup cilantro, garlic, and jalapeño and serrano peppers in 2 tablespoons butter over medium heat for 4 to 5 minutes. Add stock, tequila, and lime juice and bring to a boil. Cook until mixture is reduced to a paste-like consistency; set aside. Pour soy sauce over diced chicken; set aside for 5 minutes. Meanwhile, cook onions and all bell peppers in 1 tablespoon butter, stirring occasionally over medium heat. When vegetables become limp, toss in chicken mixture. Add tequila/lime paste and cream and bring to a boil. Boil gently for 3 minutes or until chicken is heated through and sauce is thick. When sauce is done, toss with well-drained pasta and 2 tablespoons cilantro. Serve family style or transfer to individual serving dishes, evenly distributing chicken and vegetables.

NUTRITION INFORMATION: 661 calories, 32 g fat, 18 g saturated fat, 143 mg cholesterol, 1258 mg sodium, 62 g carbohydrate, 5 g sugars, 4 g fiber, 32 g protein.

Beef Pairing: British-style ales and Special Bitters complement this rich and smooth meal.

Wine Pairing: A Vernaccia that is from the San Gimignagno in Italy would be an excellent complement to this fettuccini dish. It has the crisp citrus flavors but enough body to go with the marinade.

fresh pesto with pasta

Serves: *6 portions*

Prep: less than 30 minutes

½   pint grape tomatoes, halved

6   ounces fresh bite-size mozzarella cheese (bocconcini)

1   teaspoon salt

PESTO

3-4   cloves garlic

½   cup pine nuts

½   cup walnuts

3   cups loosely packed fresh basil

1   teaspoon salt

black pepper to taste

½   tablespoon olive oil

½   pound campanelle pasta

½   teaspoon black pepper

6   tablespoons Parmesan cheese

6   tablespoons grated Asiago cheese

1   cup olive oil

Combine tomatoes, mozzarella cheese, salt, pepper, and olive oil; let stand for 30 minutes. Cook pasta in boiling water until al dente; drain.

For pesto, mince garlic in a food processor. Add pine nuts, walnuts, basil, 1 teaspoon salt, and ½ teaspoon pepper and process until well mixed. Add Parmesan and asiago cheeses and process until smooth. With the food processor running, slowly add 1 cup olive oil and process until smooth. Toss tomato mixture with pasta and ¾ cup basil pesto. Serve at room temperature or chilled.

Pesto recipe makes 2¼ cups of sauce. Leftover pesto can be refrigerated up to one week or frozen up to three months.

NUTRITION INFORMATION: 400 calories, 26 g fat, 7 g saturated fat, 24 mg cholesterol, 586 mg sodium, 31 g carbohydrate, 3 g sugars, 2 g fiber, 13 g protein.

Wine Pairing: Vermentino is one of the white wine grapes of the Cinque Terre. It would also be delightful with this meal. It has crisp citrus and pear fruit flavors that would go well with the nuttiness and the cheese tastes.

pesto ratatouille

Serves: *6 portions*

Prep: less than 30 minutes | Bake: 25-30 minutes

3 tablespoons extra virgin olive oil

2-3 cloves garlic, minced

1 yellow squash, chopped

1 Mexican Autumn squash, chopped

1 zucchini squash, chopped

1 red bell pepper, chopped into ½-inch pieces

1 green bell pepper, chopped into ½-inch pieces

1 orange bell pepper, chopped into ½-inch pieces

1 yellow bell pepper, chopped into ½-inch pieces

1 10 ounce jar marinated artichoke hearts, drained

1 large tomato, diced, or 1 (14½ ounce) can diced tomatoes

1 small red or white onion, chopped

3-4 tablespoons pesto

1½ cups shredded mozzarella cheese

Preheat oven to 350 degrees. Combine oil and garlic in a skillet over medium-low heat. Add all squash to pan and cook until soft and lightly browned. Place all peppers in a large mixing bowl. Add artichoke hearts, tomatoes, and onions to bowl. Add squash mixture and mix all vegetables together. Add pesto and mix to lightly coat vegetables. Transfer mixture to an ungreased 13x9x2-inch pan. Top with mozzarella cheese. Bake for 25 to 30 minutes or until cheese in melted and vegetables are warmed. Serve over warm crusty sourdough baguette or over pasta of your choice.

NUTRITION INFORMATION: 251 calories, 19 g fat, 5 g saturated fat, 20 mg cholesterol, 386 mg sodium, 15 g carbohydrate, 6 g sugars, 5 g fiber, 10 g protein.

pasta with shrimp and fresh asparagus

Serves: *6 portions*

Prep: less than 30 minutes | Cook: 15 minutes

5 cloves garlic, minced

½ cup olive oil

1 pound raw shrimp, peeled

3 Roma tomatoes, diced

8 spears asparagus, lightly cooked and cut into 1-inch pieces

4 green onions, sliced

½ cup freshly grated Parmesan cheese

salt and pepper to taste

12 ounces dry pasta of choice, cooked, drained, and kept warm

sliced fresh basil and Parmesan cheese for topping

Lightly sauté garlic in olive oil. Add shrimp and cook until pink throughout. Add diced tomatoes, asparagus, and green onions and lightly sauté but do not cook through. Remove from heat and add ½ cup Parmesan cheese and salt and pepper. Toss in a bowl with warm pasta. Top with basil and extra Parmesan cheese.

NUTRITION INFORMATION: 469 calories, 21 g fat, 4 g saturated fat, 104 mg cholesterol, 224 mg sodium, 47 g carbohydrate, 4 g sugars, 3 g fiber, 21 g protein.

shrimp and basil sauce with bowtie pasta

Serves: *6 portions*

Prep: less than 30 minutes, plus marinating time | Cook: 30 minutes

½ cup butter, melted	9 ounces dry bowtie pasta
1 cup chopped fresh basil	2 tablespoons butter
6 cloves garlic	¾ cup heavy cream
½ teaspoon salt	½ cup Parmesan cheese
2 teaspoons lemon pepper	salt and pepper to taste
2 pounds medium shrimp, peeled and deveined	2 tablespoons chopped fresh parsley

Process melted butter, basil, garlic, ½ teaspoon salt, and lemon pepper in a food processor until blended. Pour mixture over shrimp in a shallow dish. Cover and marinate in refrigerator for at least 1 hour or until ready to cook, stirring occasionally.

Cook pasta in boiling water until al dente, drain. Meanwhile, drain shrimp, reserving the marinade. Sauté shrimp in a skillet with 2 tablespoons butter until pink. Remove shrimp to a bowl using a slotted spoon. Add cream, Parmesan cheese, and reserved marinade to cooking juices in skillet and mix well. Cook over medium heat until heated, stirring constantly. Stir in shrimp. Season to taste with salt and pepper. Serve over pasta and sprinkle with parsley.

NUTRITION INFORMATION: 563 calories, 34 g fat, 20 g saturated fat, 293 mg cholesterol, 778 mg sodium, 34 g carbohydrate, 2 g sugars, 1 g fiber, 30 g protein.

Wine Pairing: The zesty, citrus flavors of the wines of the Rueda in Spain would complement the shrimp and basil flavors superbly.

angel hair with seafood sauce

Serves: *8 portions*

Prep: less than 30 minutes | Cook: 45 minutes

1	pound dry angel hair pasta	1	cup halved cherry tomatoes
1	cup extra virgin olive oil	4	tablespoons butter
1	cup chopped green bell pepper	16	large shrimp, peeled and deveined
1	cup chopped red bell pepper	16	leaves basil, torn
6	cloves garlic, finely chopped		kosher salt and freshly ground black pepper to taste
1	large yellow onion, chopped		
⅔	cup white wine	1	cup grated Asiago cheese
16	mussels, scrubbed and debearded		torn fresh basil and lemon wedges for garnish

Bring a pot of salted water to a boil over high heat. Add pasta and cook 8 to 10 minutes or until al dente. Drain pasta, reserving ½ cup pasta water. Meanwhile, heat olive oil in a 12-inch skillet over medium-high heat. Add green and red bell peppers, garlic, and onions and sauté 3 minutes or until vegetables begin to soften. Add wine and mussels and cook, covered, for 2 minutes or until mussels open. Add reserved pasta water, tomatoes, butter, and shrimp and cook and stir for 1 minute or until shrimp are just pink. Add cooked pasta, toss to combine, and cook, stirring occasionally, until the sauce thickens and clings to pasta. Stir in basil and season with salt and pepper. Divide pasta between bowls. Sprinkle with Asiago, and garnish with extra basil and lemon wedges.

NUTRITION INFORMATION: 654 calories, 39 g fat, 10 g saturated fat, 100 mg cholesterol, 350 mg sodium, 50 g carbohydrate, 5 g sugars, 3 g fiber, 22 g protein.

Wine Pairing: A crisp, flavorful lighter white wine marry well the seafood and spices in this dish. Frascati is a delightful Italian white.

penne with tomato vodka sauce

Serves: *6 portions*

Prep: less than 30 minutes | Cook: 30 minutes

3	cloves garlic, chopped	1	pound dry penne pasta
	pinch of red pepper flakes	1	cup heavy cream
2-3	tablespoons olive oil		splash of vodka
2	14½ ounce cans diced tomatoes	½	cup Parmesan cheese
½	teaspoon sugar		fresh basil and Parmesan cheese for topping
1	8 ounce can tomato sauce		

Brown garlic and red pepper flakes in olive oil. Add tomatoes, sugar, and tomato sauce and simmer for 30 minutes.

Meanwhile, cook pasta until al dente; drain. Add cream and vodka to tomato mixture, mix thoroughly. Toss pasta, tomato mixture, and ½ cup Parmesan cheese. Top with fresh basil and extra Parmesan cheese.

Grilled shrimp or chicken can be added for a complete meal.

NUTRITION INFORMATION: 531 calories, 22 g fat, 11 g saturated fat, 60 mg cholesterol, 516 mg sodium, 67 g carbohydrate, 9 g sugars, 4 g fiber, 15 g protein.

Beer Pairing: A smooth Rye Ale goes down well with this thick pasta, and brings out the sweet tomato.

orzo with shrimp and grilled vegetables

Serves: *6 portions*

Prep: less than 30 minutes I Cook: 20 minutes

PASTA

1⅓ cups dry orzo

1 tablespoon extra virgin olive oil

VEGETABLES

¼ cup red wine vinegar

2 tablespoons extra virgin olive oil

2 medium zucchini or summer squash (about 9 ounces total), cut lengthwise into ¼-inch thick slices

1 red or yellow bell pepper, quartered

salt and pepper to taste

PESTO VINAIGRETTE

¼ cup purchased basil pesto

2 tablespoons fresh lime juice

3½ tablespoons extra virgin olive oil

2 tablespoons red wine vinegar

1 pound raw large shrimp, peeled

salt and pepper to taste

2 heirloom tomatoes (8 to 10 ounces total), cored and cut into ½-inch cubes

½ cup thinly sliced fresh basil leaves

6-8 ounces Parmesan cheese, shredded

sprigs of fresh basil for garnish

Cook orzo in a large pot of boiling salted water, stirring occasionally, until tender but still firm to bite. Drain, rinse with cold water, and drain well. Transfer pasta to a large bowl and toss with 1 tablespoon olive oil.

To prepare vegetables, whisk vinegar and olive oil in a small bowl. Brush zucchini and bell peppers with oil mixture, then sprinkle with salt and pepper.

To make vinaigrette, whisk pesto, lime juice, olive oil, and vinegar in a small bowl.

Preheat grill over medium-high heat. Place shrimp in a medium bowl. Add 2 tablespoons Pesto Vinaigrette and toss to coat. Grill zucchini and bell pepper until crisp-tender, about 3 minutes per side for zucchini and 4 minutes per side for bell pepper. Transfer vegetables to a work surface. Sprinkle shrimp with salt and pepper and grill 2 to 3 minutes on each side or until charred and cooked through. Place shrimp in bowl with orzo. Chop zucchini and bell pepper and add to bowl with orzo. Add remaining vinaigrette along with tomatoes, sliced basil, and Parmesan and toss to combine. Season to taste with salt and pepper. Serve immediately, or cover and chill for up to 2 hours. Garnish with basil sprigs and serve cold or at room temperature.

NUTRITION INFORMATION: 519 calories, 29 g fat, 8 g saturated fat, 125 mg cholesterol, 647 mg sodium, 35 g carbohydrate, 5 g sugars, 3 g fiber, 29 g protein.

Wine Pairing: A Sauvignon Blanc and Semillon blend would be delightful with the shellfish and pasta. A white Bordeaux is a classic example of this blend. The Sauvignon Blanc is citrus flavored and the Semillon softens those flavors with its melon character.

vegetable quinoa risotto

Serves: *6 main course or 8-10 side dish portions*

Prep: 45 minutes | Cook: 30-45 minutes

2	tablespoons butter
1	tablespoon olive oil
12	ounces assorted wild mushrooms, such as chanterelles, stemmed shiitakes, oyster, and morels, thinly sliced (about 6 cups)
3	cloves garlic, minced
3	tablespoons olive oil
1	cup chopped onions
2	cups (about 13 ounces) quinoa, rinsed
½	cup dry white wine

3½	cups (or more) vegetable broth
1	pound asparagus, trimmed and cut into 1-inch pieces
1	8 ounce package frozen artichoke hearts, thawed
½	cup Parmesan cheese
	salt and pepper to taste
1	cup shaved Manchego cheese (see note below)

Melt butter with 1 tablespoon olive oil in heavy large skillet over medium-high heat. Add mushrooms and sauté for 7 minutes or until brown and tender. Add garlic and sauté for 2 minutes; set aside. Risotto can be made 2 hours ahead up to this point; let stand at room temperature until ready to proceed.

Heat 3 tablespoons olive oil in a heavy large saucepan over medium-high heat. Add onions and sauté for 5 minutes or until translucent. Add quinoa and sauté for 2 minutes. Add wine and cook 2 minutes or until liquid is almost absorbed. Add broth and cook for 10 minutes. Add asparagus and artichoke hearts. Simmer for 7 minutes or until quinoa and vegetables are tender; stirring often and adding more broth in ¼-cup intervals, if needed. Add Parmesan cheese and reserved mushrooms. Stir for 2 minutes or until cheese melts and mushrooms are heated through. Season with salt and pepper. To serve, divide risotto among bowls and garnish with shaved Manchego cheese.

Manchego is a Spanish cheese made from sheep's milk; it is available at specialty food stores and some supermarkets.

NUTRITION INFORMATION (for main course serving): 486 calories, 23 g fat, 8 g saturated fat, 29 mg cholesterol, 738 mg sodium, 51 g carbohydrate, 6 g sugars, 9 g fiber, 19 g protein.

risotto with artichoke hearts

Serves: *6 portions*

Prep: less than 30 minutes | Cook: approximately 30 minutes

3	cloves garlic, chopped		2	14 ounce cans artichoke hearts, drained and quartered
½	yellow onion, chopped		2	cups frozen peas, thawed
2	tablespoons olive oil		2	teaspoon chopped fresh dill
2	tablespoons butter			zest of 1 lemon
2	cups dry Arborio rice		1	cup Parmesan cheese
6	cups chicken broth			

Sauté garlic and onions in olive oil and butter until softened. Add rice and sauté until translucent. Add enough broth to cover rice. Simmer over medium heat until broth is almost completely absorbed. Continue to add broth, about 1 cup at a time, and simmer until broth is absorbed and rice is tender. Add artichokes, peas, dill, and lemon zest. Cook until heated through. Mix in Parmesan cheese and serve.

NUTRITION INFORMATION: 315 calories, 12 g fat, 5 g saturated fat, 22 mg cholesterol, 1011 mg sodium, 39 g carbohydrate, 5 g sugars, 4 g fiber, 12 g protein.

Chef Tip: If you have the broth hot, or at least warm, the process goes quicker.

Wine Pairing: A white that has fruit and acidity. An Italian white would be ideal. Arneis from the Piedmont region or Friulano Bianco from Fiuli (formerly known as Tocai Friulano).

lamb and eggplant curry over rice

Serves: *4 portions*

Prep: 45 minutes | Cook: 20 minutes

1½	cups jasmine rice		4	cloves garlic, chopped
2	tablespoons olive oil		1	14 ounce can diced tomatoes
1	pound cubed lamb, cut into ¾-inch pieces		¼	cup mango chutney
1	eggplant, peeled and cut into 1-inch squares		2	tablespoons curry powder
1	large yellow onion, chopped		1	cup vegetable broth
1	large red bell pepper, chopped			

CONDIMENTS

toasted sliced almonds	sliced green onions
shredded coconut	chutney

Prepare rice according to package instructions. Heat olive oil in large pan. Add lamb and brown on all sides. Add eggplant, onions, and bell peppers, cover, and cook 6 to 8 minutes, stirring occasionally. Uncover, add garlic, and cook 1 minute longer. Add tomatoes, chutney, curry power, and broth. Simmer over low heat, uncovered, for 5 to 10 minutes, stirring frequently.

To serve, portion rice onto plates. Ladle curry over rice. Serve condiments in bowls and allow guests to top the curry with their choice.

NUTRITION INFORMATION: 449 calories, 14 g fat, 3 g saturated fat, 65 mg cholesterol, 426 mg sodium, 56 g carbohydrate, 17 g sugars, 9 g fiber, 26 g protein.

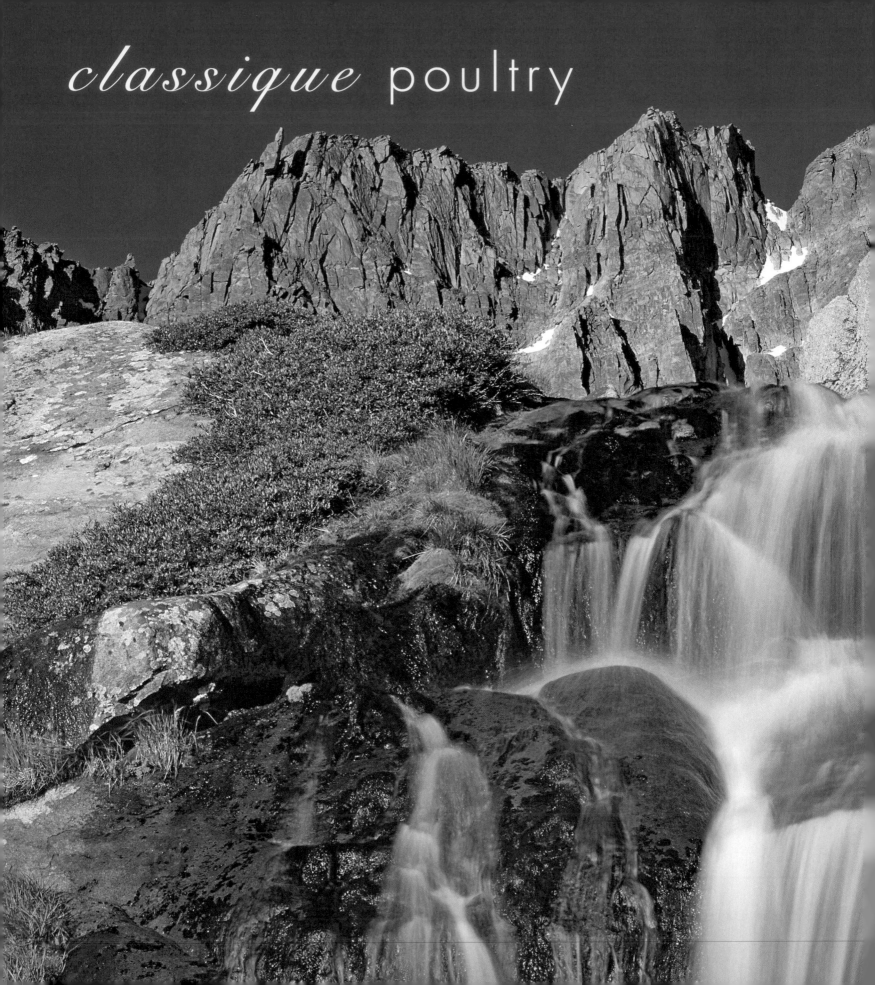

classique poultry

caribbean fajitas

Serves: *4 portions*

Prep: 30 minutes | Cook: 15 minutes

1	pound boneless, skinless chicken, cut into strips		4	1-inch slices fresh pineapple, peeled
1	small red bell pepper, cut into strips		1	tablespoon canola oil
1	small orange bell pepper, cut into strips		8	6-inch flour tortillas, warmed
1	tablespoon Jamaican Jerk seasoning			fresh chopped cilantro
⅛	teaspoon black pepper			lime wedges

Combine chicken and bell peppers in a zip-top bag. Add Jerk seasoning and pepper and toss until coated. Marinate 1 hour.

Cook pineapple slices in a skillet or on a preheated grill, turning once, for a total cooking time of 4 to 6 minutes or until done. If already using a skillet, remove cooked pineapple, but retain juices in pan. Add oil to skillet over medium-high heat. Add chicken and peppers and sauté until chicken is cooked through.

Core and chop pineapple slices. Fill warmed tortillas with chicken and peppers. Spoon chopped pineapple on top and sprinkle with cilantro. Garnish with lime wedges.

NUTRITION INFORMATION: 393 calories, 9 g fat, 2 g saturated fat, 66 mg cholesterol, 569 mg sodium, 45 g carbohydrate, 10 g sugars, 3 g fiber, 32 g protein.

Chef Tip: Give me room! Do not crowd a pan with too much chicken. If you do, it decreases the heat and you will not get the browning and quick sautéing you are looking for.

Beer Pairing: The heat of the fajitas can be chilled with a Maibock.

Wine Pairing: Marsanne and Roussanne with their flavors of peach and apricot would be delicious but the slight tropical note would be the key. The Rhône Valley of France produces some as well as California and Australia.

martini chicken

Serves: *4 portions*

Prep: less than 30 minutes | Cook: 20 minutes

2	tablespoons butter			salt and pepper to taste
2	medium cloves garlic, minced		½	cup vermouth
¼	cup diced onions		¼	cup fresh lemon juice or chicken broth
4	boneless, skinless chicken breast cutlets			

Melt butter in a skillet. Add garlic and onions and cook for 1 minute. Add chicken. Sprinkle chicken generously with salt and pepper and sauté over medium-high heat. Turn chicken and season with more salt and pepper. Remove chicken from skillet when done. Deglaze skillet with vermouth and lemon juice, or use chicken broth for a milder flavor. Increase to high heat and cook until sauce reduces by half. Serve chicken with sauce on the side in a gravy boat.

NUTRITION INFORMATION: 213 calories, 7 g fat, 4 g saturated fat, 83 mg cholesterol, 119 mg sodium, 4 g carbohydrate, 1 g sugars, 0 g fiber, 28 g protein.

margarita grilled chicken with corn cilantro salsa

Serves: *5 portions*

Prep: less than 30 minutes | Grill: 10 minutes

GRILLED MARGARITA CHICKEN

½	cup tequila blanco, or tequila of choice	2	cloves garlic, minced
	juice of 6 limes	2	teaspoons sea salt
	juice of 2 oranges	1	teaspoon freshly ground black pepper
1	tablespoon chili powder	6	boneless, skinless chicken breasts
1	jalapeño pepper, seeded and minced		

CORN CILANTRO SALSA

1¼	cups frozen or fresh corn	¼	cup chopped cilantro
¼	cup chopped red onion	2	teaspoons jalapeño, seeded and chopped
¼	cup chopped red bell pepper	2	tablespoons fresh lime juice

To prepare chicken, combine tequila, lime juice, orange juice, chili powder, jalapeño, garlic, salt, and pepper in a large plastic zip-top bag; mix until combined. Add chicken and marinate overnight.

Mix all salsa ingredients together. Cover and chill for at least 1 hour.

When ready to cook, preheat a grill to medium heat. Grill chicken over indirect heat for 4 to 5 minutes on each side or until done. Pour salsa over chicken or serve on the side, or both.

Chicken can be served as a topping on a Mexican salad. This marinade also is great with chicken tenders or raw shrimp.

NUTRITION INFORMATION: 205 calories, 2 g fat, 1 g saturated fat, 82 mg cholesterol, 560 mg sodium, 12 g carbohydrate, 2 g sugars, 1 g fiber, 34 g protein.

Beer Pairing: The aggressive aroma of the cilantro is accented well with a hoppy IPA.

Wine Pairing: A white that has the fruit to carry the salsa but with acidity for the lime and enough body for the chicken. Sounds like a tasty, fairly full Chardonnay. Try one from Colorado.

colorado chimichangas

Serves: *6 portions*

Prep: less than 30 minutes | Bake: 30 minutes

1-1½	pounds ground turkey	2	green onions, chopped
1	1¼ ounce packet taco seasoning	½	cup low-fat sour cream
1	teaspoon ground cumin	½	cup shredded Cheddar cheese
2	teaspoons chopped fresh oregano	4	tablespoons butter
2	tablespoons chopped fresh cilantro	6	fajita-size flour tortillas
1-2	4 ounce cans fire-roasted green chiles	½	cup shredded Cheddar cheese
½	cup salsa		

GARNISHES (OPTIONAL)

1	cup chopped tomatoes	1	cup guacamole
1½	cups shredded lettuce	1	cup salsa
1	cup shredded cheese	1	cup sour cream

Preheat oven to 450 degrees. Cook turkey with taco seasoning according to directions on seasoning packet. Add cumin, oregano, cilantro, chiles, salsa, green onions, sour cream, and ½ cup Cheddar cheese. Melt butter in a microwave. Lay tortillas on wax paper and brush both sides with melted butter. Spoon ⅓ cup filling into center of each tortilla and fold envelope style. Place tortillas, seam-side down, in a 13x9x2-inch pan. Bake for 20 to 25 minutes or until golden. Sprinkle with cheese and return to oven to melt cheese. Serve with garnishes as desired.

NUTRITION INFORMATION: 435 calories, 24 g fat, 12 g saturated fat, 94 mg cholesterol, 928 mg sodium, 30 g carbohydrate, 3 g sugars, 2 g fiber, 24 g protein.

huli huli chicken

Serves: *4-6 (can easily be doubled)*

Prep: less than 30 minutes | Grill: 20 minutes

4-6	boneless, skinless chicken breasts	2	tablespoons sesame oil (flavored, not refined)
½	teaspoon garlic salt	1	tablespoon sugar
½	teaspoon kosher salt	6	cloves garlic, minced
¼	cup low-sodium soy sauce	1	teaspoon paprika

Combine all ingredients in a zip-top bag. Marinate at least 1 to 2 hours or overnight.

When ready to cook, preheat grill. Remove chicken from marinade and discard liquid. Grill chicken until cooked through.

This marinade can also be used for fish and meats. It goes great with salmon, as well as pork and beef.

NUTRITION INFORMATION: 135 calories, 1 g fat, 0 g saturated fat, 68 mg cholesterol, 452 mg sodium, 1 g carbohydrate, 0 g sugars, 0 g fiber, 28 g protein.

Chef Tip: This is also great with thighs.

Beer Pairing: A sweet German-style Hefeweisen or British-style Golden Ale complete this flavor luau.

Wine Pairing: Chenin Blanc has the soft pear and peach flavors to accompany this Hawaiian dish. A South African Chenin Blanc is drier in style and would quite tasty.

chicken thighs with roasted grape tomatoes

Serves: *4 portions*

Prep: less than 30 minutes | Bake: 25 minutes

1½ tablespoons lemon zest

2 tablespoons fresh lemon juice

1 teaspoon olive oil

2 cloves garlic, minced

8 boneless Maverick Ranch Certified Organic Chicken Thighs

½ teaspoon salt

¼ teaspoon black pepper

ROASTED GRAPE TOMATOES

2 cups grape tomatoes

2 teaspoons olive oil

2 tablespoons chopped fresh parsley

1 teaspoon lemon zest

1 tablespoon fresh lemon juice

1½ tablespoons capers

⅛ teaspoon salt

⅛ teaspoon freshly ground black pepper

½ cup Parmesan cheese

Preheat and oil grill. Combine lemon zest, lemon juice, olive oil, and garlic in a large zip-top bag. Add chicken to bag and seal. Marinate in refrigerator for 15 minutes, shaking bag occasionally. Remove chicken from bag and place on a plate; discard marinade. Sprinkle chicken with salt and pepper. Grill chicken for 5 minutes on each side or until done.

To roast tomatoes, preheat oven to 425 degrees. Combine tomatoes and olive oil in an 8-inch square baking dish and toss gently. Bake for 18 minutes or until tomatoes are tender. Combine tomatoes with parsley, lemon zest, lemon juice, capers, salt, and pepper and stir gently. Serve tomatoes in a small bowl next to chicken and dip chicken in sauce of tomatoes, or spoon tomatoes over chicken. Garnish with Parmesan cheese.

NUTRITION INFORMATION: 317 calories, 18 g fat, 5 g saturated fat, 108 mg cholesterol, 715 mg sodium, 7 g carbohydrate, 3 g sugars, 1 g fiber, 32 g protein.

Chef Tip: Dark meat is better on the grill because the fat content allows it to keep moist over direct heat.

Beer Pairing: A malty Amber or Brown Ale matches well with the darker meat of this chicken.

Wine Pairing: Dolcetto that is from the Piedmont region of Italy would be a nice combination with tomatoes and the chicken. It has the acidity to match the tomatoes but is not too intense to overpower the chicken.

sun-dried tomato chicken wellington

Serves: *4 portions, each with 1 tablespoon sauce*
Prep: less than 30 minutes | Bake: 30 minutes

CHICKEN WELLINGTON

1 sheet puff pastry
  (½ of a 17.3 ounce package)

4 4 ounce chicken breasts

4 tablespoons butter

salt to taste

lemon pepper to taste

4 ounces cream cheese

3-4 cloves garlic, minced

1 10 ounce jar sun-dried tomatoes,
  sliced into thin strips and divided into
  4 equal portions

1 egg, beaten

SAUCE

4 cloves garlic, minced

3 tablespoons olive oil

½ cup marinated sun-dried tomatoes,
  drained and coarsely chopped

1 cup marinated artichoke hearts,
  coarsely chopped

2 cups heavy cream

1 cup freshly grated Parmesan

salt and pepper to taste

Thaw puff pastry overnight in refrigerator. Place chicken breasts in a zip-top bag and flatten to a uniform thickness of ¾- to 1-inch; cut off thinner ends of chicken and freeze for a later use. In a skillet, melt butter over medium heat. Add chicken and sear to golden; do not overcook as chicken will finish cooking in the oven. Season with salt and lemon pepper; cool slightly. Roll out puff pastry on a floured surface to about ⅛-inch thickness. Cut in quarters. Place 2 tablespoons cream cheese, one-fourth of garlic, 1 portion of sun-dried tomatoes, and a chicken breast on each square. Fold up pastry like a package, sealing the edges with beaten egg. Trim any excess pastry before folding over ends. Turn over carefully and place on a greased baking sheet. If desired, decorate top with cutouts of remaining pastry. Brush the top with egg for a golden presentation. At this point, pastries can be refrigerated until ready to bake; remove from refrigerator and allow to stand for 20 minutes before proceeding.

Preheat oven to 350 degrees. Bake for 30 minutes or until pastry is golden and internal temperature of chicken breast is 160 degrees.

To make sauce, sauté garlic until golden in olive oil in a small saucepan. If a smaller cut is desired, pulse tomatoes and artichokes in a food processor. Add tomatoes and artichokes to garlic and sauté for 1 to 2 minutes. Add the cream and bring to a boil. Whisk in Parmesan cheese. Season with salt and pepper. Reduce heat and simmer for 10 minutes or until sauce begins to thicken, stirring frequently to prevent burning.

When done, remove pastries from oven and let rest for 5 minutes before slicing. Arrange on a plate and drizzle about 1 tablespoon of sauce in a vertical line to display the colors of the dish.

NUTRITION INFORMATION: 915 calories, 65 g fat, 25 g saturated fat, 205 mg cholesterol, 661 mg sodium, 47 g carbohydrate, 1 g sugars, 5 g fiber, 41 g protein.

Beer Pairing: A sweet Belgian Dubbel accents the sun-dried tomatoes.

two chile chicken

Serves: *4 portions*

Prep: 1 hour | Bake: 40 minutes

1	tablespoon vegetable oil		½	cup soy sauce
4	boneless chicken breasts, with skin or skinless		½	cup white wine vinegar
2	dried ancho chiles, stems and seeds removed		⅔	cup sugar
2	chipotle chiles, stems and seeds removed		1½	cups water
			¼	cup chopped fresh cilantro
				salt and pepper to taste

Preheat oven to 200 degrees. Heat oil in a large skillet over medium-high heat. Add chicken in a single layer, skin-side down if applicable, and cook for 5 minutes or until browned on that side. Remove with a slotted spoon and set aside. Drain oil from pan, leaving any browned bits on the bottom. Add both chiles, soy sauce, vinegar, sugar, and water to pan and bring to a boil over high heat. Reduce heat and simmer for 5 minutes or until slightly thickened. Return chicken, skin-side up, to pan. Cover and simmer for 15 minutes or until no longer pink in the center. Transfer to a serving dish, cover with foil, and keep warm in oven.

Meanwhile, simmer sauce in skillet for 25 minutes or until it is reduced and coats the back of a spoon. Remove chiles and discard. Spoon sauce over chicken and garnish with cilantro. Serve immediately with jasmine rice or sticky rice. (Do not put sauce on until ready to serve; chicken and sauce will turn syrupy if left to sit.)

Ancho and chipotle chiles may be somewhat hard to find. Look for them in the refrigerated fresh herb section of your grocery store, or in specialty stores such as Tony's Meats, Sunflower Market, or Whole Foods.

NUTRITION INFORMATION: 350 calories, 6 g fat, 1 g saturated fat, 68 mg cholesterol, 1987 mg sodium, 43 g carbohydrate, 34 g sugars, 2 g fiber, 30 g protein.

Chef Tip: If you slightly pound the breast meat so that it is all one thickness, it will cook quicker and all of the breast will be done at the same time.

Wine Pairing: The spice would require a wine with plenty of fruit. Chenin Blanc is packed with peach and pear flavors that would tame the heat of the peppers but enhance their flavors.

vietnamese chicken meatballs in lettuce wraps

Serves: *4 portions*

Prep: 45 minutes | Bake: 15 minutes

MEATBALLS

1	pound lean chicken breast, ground
3	tablespoons Asian fish sauce
3	small shallots, chopped
3	cloves garlic, grated
1	stalk fresh lemongrass, tender white inner bulb only, finely minced
1	teaspoon sesame oil
3	tablespoons chopped cilantro
2	teaspoons chopped mint
1½	teaspoons cornstarch
½	teaspoon kosher salt
½	teaspoon freshly ground black pepper
	granulated sugar (not extra fine) for rolling
	red and green lettuce leaves

ASIAN SWEET AND SOUR SAUCE

6	tablespoons rice vinegar
¼	cup Asian fish sauce
2	tablespoons light brown sugar
3	cloves garlic, grated
¼	teaspoon crushed red pepper flakes, or to taste
2	tablespoons shredded carrot

GARNISHES

½	cup fresh cilantro leaves
½	cup fresh mint leaves
½	cup sliced cucumber
½	cup thinly sliced red onion

Mix all meatball ingredients except sugar and lettuce with slightly moistened hands and form into 1½-inch diameter meatballs. If possible, refrigerate for several hours.

To make sauce, combine all ingredients and stir until sugar dissolves. Chill for at least 1 hour.

When ready to cook, preheat oven to 400 degrees. Roll meatballs in sugar and place on a baking sheet lined with parchment paper. Bake in the upper third of the oven for about 15 minutes, turning every 5 minutes for color consistency.

Serve meatballs on lettuce leaves garnished as desired. Serve Asian Sweet and Sour Sauce, peanut sauce, Asian chili sauce, or plum sauce on the side.

NUTRITION INFORMATION: 232 calories, 3 g fat, 1 g saturated fat, 66 mg cholesterol, 1897 mg sodium, 22 g carbohydrate, 18 g sugars, 0 g fiber, 27 g protein.

Beer Pairing: Red Ales and Copper Ales are fantastic with this spicy/cool combo.

Wine Pairing: This is a meal with lots of flavors and requires a wine with a touch of sweetness. Vouvray from France has the right amount of fruit to handle those spices. Chenin Blanc is the grape if a substitute is necessary.

chicken satay with spicy peanut sauce

Serves: *6 portions*

Prep: less than 30 minutes | Cook: 10 minutes

2   cloves garlic, minced

2   tablespoons minced ginger

3   tablespoons reduced-sodium soy sauce

1   tablespoon sesame oil

2   tablespoons brown sugar

3   tablespoons lime juice

2   pounds boneless, skinless chicken breasts,
     cut into about twenty (1-inch) strips

2   tablespoons olive oil

     cilantro sprigs for garnish

PEANUT SAUCE

⅓   cup creamy peanut butter

3   tablespoons Asian style chili sauce

1   tablespoon brown sugar

3   tablespoons lime juice

1   teaspoon reduced-sodium soy sauce

3   tablespoons water

Whisk together garlic, ginger, soy sauce, sesame oil, brown sugar, and lime juice in a small bowl until smooth. Pour mixture into a zip-top bag. Add chicken strips to bag and marinate for 30 minutes in refrigerator. At the same time, soak 20 bamboo skewers in water.

Heat olive oil in a large sauté or grill pan over medium-high heat. Thread chicken onto skewers. Cook chicken for 3 minutes per side or until golden brown.

Stir together all sauce ingredients in a small saucepan over low heat. Stir well and heat until warm. Serve chicken with peanut sauce and garnish with cilantro sprigs.

NUTRITION INFORMATION: 315 calories, 14 g fat, 2 g saturated fat, 88 mg cholesterol, 466 mg sodium, 9 g carbohydrate, 6 g sugars, 1 g fiber, 39 g protein.

Chef Tip: Is soaking the skewers important? Only if you do not want charred sticks that will catch fire immediately.

Wine Pairing: Gewürtztraminer which is filled with flavors of passion fruit and mango and spice would complement the spice and the peanut aspect of this dish. Alsace, Germany, California, and the Pacific Northwest produce excellent examples.

spicy grilled chicken and black bean enchiladas

Serves: *8 or 12 portions, depending on tortillas used*

Prep: 1 hour | Bake: 40 minutes

SAUCE

½	cup chopped onions
4	cloves garlic, chopped
2	teaspoons ground coriander
¼	teaspoon black pepper
1	teaspoon ground cumin
2	tablespoons butter
3	tablespoons flour

8	ounces sour cream
2-3	cups chicken broth
½-1	4 ounce can jalapeño peppers
1	4 ounce can chopped green chiles or fire-roasted chiles
1	cup shredded Monterey Jack cheese

ENCHILADAS

4	chicken breasts, grilled and cut into bite-size pieces
8	6-inch flour tortillas, or 12 corn tortillas
1-2	15 ounce cans black beans, drained

2	cups shredded Monterey Jack cheese
½	cup sliced black olives
1	cup chopped tomatoes
¼	cup sliced green onions

Preheat oven to 350 degrees. In a saucepan, sauté onions, garlic, coriander, black pepper, and cumin in butter until onions are tender. Stir flour into sour cream until well mixed and add to onion mixture. Stir in 2 cups broth, jalapeños, and chiles. Cook and stir sauce until smooth, thickened, and bubbly. Add more broth if needed. Remove from heat and stir in cheese.

To assemble enchiladas, mix ½ cup of sauce with chopped cooked chicken. Spoon about ¼ cup of chicken mixture onto each tortilla. Divide black beans among tortillas. Roll up tortillas and place in a 9x13x2-inch baking dish. Top with remaining sauce. Bake, covered, for about 35 minutes. Sprinkle with cheese. Bake, uncovered, about 5 minutes longer. Let stand 10 minutes before serving. Sprinkle with olives, tomatoes, and green onions.

NUTRITION INFORMATION: 476 calories, 24 g fat, 13 g saturated fat, 98 mg cholesterol, 1025 mg sodium, 32 g carbohydrate, 3 g sugars, 5 g fiber, 30 g protein.

Beer Pairing: Crisp dark lagers are an excellent choice with enchiladas.

charmoula chicken kebabs

Serves: *4 portions*

Prep: 45 minutes | Cook: 10 minutes

¼ cup nonfat plain yogurt

2 tablespoons chopped fresh Italian parsley, plus a little extra for garnish

2 tablespoons chopped fresh cilantro

1½ tablespoons fresh lemon juice

1 tablespoon olive oil

2 cloves garlic, finely chopped

1½ teaspoons paprika

¾ teaspoon ground cumin

½-¾ teaspoon salt

¼ teaspoon freshly ground black pepper

¼-½ teaspoon red pepper flakes

2 8 ounce boneless, skinless chicken breasts, cut into 1-inch pieces

1 large red or yellow bell pepper, cut into 1½-inch pieces

1 medium zucchini or pattypan squash, cut into ¼-inch thick rounds

1 cup sliced mushrooms

1 handful cherry peppers

1 cup Mediterranean or Israeli couscous

PEPPER YOGURT SAUCE

1 cup Greek yogurt

2-4 cherry peppers, or more for added spice

3 cloves garlic, coarsely chopped

1 teaspoon lemon zest

1-2 teaspoons chopped fresh cilantro

salt and pepper to taste

Stir together yogurt, 2 tablespoons parsley, cilantro, lemon juice, olive oil, garlic, paprika, cumin, ½ teaspoon salt, black pepper, and pepper flakes. Add chicken and toss to coat. Cover with plastic wrap and marinate in refrigerator for a minimum of 20 minutes or overnight. If using wooden skewers, soak them in the water.

Preheat grill or broiler. Blanch bell peppers in boiling salted water for 3 minutes. Remove with a slotted spoon and refresh with cold water. Blanch squash for 1 minute. Drain and refresh with cold water. Thread kebabs by alternating chicken cubes, bell peppers, zucchini, mushrooms, and cherry peppers. Grill or broil for 3 to 4 minutes or until chicken is done.

Meanwhile, cook couscous according to directions. To serve, mound couscous on a platter or individual plates and place kebabs over couscous.

To make sauce, combine yogurt, peppers, garlic, zest, and cilantro in a blender and process until smooth. Add salt and pepper to taste. Spoon yogurt sauce over kebabs. Garnish with a sprinkle of chopped parsley or cilantro.

NUTRITION INFORMATION: 365 calories, 4 g fat, 1 g saturated fat, 66 mg cholesterol, 261 mg sodium, 42 g carbohydrate, 6 g sugars, 4 g fiber, 39 g protein.

Wine Pairing: The multitude of flavors this dish offers would require a wine with some complexity. Chardonnay would be the selection. Meursault from France or something from the Russian River in California will have the depth to honor this meal.

sautéed chicken with mushroom sherry sauce

Serves: *3 portions*

Prep: 45 minutes | Cook: 30 minutes

1 tablespoon butter	salt and pepper to taste
3 boneless, skinless chicken breast halves	½ cup dry sherry
1½ tablespoons butter	½ cup chicken broth
8 ounces large mushrooms, quartered	⅔ cup heavy cream
2 green onions, chopped and divided	

Melt 1 tablespoon butter in a heavy large skillet over medium heat. Add chicken and sauté for 12 minutes or until cooked through, turning occasionally. Transfer chicken to a plate and cover to keep warm. Pour off fat from skillet. Melt 1½ tablespoons butter in same skillet over medium-high heat. Add mushrooms and two-thirds of green onions. Season with salt and pepper. Sauté for 2 minutes or until mushrooms begin to turn color. Add sherry and broth and boil for 5 minutes or until reduced to a syrupy consistency, scraping up any browned bits. Add cream and boil for 2 to 5 minutes or until sauce begins to thicken. Return chicken and any accumulated juices on plate to skillet. Simmer for 1 minute or until chicken is heated through and sauce thickens. Adjust seasoning as desired. Serve over cooked rice. Top with remaining green onions.

NUTRITION INFORMATION: 438 calories, 31 g fat, 19 g saturated fat, 166 mg cholesterol, 255 mg sodium, 6 g carbohydrate, 2 g sugars, 1 g fiber, 31 g protein.

Beer Pairing: A Robust Porter will accent the rich sauce for an aggressive pairing.

chicken eggplant parmesan

Serves: *6 portions*

Prep: less than 30 minutes | Bake: 30 minutes

1 small eggplant, sliced into ¼-inch thick rounds	1 15 ounce can crushed tomatoes
6-8 tablespoons olive oil, divided	2 6 ounce packages sliced mozzarella cheese
2 teaspoons salt, divided	½ cup Parmesan cheese
1 teaspoon freshly ground black pepper, divided	¼ cup lightly packed fresh basil leaves
4 boneless, skinless chicken breasts, cut into ¼-inch slices	

Preheat broiler. Coat both sides of eggplant rounds with some of olive oil, salt, and pepper. Arrange eggplant on a baking sheet and broil about 5 minutes on each side or until browned; set aside. Turn oven to 425 degrees. Heat 1 tablespoon olive oil over medium heat in a large skillet. Season chicken with salt and pepper and sauté in hot oil. Layer a greased baking dish with half of eggplant, half of chicken, half of tomatoes, half of mozzarella cheese, half of Parmesan cheese, and half of basil leaves. Repeat layers. Drizzle top with ½ tablespoon olive oil. Bake, uncovered, for 20 to 25 minutes. Let stand 5 minutes before serving.

NUTRITION INFORMATION: 417 calories, 26 g fat, 9 g saturated fat, 88 mg cholesterol, 1391 mg sodium, 10 g carbohydrate, 4 g sugars, 3 g fiber, 36 g protein.

parmesan chicken in mushroom cream sauce

Serves: *4 portions*

Prep: 45 minutes | Bake: 30 minutes

2   large or 4 small boneless, skinless chicken breasts (if using 2 large chicken breasts, cut each in half)

1   cup buttermilk

1   tablespoon hot pepper sauce

1   cup panko or homemade bread crumbs (see note below)

1   cup Parmesan cheese

1   teaspoon salt or smoked salt

2   eggs, beaten

    flour for dusting

4   tablespoons unsalted butter

MUSHROOM CREAM SAUCE

5   ounces fresh mushrooms, stemmed and quartered

1   tablespoon unsalted butter

1   small shallot, chopped

½   cup chicken broth

½   cup vermouth

¾   cup heavy cream

Marinate chicken in buttermilk and hot sauce in a zip-top bag overnight or up to 24 hours, turning once.

Preheat oven to 375 degrees. Combine bread crumbs, cheese, and salt in a shallow dish. Place beaten eggs in a separate shallow dish. Remove chicken from marinade. Dust chicken in flour. Dip chicken in eggs, then roll in bread crumb mixture, coating thoroughly. Melt butter in a skillet over medium heat. Add chicken and cook until lightly browned on both sides, being careful to not scorch coating. Transfer browned chicken to a baking sheet. Bake for 10 to 15 minutes or until done.

While chicken bakes, prepare sauce. Sauté mushrooms in butter in a skillet; set aside. Add shallots to skillet and sauté lightly. Add broth and vermouth to skillet and reduce to 2 tablespoons. Return mushrooms to skillet and stir in cream. Reduce sauce to desired consistency. To preserve crispy coating, serve chicken with sauce on the side.

Homemade bread crumbs: Chop French bread into pieces and place on a baking sheet. Toast in oven at 350 degrees for 10 minutes or until lightly browned. Place toasted bread in zip-top bag and crush; or grind toasted bread in a food processor.

NUTRITION INFORMATION: 515 calories, 36 g fat, 22 g saturated fat, 200 mg cholesterol, 720 mg sodium, 10 g carbohydrate, 1 g sugars, 1 g fiber, 34 g protein.

under the tuscan sun chicken

Serves: *6 portions*

Prep: 45 minutes | Bake: 40 minutes

6	6 ounce boneless, skinless chicken breasts
2	large shallots, finely minced
2	large cloves garlic, finely minced
2	tablespoons unsalted butter
1	cup whole milk ricotta cheese
1	cup grated Italian fontina cheese
½	cup chopped dried Mission figs, or other dried fruit, such as cranberries
2	tablespoons finely chopped flat-leaf Italian parsley
½	teaspoon kosher salt
½	teaspoon freshly ground black pepper
12	leaves fresh sage
6	thin slices pancetta
	extra virgin olive oil
1	cup unsalted chicken broth
1	cup dry Italian Marsala wine
3	tablespoons unsalted butter, chilled
	Italian parsley sprigs and fresh cut figs for garnish

Flatten chicken breasts to about ¼-inch thickness using the flat end of a meat tenderizer; placing chicken in a large plastic freezer bag before flattening works well. Refrigerate chicken while preparing filling. Sauté shallots and garlic in 2 tablespoons unsalted butter just until tender; cool slightly. Mix together ricotta and fontina cheeses. Add shallots mixture and chopped figs and mix well. Stir in parsley, salt, and pepper. Fill each prepared chicken breast with 2 tablespoons cheese filling and roll up. Place 2 whole sage leaves on top of each chicken breast, then wrap each breast with 1 slice of pancetta. Place chicken rolls in large baking dish that has been drizzled with olive oil. This portion of the recipe may be prepared up to a day ahead of time.

Preheat oven to 350 degrees. Before baking, drizzle chicken breasts with olive oil and sprinkle with cracked black pepper. Bake for 30 to 40 minutes. Remove chicken to a platter and cover with foil. Deglaze baking pan over medium heat with broth and wine and cook until reduced by about half. Swirl in 3 tablespoons cold butter. Pour sauce over chicken and garnish with sprigs of Italian parsley and fresh cut figs.

NUTRITION INFORMATION: 526 calories, 26 g fat, 14 g saturated fat, 174 mg cholesterol, 634 mg sodium, 14 g carbohydrate, 8 g sugars, 1 g fiber, 52 g protein.

"roastisserie" style chicken

Serves: *8 portions*

Prep: less than 30 minutes | Bake: 5 hours

4	teaspoons salt	1	teaspoon black pepper
4	teaspoons paprika	1	teaspoon garlic powder
2	teaspoons onion powder	2	4 pound whole Maverick Ranch™ Free-Range Air-Chilled Chickens, giblets discarded
2	teaspoons dried thyme		
2	teaspoons white pepper	2	small or 1 large onion, cut into or quarters
1	teaspoon cayenne pepper		

In a small bowl, combine all ingredients except chicken and onion. Rinse each chicken cavity and pat dry with paper towel. Rub each chicken inside and out with spice mixture. Divide onion quarters between chicken cavities. Place chickens in a large zip-top bag or double wrap with plastic wrap. Refrigerate 4 to 6 hours or overnight.

Preheat oven to 250 degrees. Remove chickens from plastic and place in a roasting pan. Bake, uncovered, for 5 hours or to a minimum internal temperature of 180 degrees. Remove from oven and let stand for 10 minutes before carving.

No basting is needed, but you can baste in the first hour, if desired. Chicken will be very moist - fall off the bone moist. Chicken does not need to be tended to the entire 5 hours of cooking unless you baste in the first hour. If only cooking one chicken, ingredients can easily be halved.

NUTRITION INFORMATION: 525 calories, 30 g fat, 8 g saturated fat, 190 mg cholesterol, 1341 mg sodium, 2 g carbohydrate, 0 g sugars, 1 g fiber, 59 g protein.

grilled tzatziki chicken burgers

Serves: *4 portions*

Prep: 30 minutes | Grill: 10 minutes

BURGERS

1¼	pounds ground chicken breast		2	teaspoons ground cumin
4	green onions, finely chopped		¼	teaspoon cayenne pepper
3	tablespoons chopped fresh ginger		¾	teaspoon salt
2	tablespoons fresh lemon or lime juice		½	teaspoon black pepper
1	tablespoon paprika			

SAUCE

1	large cucumber, seeds removed		1	tablespoon fresh squeezed lemon or lime juice
2	cups plain whole milk yogurt			salt and pepper to taste
2	tablespoons chopped fresh cilantro		2	medium cloves garlic, minced
2	tablespoons chopped fresh mint			

Preheat grill to medium-high heat and spray a rack with smaller holes with high-temperature cooking spray. Mix together all burger ingredients and form into patties. Grill patties for 3 to 4 minutes on each side or until done.

To make sauce, blend all ingredients in a food processor.

Serve burgers with pita bread, tortillas (as a wrap), or burger buns, thinly sliced purple onion and cucumber, chopped home-grown tomatoes, kalamata olives, feta cheese, and cilantro to garnish.

NUTRITION INFORMATION: 269 calories, 6 g fat, 3 g saturated fat, 98 mg cholesterol, 596 mg sodium, 13 g carbohydrate, 9 g sugars, 3 g fiber, 38 g protein.

Wine Pairing: Beaujolais would have the soft fruitiness to accompany the sauce and light enough to go with the chicken. Pinot Noir would be quite good as well.

baked lemon turkey

Serves: *6-8 portions*

Prep: 15 minutes | **Bake:** about 1½ hours

½	bone-in turkey breast, about 2½ to 3 pounds
1	lemon, ½ thinly sliced, ½ juiced
2-3	sprigs fresh sage
1	tablespoon olive oil

1	heaping tablespoon fresh rosemary, or 1 to 1½ teaspoons dried
	freshly ground salt and pepper to taste
4	tablespoons butter

Preheat oven to 350 degrees. Clean turkey breast and pat dry. Loosen skin of breast. Slide lemon slices and sage sprigs under skin. Secure skin to breast with 1 to 2 turkey skewers. Rub turkey breast all over with olive oil. Rub rosemary into oil and season turkey on all sides with salt and pepper. Place turkey in a roasting pan. Cover and bake for 1 hour, 15 minutes to 1 hour, 30 minutes or to an internal temperature of 160 degrees on a meat thermometer.

Meanwhile, melt butter and combine with lemon juice. While baking, baste turkey with butter mixture every 30 minutes or so; the more the turkey is basted, the moister it will be. When done baking, remove and discard skin and sage and lemon slices under skin. Carve meat into thin slices and serve. Great leftover and cold.

NUTRITION INFORMATION: 199 calories, 7 g fat, 3 g saturated fat, 99 mg cholesterol, 85 mg sodium, 0 g carbohydrate, 0 g sugars, 0 g fiber, 31 g protein.

Beer Pairing: A strong Golden Ale or Belgian Trippel go together well with grilled turkey.

chicken skewers with lemon butter sauce

Serves: *6 portions*

Prep: less than 30 minutes | **Cook:** 12 minutes

½	cup olive oil
½	cup white wine
1	tablespoon chopped fresh parsley
⅛	teaspoon salt
¼	teaspoon black pepper
⅛	teaspoon crushed red pepper flakes

6	boneless, skinless chicken breast halves, cut into 1-inch strips
¾	cup dry white bread crumbs
¾	cup freshly grated Parmesan cheese
4	tablespoons butter
2	tablespoons fresh lemon juice

Mix olive oil, wine, parsley, salt, black pepper, and pepper flakes in a large bowl. Add chicken and toss to coat. Cover and refrigerate 3 hours.

Preheat broiler. Combine breadcrumbs and cheese in another large bowl. Remove chicken from marinade. Add chicken to breadcrumb mixture and toss to coat. Thread chicken onto twelve 8-inch bamboo skewers that have been soaked in water for 30 minutes, or metal skewers. Broil for 12 minutes or until cooked through, turning regularly.

Melt butter in a small saucepan over medium heat. Remove from heat and mix in lemon juice. Drizzle lemon butter over chicken.

NUTRITION INFORMATION: 288 calories, 13 g fat, 7 g saturated fat, 96 mg cholesterol, 364 mg sodium, 9 g carbohydrate, 1 g sugars, 1 g fiber, 32 g protein.

Beer Pairing: American wheat beers are a great garnish for this lemon chicken.

classique
meats

Best of Beef Tips

Brought to you by:

Colorado Beef Council

"Proudly representing the farming and ranching families of Colorado; the true environmental stewards of the land."

DID YOU KNOW...a 3 ounce cooked portion of beef is about the size of a deck of cards. A 3 ounce cooked hamburger is about the size of a hockey puck.

Is it lean?

One tip to quickly find a lean cut of beef at the grocery store is to look for the words loin or round in the name, such as tenderloin, sirloin, top round, and round steak. Other cuts, such as flank, strip steak, brisket, T-bone, and eye round roast are also considered lean. Beef qualifies as lean if it has the following per serving (3.5 ounces):

1. Less than 10 grams of total fat

2. 4.5 grams or less saturated fat

3. less than 95 milligrams cholesterol

Beef has "umami"

Umami is a Japanese word for "delicious". This fifth taste is described as meaty and savory. Pairing beef with other umami-rich foods can produce eight times as much flavor. Ingredients such as wine, mushrooms, blue cheese, and tomatoes magnify the flavor of your beef dish. Give it a try!

Make it tender

Turn steaks with tongs. A fork pierces the beef, allowing the loss of flavorful juices. Season beef with herbs or spices as desired. Salt draws out moisture and inhibits browning, so salt after grilling. If you choose to marinate, do so in a plastic bag or glass container in the refrigerator, never at room temperature. Grill and enjoy!

www.BeefItsWhatsForDinner.com
www.cobeef.com

162 meats

spicy flank steak with tomato jam

Serves: *8 portions*

Prep: 1 hour | Grill: 45 minutes

JAM

6	large ripe tomatoes, cored and cut in half crosswise	2	jalapeño peppers, minced
⅓	cup sugar	¼	cup chopped fresh cilantro or mint
⅓	cup grated onion	3	tablespoons fresh lime juice
3	cloves garlic, minced	½	teaspoon salt

STEAK

⅓	cup fresh lime juice	2	cloves garlic, minced
¼	cup olive oil	2-2½	pounds flank steak, trimmed
2	jalapeño peppers, minced	½	teaspoon salt

To make jam, grate tomatoes, flesh-side down, over a large bowl to yield 4 to 5 cups pulp; discard skins. Combine tomato pulp with sugar, onion, garlic, and jalapeños in a medium saucepan. Bring to a boil. Reduce heat and simmer 30 minutes or until reduced to 2¼ cups, stirring occasionally. Cool to room temperature. Stir in cilantro or mint, lime juice, and salt. Cover and store in refrigerator for up to 2 days, but serve at room temperature.

For steak, combine lime juice, olive oil, jalapeños, and garlic in a large zip-top plastic bag. Add steak and seal. Marinate in refrigerator for 8 hours or overnight, turning bag occasionally.

When ready to cook, preheat grill. Remove steak from bag and discard marinade. Sprinkle both sides of steak evenly with salt. Grill steak 4 to 5 minutes on each side or until cooked to desired doneness. Let stand 5 minutes. Cut steak diagonally across the grain into thin slices. Serve with jam.

Tomato jam is a great topping for chicken and fish, or used as a dip with chips. For an appetizer, slice grilled steak thinly into 1-inch length pieces. Serve steak on crackers with a dollop of jam on top.

NUTRITION INFORMATION: 221 calories, 7 g fat, 3 g saturated fat, 45 mg cholesterol, 344 mg sodium, 15 g carbohydrate, 13 g sugars, 2 g fiber, 24 g protein.

Beer Pairing: A hearty stout accents this steak well.

Wine Pairing: Aglianico from the Campania in Italy has the fruit and the structure to handle this spicy, flavorful meal. Nero D'Avola from Sicily would be a good second choice.

barbeque pork ribs with dipping sauce

Serves: *8 portions*

Prep: 45 minutes | Bake: 2 hours, 30 minutes

BASIC RUB AND RIBS
(MAKES ENOUGH FOR 2 RACKS OF MAVERICK RANCH ™ NATURALLY RAISED PORK RIBS)

1	tablespoon kosher salt		1	tablespoon ground oregano
1	tablespoon black pepper		1	tablespoon dried thyme
2	tablespoons chili powder		2	racks of pork baby back ribs or 4 pounds country ribs
1	tablespoon paprika			

DIPPING SAUCE

1	cup chopped yellow onion		½	cup brown sugar
2	tablespoons olive oil		¼	cup prepared yellow mustard
2	tablespoons minced garlic		¼	cup fresh lime juice
1	cup ketchup		3	canned chipotle peppers in adobo sauce
1	cup orange marmalade		¼	cup chopped fresh cilantro
¾	cup apple cider vinegar			

Combine all Basic Rub ingredients. Rub mixture over ribs. Cover and refrigerate for at least 1 hour before roasting.

Preheat oven to 300 degrees. Wrap ribs tightly in aluminum foil and bake for 2 hours, 30 minutes. Place ribs on platter and coat with warm sauce. Serve with additional sauce.

To make sauce, sauté onion in olive oil until softened. Add garlic, ketchup, marmalade, vinegar, brown sugar, mustard, lime juice, and peppers. Simmer on low heat for 25 to 35 minutes or until sauce thickens. Remove from heat and stir in the cilantro.

NUTRITION INFORMATION: 634 calories, 35 g fat, 12 g saturated fat, 122 mg cholesterol, 1341 mg sodium, 55 g carbohydrate, 46 g sugars, 3 g fiber, 27 g protein.

Beer Pairing: The lightly malted sweetness of a Copper Ale harmonizes like the trumpet of an uptempo jazz combo with this dipping sauce.

Wine Pairing: A Red Zinfandel from California is the perfect wine to go with barbecued ribs. It has the intense bramble flavors and spice that will enhance the rub used on the meat and the sauce as well.

grilled flank steak with asian slaw

Serves: *4 portions*

Prep: less than 30 minutes | Grill: 15 minutes

¼ cup soy sauce	2 jalapeño peppers, red or green, thinly sliced into rounds
¼ cup vegetable oil	
1 tablespoon grated fresh ginger	2 teaspoons soy sauce
1 clove garlic, minced	1 tablespoon grated fresh ginger
1-1½ pounds flank steak	5 cups thinly sliced Napa cabbage (about 9 ounces)
3 tablespoons sugar	1 cup julienned carrots
¼ cup seasoned rice vinegar	½ cup chopped mint (optional)
	salt and pepper to taste

Mix ¼ cup soy sauce, oil, 1 tablespoon ginger, and garlic in zip-top plastic bag. Add flank steak and marinate in refrigerator for 1 to 3 hours, turning occasionally.

When ready to cook, preheat grill. Stir sugar and vinegar in a small saucepan over medium heat until sugar dissolves. Remove from heat and add jalapeños, 2 teaspoons soy sauce, and 1 tablespoon ginger. Place cabbage, carrots, and mint in a medium bowl. Pour vinegar mixture over vegetables and toss to coat. Season with salt and pepper.

Grill steak about 4 minutes per side for medium-rare, or until cooked to desired doneness. Allow to rest for 10 minutes before carving into thin slices. Divide slaw between plates and top with beef.

NUTRITION INFORMATION: 230 calories, 7 g fat, 3 g saturated fat, 45 mg cholesterol, 287 mg sodium, 16 g carbohydrate, 13 g sugars, 2 g fiber, 24 g protein.

Chef Tip: Flank steak or skirt steak, can I interchange? Though they are not the same cut, they can be substituted if you prefer one cut to the other.

Wine Pairing: The steak marinade and the spices and the vinegar need a wine with substantial body and fruit. Shiraz from Australia would supply both of those. A Shiraz from the Barossa would have the body and one from the McLaren Vale would have the fruit, either would work.

porcini crusted filet mignon with herb butter

Serves: *6 portions*

Prep: less than 30 minutes | Cook: 10-12 minutes

¾ cup butter, softened

3 tablespoons snipped fresh chives

1½ tablespoons finely chopped fresh tarragon, or ½ tablespoon dried

¾ teaspoon minced garlic

salt and freshly ground black pepper to taste

¾ ounce dried porcini mushrooms, unwashed, debris and stems removed.

6 5-6 ounce, 1-inch thick filet mignons

Mix butter with chives, tarragon, and garlic in a small bowl. Add salt and pepper to taste; set aside. Place dried mushrooms in a spice processor or blender and process until reduced to powder. Pour powder into a pie plate. Season filet mignons with salt and pepper as desired. Dredge both sides of filets in porcini powder until evenly coated.

Melt 3 tablespoons of the herb butter in a large nonstick skillet over medium to medium-high heat, taking care not to burn the butter. Add filet mignons to skillet and cook 5 to 6 minutes per side for medium-rare, or to desired doneness; do not overcook. Place cooked filet mignons on a serving platter. Top each filet with a mound of remaining herb butter.

Dried porcini mushrooms have a long shelf life.

For a festive look, squeeze herb butter through a pastry bag with a decorative tip. Serve immediately.

NUTRITION INFORMATION: 419 calories, 31 g fat, 18 g saturated fat, 144 mg cholesterol, 225 mg sodium, 2 g carbohydrate, 0 g sugars, 1 g fiber, 32 g protein.

Chef Tip: Why do recipes always say "snipped" for chives? Snipped chives do not brown like they will if cut.

Wine Pairing: A full-bodied Cabernet Sauvignon that is from the New World. The ripeness will make the filet melt in the mouth.

Colorado's Best Beef Company

The importance of searing

For fine cuts, such as this filet mignon, or any steak or roast, searing the meat with high intense heat or flame for a short period of time seals in the flavor and juices. Reduce to a low heat or flame to complete the cooking.

Never cut to test for doneness!

With practice, you should be able to determine doneness by touch. Cutting into meat while it is cooking causes all of the wonderful juices to spill into the pan or fire. Always let meat rest before cutting. Resting allows the bubbling juices to return to the center of the meat so the juices are less likely to 'spill' out when cut.

Cover it up!

After cooking, place your steaks into a covered container to rest. The steam from the meat will drip back into the container providing a natural 'au jus'.

Beef Tips

Brought to you by:

Colorado's Best Beef Company

"...from our ranch, to your table."

DID YOU KNOW...The purebred white Charolais (Shar-o-lay) and Charolais-influenced beef came to the United States from Mexico in 1936, but originated in France. To many tastes, Charolais is some of the most mouth-watering, perfectly marbled, meltingly tender beef anywhere. It's juicy and buttery without being fatty, spreading an irresistible nutty flavor across the tongue and palate. The quality of the meat is due, not only to the aging of the beef for 14-21 days (which adds to the tenderness and flavor), but also an already inherent predisposition for the tenderness.

There are 4 variables that make up a good piece of beef:

1. The source and breed of cattle (we raise Charolais)

2. The way they are fed (our beef is corn finished)

3. The way it is processed (we dry-age our beef 14-21 days)

4. And the way it is cooked

www.naturalbeef.com

garlic new york strip steak

Serves: *4 portions*

Prep: less than 30 minutes I Grill: 10 minutes

3	cloves garlic, peeled, chopped		2	teaspoons black pepper
½	teaspoon kosher salt		¼	cup extra virgin olive oil
1	tablespoon finely chopped fresh rosemary		4	8 ounce New York Strip steaks

Preheat grill. Using a mortar and pestle or a small bowl, crush garlic and salt until a paste forms. Add rosemary and pepper. Whisk in oil and stir well. Spread garlic mixture over both sides of steaks. Grill steaks 8 to 9 minutes for rare, or more depending on desired doneness.

NUTRITION INFORMATION: 434 calories, 24 g fat, 6 g saturated fat, 110 mg cholesterol, 376 mg sodium, 2 g carbohydrate, 0 g sugars, 0 g fiber, 51 g protein.

beef tenderloin

Serves: *8 portions*

Prep: 45 minutes I Bake: 1 hour

1	(about 3 pound) beef tenderloin		½	cup finely chopped fennel bulb
1	cup finely chopped onion		4	tablespoons butter, melted
¼	cup finely chopped celery			salt and pepper to taste
½	cup finely chopped carrot			

RED WINE SAUCE

½	cup chopped shallots		2	tablespoons butter
½	cup red wine			

Preheat oven to 325 degrees. Trim excess muscle and fat from tenderloin. Place meat in a roasting pan, preferably on a rack. Mix together onion, celery, carrot, and fennel in a medium bowl. Drizzle half of melted butter over tenderloin and sprinkle with salt and pepper. Pat vegetable mixture over top of tenderloin. Drizzle with remaining butter and sprinkle with more salt and pepper. Bake for 1 hour. Let beef rest for 10 to 15 minutes before serving. Serve with Red Wine Sauce or a béarnaise sauce, if desired.

To make Red Wine Sauce, remove beef from pan. Add shallots to pan drippings and sauté in pan on the stove. Add red wine to deglaze pan. Stir in butter until melted. Drizzle sauce over beef.

NUTRITION INFORMATION: 354 calories, 19 g fat, 9 g saturated fat, 123 mg cholesterol, 151 mg sodium, 6 g carbohydrate, 2 g sugars, 1 g fiber, 37 g protein.

Beer Pairing: For the adventurous, a Smoked Porter with this rich dish is a perfect accent.

Wine Pairing: A big full-bodied red is perfect with beef. Cabernet Sauvignon is among the biggest. California, Washington, and Australia produce some great ones.

rib-eye with vietnamese chimichurri sauce

Serves: *4-6 portions*

Prep: less than 30 minutes | Grill: 10 minutes

1	tablespoon Thai fish sauce (nam pla)	2	teaspoons chopped garlic
1	teaspoon cracked or coarsely ground black pepper	2	medium shallots, chopped
1	teaspoon sugar	½	cup chopped mint, or more to taste
½	jalapeño pepper, chopped, or ½ teaspoon crushed red pepper flakes	½	cup chopped fresh cilantro
			salt and pepper to taste
2	tablespoons fresh lime juice	2	pounds rib-eye steak

Preheat grill. Combine fish sauce, black pepper, sugar, jalapeño, lime juice, garlic, and shallots in a blender or food processor and purée. Add mint and cilantro and pulse until finely chopped but not quite puréed. Season with salt and pepper.

Cook steaks on grill. Top steaks with sauce.

NUTRITION INFORMATION: 393 calories, 18 g fat, 7 g saturated fat, 113 mg cholesterol, 482 mg sodium, 5 g carbohydrate, 2 g sugars, 1 g fiber, 52 g protein.

Chef Tip: Let it be! Make sure to always let meat rest before slicing into it. Let the juices stay in the meat instead of all over your cutting board. How long? 5 to 10 minutes for a steak, up to 30 minutes for a whole turkey or prime rib.

tandoori grilled flank steak

Serves: *8 portions*

Prep: less than 30 minutes | Grill: 8-12 minutes

½	cup olive oil	1	teaspoon dried oregano
⅓	cup lemon juice	1	teaspoon black pepper
1½	tablespoons minced ginger	2	large cloves garlic, minced
1	tablespoon ground cumin	3	pounds flank steak
1	tablespoon chili powder		coarse salt to taste
1	teaspoon turmeric		

Combine oil, lemon juice, ginger, cumin, chili powder, turmeric, oregano, pepper, and garlic in a medium bowl. Place flank steak in a large zip-top bag, add marinade, and seal. Refrigerate for at least 4 to 6 hours, or overnight.

Before grilling, drain steaks, discard marinade, and bring steaks to room temperature. Preheat grill. Season steaks with coarse salt. Grill to desired doneness, about 4 minutes per side for medium rare.

NUTRITION INFORMATION: 236 calories, 10 g fat, 4 g saturated fat, 67 mg cholesterol, 68 mg sodium, 0 g carbohydrate, 0 g sugars, 0 g fiber, 34 g protein.

Wine Pairing: A Cabernet Sauvignon with its currant and berry fruit would match the steak perfectly. A "Cab" from California or Colorado would be tops on the list for this meal.

oaxacan pork tenderloin

Serves: *4-6 portions*

Prep: 45 minutes | Grill: 1 hour

2	1 pound Maverick Ranch™ Naturally Raised Pork Tenderloins		2	teaspoons black pepper
2	teaspoons sea salt		2	cups orange juice

SAUCE

3	tablespoons olive oil		2	tablespoons chopped fresh chives
¼	cup minced shallots		1-2	tablespoons minced canned chipotle peppers in adobo sauce, optional
1	cup dry white wine		¼	cup toasted pine nuts
2	cup orange juice			finely grated zest of ½ lemon
1½	cups chicken broth			
¼	cup chopped fresh cilantro			

Season tenderloins with salt and pepper. Place in a plastic bag with orange juice and marinate at least 6 hours or overnight.

For the sauce, heat olive oil in a medium saucepan. Add shallots and sauté until soft. Add wine and boil for 10 minutes or until reduced to a glaze. Add orange juice and broth and boil 20 to 40 minutes or until reduced to 1½ cups.

When ready to cook, preheat grill to medium heat. Drain pork and pat dry. Grill pork, turning often, until meat reaches desired doneness, about 25 to 30 minutes for medium. Remove from grill and let stand for 5 minutes.

To serve, reheat sauce and add cilantro, chives, and chipotle peppers. Slice pork and arrange on a platter. Pour sauce over sliced pork and top with pine nuts and lemon zest.

NUTRITION INFORMATION: 478 calories, 21 g fat, 4 g saturated fat, 117 mg cholesterol, 1104 mg sodium, 17 g carbohydrate, 12 g sugars, 1 g fiber, 46 g protein.

Chef Tip: Did you know chipotle peppers are dried, smoked jalapeño peppers?

Wine Pairing: Barbera from Italy has the fruit to match the spices with the pork and the acidity to handle the sauce.

pork tenderloin with cranberry chutney

Serves: *8 portions*

Prep: 45 minutes | Bake: 45-50 minutes

2	pounds pork tenderloin		1½	teaspoons ground ginger
	salt and pepper to taste		1	teaspoon ground cloves
4	cups fresh cranberries		½	teaspoon ground allspice
¾	cup granulated sugar		1	cup unpeeled and chopped tart apples, such as Granny Smith
1	cup water		½	cup golden raisins
½	cup brown sugar		½	cup diced celery
2	teaspoons ground cinnamon			

Preheat oven to 400 degrees. Place pork tenderloin in a roasting pan or casserole dish and sprinkle with salt and pepper. In a large saucepan, combine cranberries, granulated sugar, water, brown sugar, cinnamon, ginger, cloves, and allspice. Bring to a boil. Reduce heat and simmer, uncovered, for 20 minutes, stirring occasionally. Add apples, raisins, and celery. Simmer uncovered for 15 minutes or until thickened.

Pour chutney sauce over pork and cover pan. Bake for 30 minutes. Uncover and spoon the cranberry sauce mixture over tenderloin. Return to the oven, uncovered, and bake for 15 to 20 minutes longer or until pork tenderloin is browned and cooked through; a meat thermometer in the center should register 160 degrees.

NUTRITION INFORMATION: 306 calories, 3 g fat, 1 g saturated fat, 58 mg cholesterol, 58 mg sodium, 50 g carbohydrate, 42 g sugars, 4 g fiber, 22 g protein.

Wine Pairing: Pinot Noir with its vibrant cherry flavors would be ideal with this pork dish. Red Burgundy would be a great choice but any Pinot Noir would work.

southwest pork tenderloin

Serves: *4-6 portions*

Prep: less than 30 minutes | Grill: 20 minutes

½	cup fresh lime juice		1	tablespoon minced garlic
6	tablespoons low sodium soy sauce		½	cup chopped fresh cilantro
¼	cup olive oil		½	teaspoon cayenne pepper
2	tablespoons sugar		1½	teaspoons chili powder
2	tablespoons chopped fresh oregano			freshly ground pepper
2	tablespoons chopped fresh rosemary		2	1 pound pork tenderloins, trimmed

Combine all ingredients except pork in a bowl and whisk together. Set aside ¼ cup of marinade for sauce. Pour remainder of marinade into a gallon-size zip-top bag. Add pork to bag and seal. Refrigerate overnight, turning bag once.

When ready to cook, preheat grill. Remove pork from bag; discard marinade in bag. Grill pork for 20 minutes or until barely pink in the center. Let meat rest for 5 minutes after removing from grill. Slice and serve with reserved marinade drizzled over the top.

This marinade works great on chicken, too.

NUTRITION INFORMATION: 275 calories, 9 g fat, 2 g saturated fat, 117 mg cholesterol, 384 mg sodium, 3 g carbohydrate, 2 g sugars, 0 g fiber, 43 g protein.

Beer Pairing: The light, caramelly flavor of a German Marzen style beer act as a foil for the sauce of this pork dish.

Wine Pairing: The spices and grilled aspect of the meat would be a superb match to a fruit forward Garnacha. The Spanish ones are quite good.

pork tenderloin with walnut curry stuffing

Serves: *4 portions*

Prep: 45 minutes | Bake: 40 minutes

PORK

2	tablespoons butter		1½	pounds pork tenderloin
1	cup walnuts		1½	teaspoons ground coriander
1	teaspoon curry powder		1	teaspoon ground cumin
1½	tablespoons olive oil		1	teaspoon salt
1	large clove garlic, peeled		½	teaspoon black pepper

GLAZE

1	12 ounce jar red currant jelly		½	teaspoon ground ginger
1	tablespoon red wine vinegar		2	tablespoons diced shallots
½	teaspoon crushed red pepper flakes			

Preheat oven to 350 degrees. Melt butter in a small skillet over medium heat. Add walnuts and cook, stirring frequently, for 1 to 2 minutes or until lightly toasted. Place walnuts, curry powder, olive oil, and garlic in a food processor and process until finely ground. Butterfly pork tenderloin by cutting along the length with a sharp knife to within ½ inch. Press open and spread walnut mixture down the center. Pull pork together and secure with skewers or tie with string. Combine coriander, cumin, salt, and pepper in small bowl. Rub mixture over pork. Place pork, seam-side down, in a baking pan. Bake for 30 minutes. Remove from oven and rest for 5 to 10 minutes.

Combine all glaze ingredients in a small saucepan and bring to a boil. Reduce heat and simmer for 5 minutes, stirring occasionally. Slice pork into ½-inch slices and arrange on a serving plate. Spoon glaze over pork.

NUTRITION INFORMATION: 654 calories, 32 g fat, 7 g saturated fat, 103 mg cholesterol, 693 mg sodium, 61 g carbohydrate, 52 g sugars, 2 g fiber, 36 g protein.

Wine Pairing: Pinot Noir would work well. A California Pinot Noir which has some ripe berry and cherry fruit would be ideal.

moroccan lamb stew with apricots

Serves: 6-8 portions

Prep: 45 minutes | Cook: 1 hour 30 minutes

1	tablespoon ground cumin	1	tablespoon tomato paste
2	teaspoons ground coriander	2	cups chicken broth
1½	teaspoons salt	1	15 ounce can garbanzo beans, drained
2	teaspoons fennel seeds	1	cup whole dried apricots
½	teaspoon cayenne pepper	2	plum tomatoes, chopped
½	teaspoon black pepper	2	4-inch long cinnamon sticks
2½	pounds lamb shoulder or leg, cubed	1	tablespoon minced peeled fresh ginger
4	tablespoons olive oil, divided	2	teaspoons lemon zest
1	large onion, finely chopped		

Mix together cumin, coriander, salt, fennel seeds, cayenne pepper, and black pepper in a large bowl. Add lamb and toss to coat. In a heavy large skillet, heat 2 tablespoons oil over medium-high heat. Add lamb in batches, cooking until browned on all sides, using remaining 2 tablespoons oil as needed. Transfer lamb to a large bowl after each batch is cooked.

Add onions to drippings in skillet and sauté over medium heat for 5 to 8 minutes or until soft. Add tomato paste, broth, beans, apricots, tomatoes, cinnamon sticks, ginger, and lemon zest. Bring to boil, scraping up browned bits. Return lamb to skillet and return to a boil. Reduce heat to low, cover, and simmer 1 hour or until lamb is tender. Uncover and simmer 20 minutes or until sauce thickens. Serve with couscous or rice.

NUTRITION INFORMATION: 482 calories, 24 g fat, 6 g saturated fat, 113 mg cholesterol, 1215 mg sodium, 29 g carbohydrate, 16 g sugars, 5 g fiber, 39 g protein.

lamb chops with balsamic cherry sauce

Serves: *4 portions*

Prep: less than 30 minutes | Bake: 20 minutes

4	lamb loin chops		1	teaspoon dried thyme
2	tablespoons olive oil			salt and pepper to taste
1	medium clove garlic, minced		2	ounces goat cheese, cut into 4 slices

BALSAMIC CHERRY SAUCE

1	cup dried tart cherries		2	tablespoons brown sugar
1	cup balsamic vinegar		2-3	tablespoons butter (optional)
½	cup chicken broth			salt and pepper to taste

Preheat oven to 400 degrees. Rub lamb chops with olive oil and sprinkle with garlic, thyme, and salt and pepper. Place in a baking pan and bake for 10 minutes. Top each chop with a slice of goat cheese and bake 4 to 5 minutes longer for medium-rare.

To make sauce, combine cherries, vinegar, broth, and brown sugar in a saucepan. Simmer for 15 minutes or until reduced. Stir in butter and season with salt and pepper. Serve over lamb chops.

NUTRITION INFORMATION: 443 calories, 17 g fat, 5 g saturated fat, 70 mg cholesterol, 251 mg sodium, 46 g carbohydrate, 37 g sugars, 2 g fiber, 25 g protein

Wine Pairing: The red fruit flavors of Rioja would accentuate the flavors of this lamb dish.

american lamb board's
lamb sirloin with arugula and blackberry vinaigrette

3	tablespoons Dijon mustard		½	cup olive oil
¼	cup blackberry vinegar		3	tablespoons chopped fresh basil and thyme
1	tablespoon sugar			kosher salt to taste
3	tablespoons blackberry preserves			

For vinaigrette, whisk all ingredients, except oil, in a bowl and mix well. While whisking slowly, add oil until emulsified. Serve with lamb loin, on a bed of arugula, with fresh blackberries, goat cheese, and toasted pecans.

Lamb Tips

Brought to you by:

"American Lamb Board"

DID YOU KNOW...American Lamb, raised right here in America, is the freshest lamb available; up to 10,000 miles and about 30 days fresher than lamb from Australia or New Zealand!

American Lamb is lean and tender and on average, a 3-ounce serving of lamb has just 175 calories and contains many essential nutrients like protein, vitamin B12, niacin, zinc, iron, and selenium. Lamb is produced in nearly every state and is freshly available year-round. Colorado Lamb is the fourth largest producer of Lamb. American Lamb has a distinctive, mild flavor that marries well with a variety of spices, herbs, and marinade.

Lamb always benefits from rest before serving - the rest allows the meat's juices to settle. Give thin cuts like chops 5 minutes before serving and allow 20 minutes before carving roasts. As the meat rests, its internal temperature typically rises 5-10 degrees. Remove lamb from cooking heat when the thermometer reads 5-10 degrees less than your desired temperature. Do not cut into a roast or chop to check for doneness. Use an instant read thermometer to give you a quick, accurate reading. Lamb roasts and chops should be cooked:

Medium rare: 145 degrees

Medium: 160 degrees

Well done: 170 degrees

www.americanlamb.com

lamb kebabs with minted tomato sauce

Serves: *4-6 portions*

Prep: 45 minutes | Grill: 10-15 minutes

2   pounds lamb shoulder or leg, cut into 1-inch pieces

MARINADE

1 tablespoon dried oregano, or 3 tablespoons fresh, chopped	1 large clove garlic, minced
1½ cups olive oil	2 teaspoons salt
¼ cup lemon juice	2 teaspoons black pepper
	1 teaspoon lemon zest

AMOGIO SAUCE

1 clove garlic, crushed with a little salt	1-2 tablespoons red wine vinegar
¼ cup water	2-3 tomatoes, crushed
2 tablespoons olive oil	1 tablespoon lemon juice
½ teaspoon dried oregano, or 1½ teaspoons fresh, chopped	1 tablespoon chopped mint

Place lamb pieces in a plastic zip-top bag or sealable container. Combine all marinade ingredients and add to meat. Marinate for at least 24 hours or up to 48 hours in refrigerator, turning occasionally.

When ready to cook, preheat grill over hot coals. Combine all sauce ingredients. Drain off marinade and thread meat onto metal skewers. Grill kebabs about 10 minutes, turning once or twice. Serve with rice and grilled bell peppers or other vegetables, spooning sauce over meat.

This recipe can also be served in the manner of the traditional Italian dish called Spiedi. For this presentation, make a mint brush by tying together several mint sprigs. Bring grilled kebabs to the table. Have each person take a piece of Italian bread or half a pita round. Wrap the bread or pita around the skewered meat and remove 4 to 5 pieces of meat, creating a sandwich. Dip the mint brush into the sauce and brush the sauce over the meat.

NUTRITION INFORMATION: 441 calories, 29 g fat, 8 g saturated fat, 136 mg cholesterol, 707 mg sodium, 3 g carbohydrate, 2 g sugars, 1 g fiber, 40 g protein.

Chef Tip: Why the shoulder or leg? They have the most flavor and fat to keep moist during the cooking method. The cut can also handle the marinade without getting mushy.

Wine Pairing: The St. Emilion region of France produces some excellent Merlot-based reds. They have a slight hebaceous quality that would be great with the mint. There is plenty of body there to handle the kebabs.

lamb curry with sweet potatoes

Serves: *4-6 portions*

Prep: 1 hour | Cook: 1 hour, 30 minutes

1-1¼	pounds lamb shoulder or leg, cut into ¾-inch cubes		1	cup sliced carrot, cut into ½-inch rounds
⅓	cup flour		1	medium-size green bell pepper, chopped
1	teaspoon salt		2	cups peeled and cubed sweet potatoes
½	teaspoon black pepper		1½	cups halved mushrooms
1	tablespoon vegetable oil		4	teaspoons curry powder
2	teaspoons minced garlic		2½	cups beef stock
1	cup chopped onion		⅓	cup red wine
			3	tablespoons tomato paste

Dust lamb with flour, salt, and pepper. In a large nonstick pan with a cover, heat oil. Sauté lamb in hot oil for 2 minutes or just until seared. Remove lamb and set aside. Add garlic, onions, carrots, bell peppers, and sweet potatoes to pan and cook, stirring often, for 8 to 10 minutes or until tender. Add mushrooms and curry powder and cook about 3 minutes. Add stock, wine, tomato paste, and lamb to pan. Cover and simmer for 1 hour, 30 minutes, stirring occasionally. Season with salt and pepper to taste. Serve with rice, linguini, or couscous.

NUTRITION INFORMATION: 371 calories, 12 g fat, 3 g saturated fat, 68 mg cholesterol, 1298 mg sodium, 34 g carbohydrate, 9 g sugars, 6 g fiber, 27 g protein.

Chef Tip: In many countries around the world, meat is used more as a condiment in dishes such as curries, rather than the main ingredient. Try making this dish with less meat (about ¾ pound) and increase the amount of rice and vegetables per serving. The meat will provide flavor for a delicious and satisfying meal.

Wine Pairing: The Rhône Valley of France produces wines with fullness and flavor that would be ideal with this dish. The Southern Rhône would be better with Gigondas, Vacqueryas, or a Côtes du Rhône.

venison tenderloin

Serves: *4-6 servings*

Prep: less than 30 minutes | Bake: 30 minutes

1½ pounds venison tenderloin, 1½ inches in diameter, trimmed, at room temperature 30 minutes

¾ teaspoon coarsely ground black pepper

¼ teaspoon salt

2 tablespoons vegetable or olive oil

¼ cup finely chopped shallots

¼ cup port, Marsala, or sherry wine

⅓ cup beef or veal demi-glace

1 teaspoon green peppercorns in brine, drained and coarsely chopped

1 teaspoon unsalted butter

¼ teaspoon salt

Preheat oven to 425 degrees, place oven rack in center of oven. Pat venison dry and sprinkle with black pepper and ¼ teaspoon salt. Heat oil in an ovenproof 12-inch heavy skillet over medium-high heat until just smoking. Add venison to oil and cook 3 minutes or until brown on all sides except ends. Transfer venison in skillet to oven. Roast 10 to 15 minutes or until a meat thermometer registers 130 degrees. Transfer venison to a plate and let stand, loosely covered with foil, for 5 minutes; temperature will rise to 145 degrees for medium-rare.

While meat rests, add shallots to pan drippings in skillet and cook and stir over medium heat for 2 minutes or until golden. Add wine and deglaze skillet by stirring and scraping up brown bits. Boil for 1 minute or until liquid is reduced by half. Add demi-glace and boil, stirring, for 1 minute or until sauce is slightly thickened. Stir in peppercorns, butter, ¼ teaspoon salt, and any meat juices that have accumulated on plate, then remove from heat. Cut venison into ½-inch thick slices and serve with sauce.

NUTRITION INFORMATION: 310 calories, 12 g fat, 3 g saturated fat, 118 mg cholesterol, 461 mg sodium, 5 g carbohydrate, 2 g sugars, 1 g fiber, 39 g protein.

Chef Tip: Gourmet stores carry demi-glaces that are fantastic. Demi-glaces have more flavor than bases made from powders.

Beer Pairing: Roasty malts of a Colorado Amber Ale bring this Rocky Mountain game from the forest to your table.

Wine Pairing: Gamey meats go very well with its intense complex red berry flavors of Châteauneuf-du-Pape. The Priorat region of Spain would be a suitable alternative.

silver spur ranch blue cheese burgers

Serves: *6 portions*

Prep: less than 30 minutes | Grill: 10-12 minutes

2	pounds lean ground beef	¾	teaspoon coarsely ground black pepper
3	ounces blue cheese, crumbled	1	teaspoon salt
⅓	cup chopped fresh chives	1	teaspoon dry mustard
½	teaspoon hot pepper sauce	6	rolls or buns, toasted
1	teaspoon Worcestershire sauce		

In a large bowl, mix ground beef, blue cheese, chives, hot pepper sauce, Worcestershire sauce, black pepper, salt, and mustard. Form mixture into 6 burgers. Cover and refrigerate for at least 2 hours or overnight.

Preheat grill or broiler. Cook burgers 5 to 6 minutes per side or until cooked to desired doneness. Serve on toasted rolls.

NUTRITION INFORMATION: 373 calories, 14 g fat, 6 g saturated fat, 94 mg cholesterol, 918 mg sodium, 22 g carbohydrate, 3 g sugars, 1 g fiber, 40 g protein.

Beer Pairing: The bitterness of blue cheese is rounded out with the malty flavors of a Strong Ale.

Wine Pairing: A French Red Bordeaux or a Meritage blend from the New World. A wine that has some body to tame the blue cheese. Typically Bordeaux is a blend of Cabernet Sauvignon and Merlot.

tangy pineapple steak marinade

Serves: *6-8 portions*

Prep: 30 minutes | Grill: 15 minutes

½	cup soy sauce	1-2	medium cloves garlic, minced
¼	cup brown sugar		black pepper to taste
¼	cup cider vinegar	2-3	pounds flank steak
¼	cup pineapple juice	6-8	thick slices fresh pineapple, optional

Combine soy sauce, brown sugar, vinegar, pineapple juice, garlic, and black pepper in a bowl. Pour marinade into a zip-top plastic bag. Add flank steak and marinate, for 5 to 6 hours.

When ready to cook, preheat grill to medium heat. Remove steak from marinade and grill for 4 minutes per side for medium-rare, or to desired doneness. Heat pineapple rings on grill, if desired, halfway through cooking steak. Slice steak thinly against the grain and garnish with grilled pineapple rings.

This marinade is also delicious with chicken.

NUTRITION INFORMATION: 215 calories, 9 g fat, 4 g saturated fat, 59 mg cholesterol, 662 mg sodium, 1 g carbohydrate, 0 g sugars, 0 g fiber, 31 g protein.

short ribs braised in red wine

Serves: *4-6 portions*

Prep: 45 minutes | Cook: 2½ hours

10	fresh parsley sprigs	4	medium carrots, coarsely chopped
3½	pounds boneless beef short ribs	4	cloves garlic, smashed
1½	teaspoons salt	1	750 ml bottle full-bodied red wine
½	teaspoon black pepper	1	teaspoon dried oregano
1	tablespoon extra virgin olive oil	2	bay leaves
1	large onion, coarsely chopped		

Pull parsley leaves off stems. Chop leaves; set aside leaves and stems. Sprinkle ribs with salt and pepper. Heat olive oil in a large pot over medium-high heat. Add seasoned ribs and cook for 12 to 15 minutes or until brown on all sides; do not let the bottom of the pot burn. Remove ribs from pot. Leave 1 to 2 tablespoons fat drippings in pot; pour out any excess. Reduce heat to medium. Add onions, carrots, and garlic and cook 8 to 10 minutes or until onions are translucent and beginning to brown. Add wine and bring to a simmer. Return ribs to pot, along with any juices. Add parsley stems, oregano, and bay leaves. Add enough water to barely cover ribs. Reduce heat to low, partially cover, and cook about 2 hours, 30 minutes, turning ribs a few times while cooking. In the last hour, check on the sauce; it should reduce by about half. If it is reducing slowly, take off the lid and let cook uncovered. When ribs are done, remove bay leaves. Stir in chopped parsley and adjust seasonings as needed. Serve over noodles with plenty of crusty bread to soak up the juices.

NUTRITION INFORMATION: 677 calories, 35 g fat, 14 g saturated fat, 161 mg cholesterol, 1030 mg sodium, 16 g carbohydrate, 7 g sugars, 3 g fiber, 55 g protein.

Brought to you by:

Rocky Mountain Buffalo Association

DID YOU KNOW…there are about 500,000 bison in the US; and many thousands of them here in the Rocky Mountain region of Colorado, Utah, New Mexico, and Wyoming?

Species	Fat	Calories
BISON	2.42	143
Beef (choice)	10.15	219
Beef (select)	8.09	210
Pork	9.66	212
Chicken	7.41	190
Salmon	10.97	216

Bison, commonly known as buffalo, is lower in fat, calories, and cholesterol than beef, pork, and chicken (even half the fat of turkey.) Substitute buffalo for any beef recipe.

Nutritional Comparison

Per 100 grams of cooked meat

Source: National Bison Association 2002 Cookbook

Buffalo steaks should be cooked to no more than medium (135-140 degrees), so please use a meat thermometer and think pink.

Buffalo roasts should have liquid added (soups, broths, salsa, wine, etc.) and can often be cooked in the crock pot all day on a low temperature, or prepare your specialty roasts in the oven at a low temperature (275 degrees) and again use a meat thermometer and keep the inside pink.

Ground buffalo is so lean, you may need to turn your skillet down or spray it with nonstick spray.

Just remember these 4 tips:

1. Lower heat
2. Cook slower
3. Think pink
4. Don't overcook

www.buffaloranchers.com

gourmet buffalo burgers

Serves: *4 portions*

Prep: less than 30 minutes | Cook: 10-15 minutes

BURGERS

1	tablespoon vegetable oil		½	teaspoon salt
1	cup diced onion		¼	teaspoon black pepper
1	egg, beaten		1	pound Maverick Ranch™ Naturally Raised Ground Buffalo Meat
1	teaspoon dried rosemary			
1	teaspoon dried thyme		4	hamburger buns, toasted
2	teaspoons Worcestershire sauce			lettuce and tomato slices for garnish
2	teaspoons brown sugar			

SAUCE

¼	cup BBQ sauce		¼	cup mayonnaise
¼	cup ketchup			

Heat oil in a skillet over medium heat. Add onions and sauté, stirring occasionally, for 5 minutes or until softened; set aside to cool. In a large bowl, combine egg, rosemary, thyme, Worcestershire sauce, brown sugar, salt, and pepper. Mix in cooled onion and buffalo meat. Shape mixture into four ½-inch thick patties. Chill for up to 6 hours.

When ready to cook, preheat an oiled grill to medium-high heat. Cook patties for about 5 minutes on each side.

Combine BBQ sauce, ketchup, and mayonnaise to make sauce. Spread 2 tablespoons sauce on each bun. Place patties on buns and garnish with lettuce and tomato. Serve remaining sauce on side for dipping, if desired.

Sauté 1 onion, sliced thinly into rings, in 2 tablespoons butter and 2 tablespoons Marsala wine for 10 to 15 minutes or until caramelized. Serve with burgers.

NUTRITION INFORMATION: 455 calories, 19 g fat, 3 g saturated fat, 120 mg cholesterol, 940 mg sodium, 39 g carbohydrate, 16 g sugars, 2 g fiber, 31 g protein.

Beer Pairing: Try a lightly-malted Colorado Golden Ale with this Colorado Buffalo.

Wine Pairing: Malbec from Argentina would have the red and black fruits and the body to go well with the buffalo burgers.

classique seafood

shrimp scampi

Serves: *2 portions*

Prep: less than 30 minutes | Grill: 30 minutes

¼	cup olive oil	½	teaspoon dried tarragon
3	cloves garlic, minced	1	teaspoon minced fresh parsley
¼	onion, finely minced		splash of Worcestershire sauce
2	tablespoons fresh lemon juice	½	teaspoon dry mustard
1	teaspoon salt	12	large shrimp, shelled and deveined
½	teaspoon dried basil	½	cup sour cream

Combine olive oil, garlic, onions, lemon juice, salt, basil, tarragon, parsley, Worcestershire sauce, and mustard. Pour oil mixture over shrimp and marinate for 1 hour.

When ready to cook, preheat grill. Thread shrimp onto skewers and drizzle half of oil mixture over shrimp. Grill 5 minutes or until shrimp becomes pink and opaque. Pour leftover marinade into a saucepan and cook over medium-high heat for 1 to 2 minutes. Add sour cream and cook and stir for 1 to 2 minutes longer; remove from heat. When shrimp is done, pour sauce over shrimp and serve with rice.

NUTRITION INFORMATION: 377 calories, 25 g fat, 9 g saturated fat, 292 mg cholesterol, 892 mg sodium, 4 g carbohydrate, 3 g sugars, 0 g fiber, 29 g protein.

silverthorne shrimp and tomato curry

Serves: *8 portions*

Prep: 1 hour | Cook: 30 minutes

2	tablespoons olive oil	¾	teaspoon turmeric
2	teaspoons black mustard seeds	¾	teaspoon salt
2	cups chopped plum tomatoes	¼	teaspoon chili powder or cayenne pepper
7	cloves garlic, minced	1½	cups unsweetened coconut milk
2	tablespoons grated fresh ginger	¼	cup finely chopped fresh cilantro
2	pounds raw large shrimp, peeled and deveined		salt and pepper to taste

Heat olive oil in heavy large skillet over medium heat. Add mustard seeds and sauté 4 minutes or until seeds begin to crack. Add tomatoes, garlic, and ginger and sauté 3 minutes or until tomatoes begin to soften. Add shrimp and sauté 5 minutes or until just opaque in the center. Transfer shrimp to medium bowl, keeping liquid in skillet. Add turmeric, salt, and chili powder to liquid and stir 1 minute. Add coconut milk and simmer 3 minutes or until sauce thickens slightly. Return shrimp and any juices to skillet. Stir in cilantro until blended and season with salt and pepper. Transfer to platter. Serve over jasmine rice.

NUTRITION INFORMATION: 206 calories, 14 g fat, 9 g saturated fat, 147 mg cholesterol, 397 mg sodium, 5 g carbohydrate, 1 g sugars, 1 g fiber, 17 g protein.

Beer Pairing: An India Pale Ale is a refreshing curry companion, especially with shrimp.

baked shrimp with tomatoes and feta cheese

Serves: *6-8 portions*

Prep: less than 30 minutes | Bake: 40 minutes

⅓ cup olive oil	2 tablespoons olive oil
3 medium onions, chopped	2 pounds raw large or medium, peeled, deveined, and tails removed
2 14½ ounce cans diced tomatoes in juice	½ cup ouzo (unsweetened anise liqueur); optional
3 tablespoons chopped fresh parsley	¼ cup kalamata olives, halved
1 tablespoon dried oregano	8 ounces feta cheese, crumbled
5 cloves garlic, minced	1 tablespoon chopped fresh parsley
½ teaspoon cayenne pepper	
salt and pepper to taste	

Heat ⅓ cup olive oil in large saucepan over medium heat. Add onions and sauté for 10 minutes or until golden. Add undrained tomatoes, 3 tablespoons parsley, oregano, garlic, and cayenne. Bring to a boil. Reduce heat to medium-low, cover, and simmer for 15 to 20 minutes or until sauce thickens. Season sauce with salt and pepper and transfer to a medium bowl. Sauce can be made up to 1 day ahead, covered, and chilled; then rewarmed before continuing.

Preheat oven to 400 degrees. Heat 2 tablespoons oil in a heavy large skillet over medium-high heat. Sprinkle shrimp with salt and pepper and add to skillet. Sauté shrimp for 3 minutes or until almost opaque in the center. Remove skillet from heat and add ouzo. Carefully ignite ouzo with a match. Return skillet to medium heat and cook until flames subside. Stir in tomato sauce and olives. Transfer mixture to a 10- to 12-cup baking dish. Sprinkle cheese over the top. Bake 10 minutes or until shrimp are cooked through. Sprinkle with 1 tablespoon parsley. Serve immediately with toasted French bread slices.

NUTRITION INFORMATION: 418 calories, 27 g fat, 8 g saturated fat, 230 mg cholesterol, 918 mg sodium, 16 g carbohydrate, 10 g sugars, 4 g fiber, 28 g protein.

Wine Pairing: The flavors in the shrimp and the red sauce and olives should pair with a lighter red wine. An Italian red from the Montepulciano grape is an excellent choice, a Valipolicella from the Veneto in Italy is a suitable choice as well.

pistachio crusted salmon

Serves: *4-6 portions*

Prep: less than 30 minutes | Bake: 12-15 minutes

4-6	5 ounce salmon fillets, skin on, uniform in thickness		4	teaspoons honey
	salt and pepper		¼	cup bread crumbs
2	tablespoons Dijon mustard		¼	cup finely chopped pistachios
2	tablespoons butter, melted		2	teaspoons chopped fresh cilantro

Preheat oven to 450 degrees. Lightly season salmon with salt and pepper and place on a lightly greased foil-lined pan, skin-side down. Mix mustard, butter, and honey together and brush on top of salmon. Combine bread crumbs, pistachios, and cilantro in a small food processor until thoroughly blended. Sprinkle crumb mixture on top of fillets. Bake for 12 to 15 minutes or until salmon is opaque in the center and begins to flake; do not overbake. Serve immediately.

NUTRITION INFORMATION: 333 calories, 16 g fat, 5 g saturated fat, 96 mg cholesterol, 348 mg sodium, 14 g carbohydrate, 7 g sugars, 1 g fiber, 34 g protein.

spicy prosciutto wrapped shrimp

Serves: *2 portions*

Prep: 45 minutes | Bake: 10 minutes

2	large lemons, divided		8-12	raw jumbo shrimp; peeled and deveined
1	teaspoon cayenne pepper		8-12	thin slices prosciutto
1	tablespoon minced garlic		8-12	small chunks pineapple

Juice 1 lemon into a resealable plastic bag. Add cayenne pepper and garlic to bag. Place shrimp in bag, seal, and turn bag to coat; let stand for 15 minutes. Wrap prosciutto around each shrimp. Cut second lemon into 8-12 wedges and alternately thread lemon wedges, shrimp, and pineapple onto skewers.

Preheat grill over medium heat. Grill shrimp, turning occasionally, for 5 to 7 minutes or until prosciutto is crisp and shrimp are pink and opaque. Squeeze the hot lemon wedges over the shrimp and serve over couscous and grilled vegetables.

NUTRITION INFORMATION: 242 calories, 9 g fat, 3 g saturated fat, 218 mg cholesterol, 1210 mg sodium, 6 g carbohydrate, 6 g sugars, 0 g fiber, 32 g protein.

Wine Pairing: This meal should have a white with body to match up with the shrimp and the spices. Chardonnay is one that emphasizes the fruit more than oak and would be the ideal choice.

grilled salmon with soy honey glaze

Serves: *4 portions*

Prep: less than 30 minutes | Grill: 15 minutes

MARINADE

⅔	cup Mirin Japanese cooking wine		1	tablespoon fresh grated ginger
2½	tablespoons soy sauce		⅛	teaspoon red pepper flakes
2½	ounces rice wine vinegar		4	5-6 ounce salmon fillets

GLAZE

⅓	cup honey		1½	tablespoons fresh lime juice
2	tablespoons soy sauce			

Combine all marinade ingredients in a shallow dish. Lay salmon in dish, skin-side up. Allow salmon to marinate for no more than 10 to 15 minutes. Place salmon on grill, skin-side down, and grill for 7 to 10 minutes.

In the meantime, place glaze ingredients in a saucepan and bring to a boil. At the end of grilling time, brush fish with glaze and place under broiler just until the glaze begins to brown.

NUTRITION INFORMATION: 273 calories, 5 g fat, 1 g saturated fat, 81 mg cholesterol, 838 mg sodium, 25 g carbohydrate, 23 g sugars, 0 g fiber, 32 g protein.

Beer Pairing: A flavorful Red Ale tastes and looks great with this salmon dish.

Wine Pairing: Pinot Gris is an excellent mate to salmon. The salty aspect of the soy would warrant a fruitier version.

not-your-mother's tuna casserole

Serves: *4 portions*

Prep: less than 30 minutes | Bake: 30-45 minutes

1	pound fresh tuna		3	cloves garlic, minced
1	6 ounce jar marinated artichoke hearts, coarsely chopped, liquid reserved		½	teaspoon basil
			½	teaspoon summer savory
¾	cup sliced mushrooms		½	teaspoon salt
½	medium-size white or yellow onion, thinly sliced		¼	teaspoon white pepper
			1	teaspoon flour
¼	cup white wine		3	cups cooked egg noodles
1	cup heavy cream			

Preheat oven to 350 degrees. Rinse tuna and pat dry. Cut tuna into slices, about 4 inches long and 3 inches wide. Drain off oil from artichoke hearts and use to marinate tuna while preparing remaining ingredients. Coat a baking dish with artichoke marinade. Layer tuna in dish and sprinkle with mushrooms, onions, artichokes. Pour wine over vegetables. Combine cream, garlic, basil, savory, salt, pepper, and flour and pour over top. Cover and bake 10 minutes. Uncover and bake for 10 minutes longer. Serve on a bed of egg noodles.

NUTRITION INFORMATION: 544 calories, 29 g fat, 15 g saturated fat, 170 mg cholesterol, 485 mg sodium, 38 g carbohydrate, 2 g sugars, 4 g fiber, 32 g protein.

spicy salmon with tomatoes and star anise

Serves: *4 portions*

Prep: less than 30 minutes | Grill: less than 30 minutes

4	6 ounce salmon fillets		salt and pepper to taste
	olive oil		

SAUCE

1	tablespoon sesame oil	¼	teaspoon dried red pepper flakes, or more to taste
1	cup chopped red onion		
2	teaspoons minced fresh ginger	4	plum tomatoes, seeded and chopped
¾	teaspoon freshly ground star anise	2	tablespoons soy sauce
		1½	tablespoons sugar

Preheat grill. Brush salmon with olive oil and season with salt and pepper. Grill salmon until done.

For sauce, heat sesame oil in a medium skillet. Add onion, ginger, star anise, and pepper flakes. Sauté 5 minutes or until onion is golden. Stir in tomatoes, soy sauce, and sugar and cook 3 to 5 minutes or until mixture is thickened, stirring occasionally.

Star anise can be ground in a spice grinder or with a mortar and pestle.

NUTRITION INFORMATION: 297 calories, 10 g fat, 2 g saturated fat, 97 mg cholesterol, 500 mg sodium, 12 g carbohydrate, 8 g sugars, 2 g fiber, 39 g protein.

Beer Pairing: Spicy Saison is a perfect counterpoint for the sweet star anise.

chile lime cream sauce

Serves: *4 portions*

Prep: less than 30 minutes

¼ cup dry white wine

¼ cup fresh lime juice

1 tablespoon chopped fresh ginger

1 tablespoon minced shallot

⅓ cup heavy cream

2 tablespoons chili-garlic sauce

4 tablespoons unsalted butter, cut into ½-inch pieces

Combine wine, lime juice, ginger, and shallot in a heavy small saucepan. Boil over high heat for 3 minutes or until reduced by half. Add cream and boil 2 minutes longer or until reduced by half. Reduce heat to low. Mix in chili-garlic sauce. Add butter, 1 piece at a time, whisking just until melted before adding next piece.

NUTRITION INFORMATION: 192 calories, 19 g fat, 12 g saturated fat, 57 mg cholesterol, 126 mg sodium, 5 g carbohydrate, 2 g sugars, 0 g fiber, 1 g protein.

oh-so-good salmon pot pie

Serves: *4 portions*

Prep: less than 30 minutes | Bake: 30 minutes

1	17 ounce package frozen puff pastry sheets, thawed
4	leeks, white parts only, thinly sliced
2	tablespoons butter
1-1½	pounds fresh salmon, cubed

1	teaspoon sea salt
½	tablespoon chopped fresh dill
1	egg
1	teaspoon water

SAUCE

1	roasted red bell pepper
1	cup plain yogurt

cayenne pepper to taste

Roll out pastry sheets into a two 10-inch squares. Cut each square in half, making 4 pastry sheets. Sauté leeks in butter for 5 minutes. Add salmon, salt, and dill and sauté 10 minutes longer.

Spoon salmon mixture into 4 small "pot pie" dishes. Cover each dish with 1 puff pastry sheet and pinch to enclose. Cut air vents on top. Beat egg with water and brush over crust. Refrigerate 1 to 3 hours.

When ready to bake, preheat oven to 400 degrees. Bake for 25 to 30 minutes or until pastry is brown.

To make sauce, roast red pepper over an open flame on stove for 5 to 7 minutes or until skin removes easily. Skin and seed pepper and combine with yogurt and cayenne in a blender or food processor. Blend until smooth and transfer to a serving bowl. Serve pot pies hot or at room temperature with sauce on the side.

NUTRITION INFORMATION: 984 calories, 58 g fat, 17 g saturated fat, 134 mg cholesterol, 1093 mg sodium, 74 g carbohydrate, 10 g sugars, 4 g fiber, 40 g protein.

Wine Pairing: A white wine that has some body but with acidity to handle the vegetables and spices. Pinot Gris would be the optimum choice. They are best from Oregon or the Alsace region of France.

oven baked mussels

Serves: *4 portions*

Prep: 45 minutes | Bake: 20 minutes

¼	cup olive oil	¼	cup dry white wine
1	fennel bulb, thinly sliced	6	ounces arugula, washed and dried (2 cups loosely packed)
2	pounds Prince Edward Island (black) mussels, scrubbed and debearded	½	cup unsalted butter, cut into small cubes
1	cup cherry tomatoes, halved		salt and pepper to taste

Preheat oven to 450 degrees. Heat olive oil in a large, oven-safe skillet. Add fennel and sauté until it turns translucent and begins to caramelize. Add mussels, cherry tomatoes, and wine and bring to a quick boil. Remove from heat. Spread arugula over mussels. Dot with butter and season with salt and pepper. Bake for 5 to 7 minutes or until the mussels open. Remove pan from oven and place over medium heat. Boil 2 minutes or until the liquid has reduced slightly. Discard any mussels that have not opened. Arrange mussels in a circle in each serving bowl and pour arugula mixture into the center. Serve with crusty French bread for soaking up the juices.

NUTRITION INFORMATION: 468 calories, 39 g fat, 17 g saturated fat, 92 mg cholesterol, 375 mg sodium, 13 g carbohydrate, 3 g sugars, 3 g fiber, 16 g protein.

Chef Tip: When you buy mussels, look for shells to be tightly closed. If any mussels are open, tap them to see if they will close. If they stay open, throw them away — they are dead.

Wine Pairing: Sauvignon Blanc that is more apple than citrus would be superb with the mussels. Hawkes Bay in New Zealand or try one from the Entre Deux Mers in France.

halibut with korean barbecue sauce

Serves: *4 portions*

Prep: less than 30 minutes | Cook: 15 minutes

1	tablespoon olive oil	3	tablespoons unseasoned rice vinegar
2	cloves garlic, minced	3	tablespoons water
2	teaspoons Asian chile sauce	1	tablespoon Asian sesame oil
⅓	cup soy sauce	4	5-6 ounce halibut or other fish fillets
¼	cup dark brown sugar		

Heat olive oil in a heavy small saucepan over medium heat. Add garlic and chile sauce and sauté 3 minutes or until light golden. Add soy sauce, brown sugar, vinegar, and water and bring to a boil, stirring until sugar dissolves. Reduce heat to medium and simmer 5 minutes or until mixture is reduced to ¾ cup; sauce will be thin. Whisk in sesame oil. Grill or broil fish for about 10 minutes, brushing with sauce while cooking. Drizzle remaining sauce over fish on serving plates.

NUTRITION INFORMATION: 284 calories, 10 g fat, 1 g saturated fat, 45 mg cholesterol, 1325 mg sodium, 16 g carbohydrate, 14 g sugars, 0 g fiber, 31 g protein.

scallops with currants, fennel, and pine nuts

Serves: *4-6 portions*

Prep: 45 minutes | Cook: 45 minutes

½ cup currants	½ tablespoon fennel seeds, crushed
¼ teaspoon dried red pepper flakes	salt and pepper
½ cup dry white wine	1-2 tablespoons extra virgin olive oil
½ cup extra virgin olive oil	1 pound sea scallops, halved crosswise into rounds
1 cup finely chopped shallots	
2 cloves garlic, minced	8 ounces dry bucatini or penne pasta, cooked and drained
1 pound fennel bulbs, finely chopped	½ cup pine nuts, toasted

Combine currants, pepper flakes, and wine in a bowl; set aside for 30 minutes. In a heavy skillet, heat ½ cup olive oil over medium-low heat. Add shallots, garlic, fennel bulb, and fennel seeds. Season with salt and cook, covered and stirring occasionally, for 25 minutes or until the fennel is tender. Add wine mixture and simmer for 10 minutes. Transfer to a bowl.

Heat same skillet over medium-high heat. Add 1 to 2 tablespoons olive oil if necessary to coat pan. Sauté scallops in oil on both sides for 3 to 5 minutes total or until opaque. Return fennel mixture to pan along with drained pasta. Mix gently and season with salt and pepper. Transfer to a serving dish and top with pine nuts. Serve immediately.

NUTRITION INFORMATION: 796 calories, 40 g fat, 6 g saturated fat, 37 mg cholesterol, 256 mg sodium, 77 g carbohydrate, 17 g sugars, 7 g fiber, 33 g protein.

Wine Pairing: Semillon with its melon notes would work well with the fennel and the texture of the scallops. Sauvignon Blanc that has Semillon in it would work as well.

pan sautéed scallops with roasted vegetable salsa

Serves: *4 portions*

Prep: 1 hour, 15 minutes | Cook: 5 minutes

SCALLOPS

1	tablespoon extra virgin olive oil	½	teaspoon dried red pepper flakes
1	teaspoon lime zest	½	teaspoon kosher salt
1	tablespoon minced garlic	¼	teaspoon black pepper
1	tablespoon freshly squeezed lime juice	24	large sea scallops

SALSA

1	small yellow onion, thinly sliced	¼	cup loosely packed cilantro
2	tablespoons olive oil	1	clove garlic, minced
8	medium tomatillos husked and rinsed	1	teaspoon brown sugar
1	medium Anaheim pepper	½	teaspoon kosher salt

In a large zip-top bag, mix olive oil, lime zest, garlic, lime juice, pepper flakes, salt, and pepper. Add scallops and shake in bag until coated. Marinate for 1 hour only; marinating longer will cause the lime to cook the scallops too much.

Meanwhile, prepare salsa. Preheat grill on high heat. Brush both sides of onion slices with olive oil. Grill onions, tomatillos, and pepper until charred. Put the onions and tomatillos in a food processor. Skin and seed the pepper, then add it to food processor. Add cilantro, garlic, sugar, and salt and blend until smooth. Transfer salsa to a serving dish.

Pan sauté scallops until the centers are opaque. Serve warm with salsa.

NUTRITION INFORMATION: 289 calories, 12 g fat, 2 g saturated fat, 56 mg cholesterol, 758 mg sodium, 15 g carbohydrate, 6 g sugars, 3 g fiber, 30 g protein.

Chef Tip: Make sure to remove the muscle on the side of the scallop. It will only get tougher during the cooking process.

Wine Pairing: This dish has some good spice and will need a wine to stand up to it. Viognier would have the peach flavors and body to do just that. France, California, and Australia make some fine Viognier.

baked cod with creole sauce

Serves: *2 servings*

Prep: 1 hour | Bake: 15 minutes

½	onion, diced		1	small bell pepper, diced
2	cloves garlic, minced		1	medium tomato, diced
2	tablespoons butter		½	teaspoon gumbo filé
1	tablespoon flour		¼	teaspoon basil
½	cup white wine		¼	teaspoon white pepper
1	8 ounce can tomato sauce		1	teaspoon salt
2	fresh okra pods, sliced crosswise ¼-inch thick			dash of thyme
½	cup green Spanish olives, chopped		1	pound cod
			1	tablespoon butter

Sauté onions and garlic in 2 tablespoons butter over medium heat until onions are clear. Add flour and continue cooking for 1 minute. Quickly add white wine and tomato sauce. Stir in okra, olives, bell peppers, tomatoes, filé, basil, pepper, salt, and thyme. Bring to a boil and simmer 45 minutes, stirring occasionally.

Preheat oven to 375 degrees. During final 15 minutes of sauce's cooking time, season cod with salt and pepper and place in a baking dish. Dot with 1 tablespoon butter. Bake cod for 10 to 12 minutes or until firm and opaque. Remove cod with a spatula and place on a platter. Pour sauce over fish and serve.

NUTRITION INFORMATION: 472 calories, 23 g fat, 12 g saturated fat, 131 mg cholesterol, 2806 mg sodium, 19 g carbohydrate, 9 g sugars, 3 g fiber, 40 g protein.

Wine Pairing: Riesling with its vibrant apple and pear flavors would have enough fruit to handle the spice and be delicate enough for the delicacy of the fish.

grilled red snapper with tomato and caper salsa

Serves: *8 portions*

Prep: 1 hour | Grill: 10 minutes

1¼ cups seeded and chopped ripe plum tomatoes

¼ cup kalamata olives, halved

1 large garlic clove, minced

2 tablespoons minced fresh chives

2 tablespoons chopped fresh basil

1 tablespoon olive oil

1 tablespoon capers, drained

2 teaspoons lemon juice

8 6 ounce red snapper fillets

2 tablespoons olive oil

kosher salt

freshly ground black pepper

To make salsa, in a medium bowl, combine tomatoes, olives, garlic, chives, basil, 1 tablespoon olive oil, capers, and lemon juice. Cover salsa with plastic and let stand for 30 minutes at room temperature.

Preheat grill to high heat. Brush snapper fillets with remaining olive oil and season with salt and pepper. Grill fillets about 4 to 5 minutes on each side. Top grilled snapper with salsa and serve.

Rockfish may be substituted if snapper is unavailable.

NUTRITION INFORMATION: 227 calories, 8 g fat, 1 g saturated fat, 60 mg cholesterol, 176 mg sodium, 2 g carbohydrate, 1 g sugars, 0 g fiber, 34 g protein.

Chef Tip: Leave it alone! When you place meat or fish on the grill or on the pan, turn it only once. That allows for a great brown that won't stick.

Wine Pairing: This is a dish that would be well suited to an Italian white that is medium-full bodied. Vernaccia or Verdicchio would be delicious.

brazilian seafood arroz de coco

Serves: *6 portions*

Prep: less than 30 minutes | Cook: 15-20 minutes

2   tablespoons olive oil

1   small onion, diced

2   cloves garlic, minced

1   green bell pepper, diced

1   red bell pepper, diced

1   jalapeño pepper, diced

1   poblano pepper, diced

2   tablespoons tomato paste

1   13½ ounce can unsweetened coconut milk (regular or low fat)

2   pounds halibut or any firm white fish, cut in 2-inch squares

16 large shrimp, peeled and deveined

    juice of 1 lime

¼   cup chopped cilantro

    salt and pepper to taste

    jalapeño or Thai red curry paste to taste, optional

In a 4-quart skillet, heat olive oil over medium heat. Add onion, garlic, and all peppers and sauté 5 minutes or until soft. Add tomato paste and coconut milk. Reduce heat to medium-low and simmer for 8 to 10 minutes. Add fish and shrimp and simmer for 5 to 7 minutes longer. Stir in lime juice, cilantro, salt and pepper, and jalapeño or Thai red curry paste. Serve over steamed rice.

NUTRITION INFORMATION: 407 calories, 22 g fat, 13 g saturated fat, 146 mg cholesterol, 219 mg sodium, 8 g carbohydrate, 3 g sugars, 2 g fiber, 44 g protein.

Chef Tip: Open the coconut milk can upside down and that way the fat is on the bottom and you can pour the milk and use as much cream as you want.

Wine Pairing: A white wine that has a lot of personality would be required for this flavorful dish. Gewürztraminer would do very well with all the flavors involved. There are plenty of dry ones produced.

halibut with pesto mint sauce and carrots

Serves: *4 portions*

Prep: 45 minutes | Grill: less than 30 minutes

PESTO

1	cup packed fresh mint leaves		1	clove garlic, peeled
½	cup shelled pistachios, toasted			salt to taste
¼	cup olive oil			

CARROTS

½	teaspoon coriander seeds		⅛	teaspoon dried red pepper flakes
½	teaspoon cumin seeds		1	cup low-salt chicken broth
½	teaspoon fennel seeds		2	tablespoons fresh lemon juice
1	tablespoon olive oil			salt and pepper to taste
12	ounces carrots, slivered or thinly sliced into rounds			

HALIBUT

4	6 ounce halibut fillets		1	tablespoon olive oil

Combine mint leaves, pistachios, olive oil, and garlic in a food processor and coarsely purée. Season with salt and set aside.

For carrots, stir coriander, cumin, and fennel seeds in a small dry skillet over medium heat for about 1 to 2 minutes. Coarsely grind seeds with a mortar and pestle. Heat olive oil in a large skillet over medium-high heat. Add carrots, pepper flakes, and ground seeds and sauté for 5 minutes or until carrots begin to brown. Add broth and lemon juice and bring to a boil. Reduce heat to low, cover, and simmer 6 minutes or until carrots are tender. Season to taste with salt and pepper.

To cook halibut, preheat grill over high heat. Rub halibut with olive oil and season with salt and pepper. Grill for 5 to 6 minutes per side, depending on thickness of fillets. Divide warmed carrots among 4 plates. Top with halibut and spoon pesto over fish.

NUTRITION INFORMATION: 511 calories, 32 g fat, 4 g saturated fat, 54 mg cholesterol, 180 mg sodium, 16 g carbohydrate, 5 g sugars, 5 g fiber, 41 g protein.

Beer Pairing: A Black Lager is a perfect balance with pesto and this light fish.

Wine Pairing: A sparkling wine or Champagne would be fun. Prosecco from Italy or Cava from Spain. On the wild side would be a sparkling Rose.

junior league fish tacos

Serves: 4 (2-taco) portions
Prep: 30 minutes | Cook: 10 minutes

1 teaspoon chili powder	1 pound tuna, tilapia, or halibut fillets, skin removed
1 teaspoon paprika	8 6-inch corn tortillas
1 teaspoon sea salt	canola oil
⅛ teaspoon cumin	
¼ teaspoon cayenne pepper	

ACCOMPANIMENTS

8 avocado slices	1 cup salsa
1 cup chopped tomatoes	2 cups shredded lettuce or cabbage
1 cup shredded cheese	4 lime wedges
1 cup pico de gallo	

Mix chili powder, paprika, sea salt, cumin, and cayenne in a small dish. Rinse fish and pat dry and place on a plate. Sprinkle spice mixture over both sides of fish. Cover and let stand 20 to 30 minutes.

When ready to cook, preheat grill or grill pan. Cook fish about 2 minutes on each side. Break cooked fish into chunks. Warm corn tortillas in hot canola oil in a small skillet for 15 to 20 seconds on each side; keep warm. Assemble tacos as desired with fish and accompaniments.

Easy and good. Vary the accompaniments as desired.

NUTRITION INFORMATION (does not include accompaniments): 204 calories, 4 g fat, 1 g saturated fat, 53 mg cholesterol, 675 mg sodium, 14 g carbohydrate, 0 g sugars, 2 g fiber, 27 g protein.

Beer Pairing: Dry amber ales go well with tortillas and fish.

Wine Pairing: A Macabeo from Spain would be a tasty accompaniment to the tacos. It is a crisp dry white that has citrus flavors which would work well with spice and other flavors that are involved.

lobster thermidor

Serves: *2 portions*

Prep: 45 minutes | Bake: 30 minutes

1	1¼ pound cooked spiny lobster		¼	cup heavy cream
2	tablespoons butter		1	tablespoon Dijon mustard
2	tablespoons flour		1	ounce sherry
1	teaspoon lobster base		½	teaspoon salt
1	cup water			dash white pepper
2	tablespoons butter			Parmesan cheese
1	ounce brandy, warmed			

Preheat oven to 350 degrees. Carefully split lobster in half lengthwise. Separate halves and remove tail meat and coral. Chop meat and coral into ½-inch pieces and set aside. Under warm water, rinse out shells and remove brain and eye sacs; let shells dry. Melt 2 tablespoons butter in a pan. Add flour and cook for 1 minute over medium heat. Dissolve lobster base in water in a separate saucepan and bring to a boil. Add flour mixture and cook and stir until thickened; set aside.

Melt 2 tablespoons butter in a skillet. Add lobster and coral and sauté for 2 minutes. Add brandy and ignite. When flame subsides, add lobster sauce, cream, mustard, sherry, salt, and pepper. Simmer for 1 minute. Pour mixture into shells and top with cheese. Bake for 12 to 15 minutes, broiling during final 2 minutes to brown.

NUTRITION INFORMATION: *793 calories, 40 g fat, 22 g saturated fat, 357 mg cholesterol, 1855 mg sodium, 17 g carbohydrate, 1 g sugars, 1 g fiber, 77 g protein.*

Chef Tip: Is your lobster 1 pound or 1½ pounds? This recipe still works, no matter the size. The most popular lobster size is 1¼ pounds.

Beer Pairing: The sweet richness of the buttery lobster can be quenched with a floral hoppy American Pale Ale.

Wine Pairing: An intense, full-bodied Chardonnay will enhance the richness of the lobster.

island relish

Serves: *4 portions*

Prep: *less than 30 minutes*

1 mango, chopped

¾ cup chopped sweet onion

½ red bell pepper, chopped

½ orange bell pepper, chopped

⅓ cup chopped basil

1 teaspoon balsamic vinegar

1 small avocado, chopped

1 small jalapeño pepper, finely chopped

1 tablespoon extra virgin olive oil

Combine all ingredients. Refrigerate for 4 hours. Use on grilled tuna, mahi-mahi, or swordfish.

NUTRITION INFORMATION: 145 calories, 9 g fat, 1 g saturated fat, 0 mg cholesterol, 6 mg sodium, 17 g carbohydrate, 10 g sugars, 5 g fiber, 2 g protein.

mountainside crab and shrimp cakes with fresh dill

Makes: 12 cakes, Serves: 3-4 as an entrée, or 6-8 as an appetizer
Prep: 1 hour | Cook: 20 minutes

1	egg
1	egg white
1	tablespoon chopped fresh dill
2	teaspoons Worcestershire sauce
½	teaspoon dry mustard
1	cup flaked cooked crab
1	cup chopped cooked tiny shrimp
¾	cup fine dried bread crumbs

¾	cup diced red bell pepper
¼	cup light mayonnaise
½	teaspoon Old Bay seasoning
2	tablespoons sliced green onions
1½	tablespoons butter
	fresh dill sprigs
	lemon or lime wedges

In a large bowl, beat egg and egg white. Add dill, Worcestershire, mustard, crab, shrimp, bread crumbs, bell peppers, mayonnaise, Old Bay seasoning, and green onions. Shape mixture into 12 equal flat rounds, each about ½-inch thick. In a 10- or 12-inch nonstick skillet over medium heat, melt ½ tablespoon butter. Place 4 crab cakes in pan and cook for 3 to 5 minutes per side or until golden, turning halfway through cooking. Keep warm in a 200 degree oven wile cooking remaining cakes in remaining butter. Garnish with dill sprigs with lemon or lime wedges on the side.

NUTRITION INFORMATION: 370 calories, 17 g fat, 6 g saturated fat, 220 mg cholesterol, 865 mg sodium, 25 g carbohydrate, 4 g sugars, 2 g fiber, 28 g protein.

Beer Pairing: Balance the richness of this dish with an aromatic dry-hopped ale.

classique
breakfast, brunch
& breads

chilled summer fruit compote
Serves: *8-10 portions*
Prep: 20 minutes, plus 1 hour to chill

4	cups fresh watermelon chunks	2	cups green seedless grapes, halved
3-4	fresh Colorado peaches, peeled and sliced	3	tablespoons fresh lemon juice
2	cups blueberries	¼	cup sugar
1	cup blackberries	¾	cup canned unsweetened coconut milk
2	papayas, peeled, seeded, and cubed	8	mint leaves, finely chopped

Place watermelon, peaches, blueberries, blackberries, papayas, and grapes in a large serving bowl. Mix lemon juice, sugar, coconut milk, and mint together to make a dressing. Pour dressing over fruit and refrigerate for 1 hour. Pour off excess dressing before serving. Best served the day it is made.

NUTRITION INFORMATION: 204 calories, 5 g fat, 4 g saturated fat, 0 mg cholesterol, 10 mg sodium, 42 g carbohydrate, 31 g sugars, 5 g fiber, 2 g protein.

ricotta breakfast puffs
Serves: *36-40 portions*
Prep: 30 minutes | Bake: 1-2 minutes per batch

1	cup ricotta cheese	4	teaspoons baking powder
3	eggs	¼	teaspoon salt
¼	cup sugar		vegetable oil for frying
1	cup all-purpose flour		powdered sugar

In a bowl, beat together ricotta, eggs, and sugar with a wooden spoon until blended and smooth. Stir together flour, baking powder, and salt in a separate bowl. Beat dry ingredients into cheese mixture to make a smooth, thick batter.

Pour oil into a saucepan to a depth of 1½ inches. Heat oil over medium heat to 375 degrees on a deep fat frying thermometer. Drop rounded teaspoons of batter, several at a time, into hot oil. Fry 1 to 2 minutes or until golden brown on all sides. Lift out puffs using a slotted spoon and drain on paper towels. Sprinkle with powdered sugar and serve warm.

NUTRITION INFORMATION (estimate)**:** 64 calories, 4 g fat, 1 g saturated fat, 20 mg cholesterol, 76 mg sodium, 4 g carbohydrate, 2 g sugars, 0 g fiber, 2 g protein.

champagne peaches and raspberries

Serves: *4 portions*

Prep: 45 minutes, plus 30 minutes to chill

⅔	cup sugar	5	whole cloves
2	cups champagne (Can be leftover from last night's party!)	2	3-inch cinnamon sticks
1	cup water	5	firm, ripe Colorado yellow peaches, peeled and each cut into 8 slices
4	strips lemon peel	2	cups fresh raspberries
2	tablespoons fresh lemon juice		mint sprigs for garnish

Combine sugar, champagne, water, lemon peel, lemon juice, cloves, and cinnamon stick in a large saucepan over medium heat. Bring just to a boil, then reduce heat to a simmer. Cook, stirring constantly, for 5 minutes or until sugar dissolves. Add peaches and bring back just to a simmer. Remove from heat and cool peaches in liquid for 30 minutes.

Remove cooled peaches to a dish with a cover. Cook remaining liquid for about 10 minutes or until it reduces and thickens to a syrup. Discard lemon peel, cloves, and cinnamon stick, and pour syrup over peaches. Chill for 30 minutes. To serve, place peaches and a little syrup in individual dishes. Scatter raspberries over peaches and top with a mint sprig.

NUTRITION INFORMATION: 277 calories, 1 g fat, 0 g saturated fat, 0 mg cholesterol, 5 mg sodium, 60 g carbohydrate, 52 g sugars, 7 g fiber, 3 g protein.

fruit and nut scones

Serves: *16 portions*

Prep: 20 minutes | Bake: 25 minutes

4	cups all-purpose flour	½	cup fresh orange juice
⅔	cup sugar	½	cup sour cream or yogurt
2	tablespoons baking powder	2	eggs
1	teaspoon salt	2½	cups fresh or thawed frozen fruit and/or nuts
1	cup butter, chilled and cut into pieces	¼	cup raw cane sugar or granulated sugar
½	cup heavy cream		

Preheat oven to 375 degrees. Using a food processor, combine flour, ⅔ cup sugar, baking powder, and salt. Cut in butter. Remove to a large bowl and add cream, orange juice, sour cream or yogurt, eggs, and fruit or nuts. Mix with a spoon until the mixture is crumbly. Press dough into a 9-inch round cake pan to define a round shape, then turn out onto a parchment-lined baking sheet. Sprinkle with remaining sugar. Cut into 16 wedges. Bake for 25 minutes.

NUTRITION INFORMATION: 321 calories, 16 g fat, 10 g saturated fat, 72 mg cholesterol, 391 mg sodium, 39 g carbohydrate, 14 g sugars, 1 g fiber, 5 g protein.

cranberry coffee cake

Serves: *10-12 portions*

Prep: less than 30 minutes | Bake: 45 minutes

BATTER

½	cup butter, softened		2	cups unbleached flour
1	cup sugar		1	teaspoon baking powder
2	eggs		1	teaspoon baking soda
1	teaspoon vanilla extract		½	teaspoon salt
1	tablespoon orange zest		1	cup sour cream

TOPPING

2½	cups fresh whole cranberries		2	teaspoons cinnamon
¾	cup light brown sugar		2	tablespoons butter
½	cup unbleached flour			

Preheat the oven to 350 degrees. To prepare batter, cream butter and sugar together until light and fluffy. Beat in eggs, one at a time. Add vanilla and orange zest. In a separate bowl, mix together flour, baking powder, baking soda, and salt. Add dry ingredients, alternating with sour cream, to creamed mixture. The batter will be smooth and thick. Spread batter evenly in a greased and lightly floured 13x9x2-inch baking pan.

For topping, sprinkle cranberries over batter. Combine brown sugar, flour, and cinnamon in a small mixing bowl. Cut in butter with two knives or a pastry blender until the mixture is crumbly. Sprinkle sugar topping evenly over cranberries.

Bake for 45 minutes or until a cake tester inserted in the center comes out clean. Serve warm or at room temperature.

If fresh cranberries are not available or for an interesting change, try fresh blueberries.

The coffee cake is also delicious when prepared in 2 standard loaf pans. It is easier to slice into uniform pieces when baked in the loaves. (The baking time remains the same.) One loaf also can be frozen for later use if serving fewer people.

NUTRITION INFORMATION: 418 calories, 16 g fat, 10 g saturated fat, 88 mg cholesterol, 390 mg sodium, 62 g carbohydrate, 38 g sugars, 2 g fiber, 5 g protein.

Coffee Brewing Tips

Brought to you by:

The Village Roaster

DID YOU KNOW...If you like a weaker brew, it is best to add hot water after brewing. This ensures that your beans aren't over extracted with excess water during the brewing process, which can make the coffee taste bitter.

Remember these tips for the purest, fullest coffee flavor:

Enjoy coffee while it is fresh. Unlike fine wine, it won't get better with age.

Refrigerate coffee beans in an airtight container.

Use the proper grind to the brewing method (finer grinds for espresso and coarser grinds for slow-drip.)

Start with fresh, cold, or filtered water.

Use at least one full tablespoon of grounds for each 5½-ounce cup.

Clean your coffeemaker often by using a commercial descaler or white vinegar solution.

Use brand-name filters in your drip maker or convert to a permanent screen filter (then clean it frequently.)

Made too much? Keep coffee hot in a thermos. Coffee turns bitter if left to sit on a hot plate.

Midnight Sun Cooler

Serves 4

2 cups Scandinavian Blend Coffee
4 teaspoons sugar
1 teaspoon pure Dutch cocoa
4 ice cubes
1 teaspoon vanilla extract
2 scoops vanilla ice cream

Chill freshly made coffee. Rapidly froth all ingredients in a blender and enjoy.

www.villageroaster.com

Honey Tips

Brought to you by:

Beeyond the Hive

"Providing Colorado's sweetest honey since 1908."

DID YOU KNOW...Honeybees account for 80% of all insect pollination. Without such pollination, we would see a significant decrease in the yield of fruits and vegetables.

Honey is sweeter than most sweeteners. Thus, when substituting honey for other sweeteners in recipes, you should use a reduced amount.

For easy measuring, coat measuring cup or spoon with cooking spray before adding honey.

All pure honey will crystallize. To reliquify, remove lid and place container in a pan of warm water (no more than 120 degrees) and stir frequently.

Do not feed to infants less than one year of age.

Because of the multitude of floral sources from which honey originates, no two honeys are exactly alike in flavor, color, and nutritional content.

The complex mix of sugars in honey provides an energy boost, but enters the bloodstream more slowly to provide a lasting source of energy.

Beeyond the Hive

From our hives to your home, we invite your taste buds to experience a proud family tradition unlike any other. Since 1908, 4 generations of skilled beekeepers have passed their love and knowledge of the bees onto the next.

www.beeyondthehive.com

homemade granola

Serves: *12 (1-cup) portions*

Prep: less than 30 minutes | Bake: 25 minutes

5	cups oats	½	cup unprocessed bran
½	cup brown sugar	2	teaspoons cinnamon
1	cup chopped walnuts	2	teaspoons vanilla extract
⅔	cup honey	1	cup chopped dates or dried cherries
⅔	cup butter, melted	½	cup raisins

Preheat oven to 325 degrees. Combine oats, brown sugar, walnuts, honey, melted butter, bran, cinnamon, and vanilla in large bowl. Spread mixture on a lightly greased jelly roll pan or baking sheet with sides.

Bake for 25 minutes, stirring often. Remove from oven and stir in dried fruit and raisins while still warm. Store in refrigerator in a covered container.

NUTRITION INFORMATION: 442 calories, 19 g fat, 7 g saturated fat, 27 mg cholesterol, 77 mg sodium, 66 g carbohydrate, 39 g sugars, 7 g fiber, 8 g protein.

hungarian nut roll

Serves: *24-30 portions (8-10 slices per roll)*

Prep: 1 hour or more | Bake: 30-35 minutes

1	cup milk	4	cups flour
3	tablespoons sugar	1½	cups sugar
2	packages active dry yeast	3	cups ground walnuts
3	eggs, separated	1	tablespoon vanilla extract
1	cup butter, melted		powdered sugar

Warm milk with 3 tablespoons sugar to lukewarm. Add yeast and dissolve. Lightly beat egg yolks and pour into yeast mixture; stir slightly. Mix in melted butter and flour. Roll dough into a smooth ball, then divide into 3 smaller balls.

To make a filling, beat egg whites until foamy. Add 1½ cups sugar, walnuts, and vanilla. Using powdered sugar to dust the work surface, roll out each dough ball into a rectangle, about ¼-inch thick. Spread one-third of filling over each rectangle and roll up to form long rolls. Place rolls on a greased baking sheet. Let rise for 1 hour in a warm place.

When ready to bake, preheat oven to 350 degrees. Bake rolls for 30 to 35 minutes or until golden brown. When cool, dust with powdered sugar. Cut into 1-inch thick slices to serve. Baked rolls may be frozen.

NUTRITION INFORMATION: 279 calories, 15 g fat, 6 g saturated fat, 47 mg cholesterol, 68 mg sodium, 32 g carbohydrate, 15 g sugars, 1 g fiber, 5 g protein.

rolls three ways

Serves: *36 portions*

Prep: 15-20 minutes, plus 2 hours or more refrigeration | Bake: 10-12 minutes

2	packages active dry yeast	½	cup butter, softened
1½	cups warm water	½	cup mashed potatoes, warmed (packaged mashed potatoes work well)
½	cup sugar		
1	tablespoon salt	6	cups flour
2	eggs		

Gently whisk together yeast, warm water, sugar, and salt in small bowl. Let mixture stand for 10 minutes to allow yeast to become foamy. In a large mixing bowl, mix eggs, butter, and mashed potatoes for 1 minute. Stir in yeast mixture. Add 3 cups flour and beat 2 minutes or until smooth. Add remaining flour and beat until all flour is absorbed; dough will be very sticky. Place dough in a large greased bowl and refrigerate for at least 2 hours or overnight; dough will keep for up to 3 days. When ready to bake, proceed as directed below.

Dinner Rolls: Take an amount of dough equivalent to the size of a golf ball and gently smooth surface with your thumbs. Roll in melted butter and place in well greased muffin tins. Allow to rise for 20 to 30 minutes. Bake at 375 degrees for 10 to 12 minutes or until rolls are golden brown. Remove from oven and transfer to a cooling rack.

Sugary Orange Rolls: Mix zest of 4 oranges with 1½ cups sugar in a pie plate. Melt ½ cup butter in a separate pie plate. On a floured surface, cut dough into thirds and shape each into a log about 10 inches long. Using a rolling pin, gently roll each log into a 6x12-inch rectangle, ½-inch thick. Cut dough into 1-inch wide strips. Dip each strip of dough into melted butter, then into sugar-zest mixture. Gently tie strip of dough into a knot, tucking ends under knot. Place knots in well greased muffin tins and let rise 20 to 30 minutes. Bake at 375 degrees for 10 to 12 minutes, watching carefully so rolls do not burn.

Cinnamon Twists: Mix 1½ cups sugar and 2 tablespoons cinnamon in a pie plate. Melt ½ cup butter in a separate pie plate. On a floured surface, cut dough into thirds and shape each into a log about 10 inches long. Using a rolling pin, gently roll each log into a 6x12-inch rectangle, ½-inch thick. Cut dough into 1-inch wide strips. Dip each strip of dough into melted butter, then into cinnamon sugar mixture. Gently twist dough strips 2 to 3 times and place twists on a parchment paper-lined baking sheet. Let rise 20 to 30 minutes. Bake at 375 degrees for 10 to 12 minutes, watching carefully so twists do not burn.

NUTRITION INFORMATION (Basic Dinner Rolls): 116 calories, 3 g fat, 2 g saturated fat, 18 mg cholesterol, 225 mg sodium, 19 g carbohydrate, 3 g sugars, 1 g fiber, 3 g protein.

sweet potato nut muffins

Serves: *12 portions*

Prep: 30 minutes | Bake: 20-25 minutes

1	10-12 ounce sweet potato, shredded		1	teaspoon baking powder
2	tablespoons fresh lemon juice		½	teaspoon baking soda
2	eggs		¼	teaspoon salt
1	cup canola oil		1	teaspoon ground cinnamon
1	cup sugar		¾	cup coarsely chopped walnuts
1½	cups all-purpose flour			turbinado sugar

Preheat oven to 350 degrees. Toss shredded sweet potato with lemon juice in a small bowl; set aside. In a large mixing bowl, combine eggs, oil, and sugar. Beat for 1 minute or until smooth and thickened. Add flour, baking powder, baking soda, salt, and cinnamon at a low speed and beat until smooth. Fold in sweet potato and walnuts. Spoon batter into 12 greased standard-size muffin cups, filling each three-fourths full. Sprinkle tops lightly with turbinado sugar. Bake for 20 to 25 minutes or until springy and a tester inserted in the center comes out clean. Cool in pan for 5 minutes before removing muffins to a rack to cool completely.

NUTRITION INFORMATION: 368 calories, 24 g fat, 2 g saturated fat, 35 mg cholesterol, 159 mg sodium, 35 g carbohydrate, 18 g sugars, 2 g fiber, 4 g protein.

olie bollen

Serves: *24 portions*

Prep: 1 hour, 30 minutes | Cook: 30 minutes

½	cup milk		⅛	teaspoon nutmeg
2	teaspoons brown sugar		½	teaspoon cinnamon
1	teaspoon salt		¾	cup golden seedless raisins or dried cherries
¼	cup warm water (105-115 degrees)		1	teaspoon orange zest
1	package active dry yeast		1	quart vegetable oil for frying
1	egg			sugar
1½	cups all-purpose flour			

Warm milk in a small saucepan. Stir in brown sugar and salt to dissolve; cool to lukewarm. Measure warm water into a large mixing bowl. Stir in yeast to dissolve. Stir in milk mixture, egg, flour, nutmeg, and cinnamon. Beat vigorously until batter is elastic and falls in sheets from spoon. Stir in raisins and orange zest and mix well. Cover and let rise in a warm place for 30 to 60 minutes or until doubled. When doubled, do not stir down.

When ready to cook, heat oil to 350 degrees. Using two spoons, shape dough into 1-inch balls and drop immediately into hot oil. Dip spoons into hot oil and drain slightly each time before shaping dough. Fry each ball about 3 minutes or until golden brown, turning once. Drain on paper towels. Roll while warm in sugar. Serve immediately.

NUTRITION INFORMATION (estimate): 92 calories, 5 g fat, 0 g saturated fat, 9 mg cholesterol, 103 mg sodium, 11 g carbohydrate, 4 g sugars, 1 g fiber, 2 g protein.

Olie Bollen are Dutch donuts that are traditionally prepared and eaten on New Year's Eve. Similar to American funnel cake, Olie Bollen often have raisins and orange zest in the dough and are deep fried to a delicious golden color!

on the go breakfast cookies

Serves: *28 portions*

Prep: less than 30 minutes | Bake: 15 minutes

2	cups old-fashioned rolled oats		1	cup light brown sugar
1¼	cups whole wheat flour		½	cup sugar
1	cup all-purpose flour		1	tablespoon vanilla extract
1	cup Grape Nut™ cereal		1	cup almonds, toasted and coarsely chopped
½	cup wheat germ		1	cup raisins
½	cup oat bran		1	cup pitted dates, chopped
2	teaspoons baking soda		14	whole dates, pitted and halved lengthwise
2	cups unsalted butter, softened			
3	eggs			

Preheat oven to 350 degrees. Mix together oats, both flours, cereal, wheat germ, oat bran, and baking soda in a large bowl; set aside. Using an electric mixer, beat butter in a separate bowl until creamy. Add eggs, both sugars, and vanilla and beat until smooth. Add dry ingredients and mix just until blended. Stir in almonds, raisins, and chopped dates. Drop mixture by ¼-cup scoopfuls, 2 inches apart, onto 2 heavy baking sheets lined with parchment paper. Lightly press each scoop with damp fingers to ½-inch thickness. Press a date half onto the center of each cookie.

Bake 1 sheet at a time for about 15 minutes or until cookies are brown on top. Cool on baking sheet on cooling racks for about 10 minutes. Remove cookies to racks to cool completely. Serve warm or at room temperature.

NUTRITION INFORMATION: 325 calories, 17 g fat, 9 g saturated fat, 57 mg cholesterol, 128 mg sodium, 41 g carbohydrate, 22 g sugars, 4 g fiber, 5 g protein.

orange poppy seed quick bread

Serves: *12 portions*

Prep: 30 minutes | Cook: 40-50 minutes

BATTER

3 eggs

2½ cups sugar

1½ cups milk

1 cup plus 2 tablespoons canola oil

1½ teaspoons almond extract

1½ teaspoons vanilla extract

3 cups all-purpose flour

1½ teaspoons baking powder

1½ teaspoons salt

1½ tablespoons poppy seeds

2 tablespoons orange zest

GLAZE

½ teaspoon almond extract

½ teaspoon vanilla extract

¾ cup sugar

¼ cup orange juice

Preheat oven to 350 degrees. Beat eggs well. Mix in sugar. Add milk, oil, and both extracts. Sift together flour, baking powder, salt, and poppy seeds. Add dry ingredients to egg mixture and mix well. Stir in orange zest. Pour batter into 2 greased and floured loaf pans. Bake for 40 to 50 minutes or until a tester inserted in the center comes out clean.

While baking, prepare glaze by mixing all ingredients in a small saucepan. Heat until blended; do not boil. Spread glaze on baked bread while still hot; cool in pans on a rack. Remove from pans when nearly cool. May be frozen.

NUTRITION INFORMATION: 552 calories, 23 g fat, 2 g saturated fat, 53 mg cholesterol, 372 mg sodium, 81 g carbohydrate, 57 g sugars, 1 g fiber, 6 g protein.

brown sugar bacon

Serves: *8 (2-slice) portions*

Prep: 10 minutes | Cook: 25-30 minutes

1 cup brown sugar

1 tablespoon cinnamon

dash of cayenne pepper

1 pound regular sliced bacon

Preheat oven (not convection) to 350 degrees. Cover a jelly roll pan or baking sheet with sides completely with aluminum foil. Place a cooling rack in the pan. Mix brown sugar, cinnamon and cayenne. Separate bacon slices and roll each in sugar mixture. Twist each slice one or two times and place on rack on pan.

Bake on center rack of oven for 25 to 30 minutes, watching carefully after 20 minutes; do not allow bacon to get too brown or it will quickly burn. Remove from oven and place on a plate, not on paper towels. If not serving immediately, warm slightly before serving.

NUTRITION INFORMATION: 155 calories, 8 g fat, 3 g saturated fat, 21 mg cholesterol, 436 mg sodium, 14 g carbohydrate, 13 g sugars, 0 g fiber, 7 g protein.

fresh tomato tart

Serves: *8 portions*

Prep: less than 30 minutes | Bake: 45 minutes plus 50 minutes

CRUST: USE AN UNBAKED CRUST OR THE FOLLOWING RECIPE

6	tablespoons cold butter, cut into 6 pieces	¾	teaspoon salt
1½	tablespoons cold shortening	4	tablespoons ice water
1¼	cups all-purpose flour		

TART

1	small head garlic	2	medium-size yellow tomatoes, sliced ¼-inch thick
1	tablespoon olive oil		
1	tablespoon Dijon mustard		sea salt and freshly ground black pepper to taste
½	cup grated Swiss cheese		
2	medium-size red tomatoes, sliced ¼-inch thick	1	tablespoon olive oil

To prepare crust recipe, add butter and shortening to a food processor bowl. Add flour and salt and pulse until mixture resembles coarse meal. Add water, 1 tablespoon at a time, until a soft dough forms. Chill for 15 minutes. Roll crust onto a floured board to a ⅛-inch thick circle. Fit crust into a 10-inch tart pan and chill until ready to fill.

To prepare tart, preheat oven to 350 degrees. Wrap garlic, drizzled with 1 tablespoon oil, in foil and place in a baking dish. Bake for 45 minutes or until garlic is soft; cool.

Squeeze garlic cloves out of skins and mash into a paste. Spread garlic paste and mustard evenly on the bottom of chilled crust. Cover with half of grated cheese. Arrange the sliced tomatoes on top of cheese, alternating colors in a circular design. Season with salt and pepper. Top with remaining cheese. Drizzle with 1 tablespoon olive oil. Bake at 350 degrees for 45 to 50 minutes or until crust is golden. Cool for 15 minutes before serving.

NUTRITION INFORMATION: 242 calories, 17 g fat, 8 g saturated fat, 30 mg cholesterol, 375 mg sodium, 19 g carbohydrate, 2 g sugars, 1 g fiber, 5 g protein.

Chef Tip: The key to baking with tomatoes is to use ones that are not too ripe so they don't break apart in the cooking process.

colorado green chile breakfast casserole

Serves: *8 portions*

Prep: 30 minutes | Bake: 1 hour

CASSEROLE

2	4 ounce cans chopped mild green chiles		⅔	cup evaporated milk
1	pound Monterey Jack cheese, coarsely grated		1	tablespoon flour
1	pound sharp Cheddar cheese, coarsely grated		1	teaspoon salt
4	eggs, separated		⅛	teaspoon black pepper

TOPPING

2	medium tomatoes, cut into wedges		1	4 ounce can whole green chiles, or 4 fresh chiles, sliced lengthwise

Preheat oven to 325 degrees. In a large bowl, combine chopped green chiles and both cheeses. Turn mixture into a well greased 9x13x2-inch casserole dish.

In a large bowl, beat egg whites until stiff peaks form. In small bowl, combine egg yolks, evaporated milk, flour, salt, and pepper. Gently fold beaten egg whites into egg yolk mixture. Pour mixture over cheese and use a fork to gently distribute egg mixture through the cheese.

Bake for 30 minutes. Remove from oven and arrange tomato wedges and sliced chiles on top. Bake for 30 minutes longer or until a knife inserted in center comes out clean. Serve hot.

NUTRITION INFORMATION: 510 calories, 39 g fat, 24 g saturated fat, 223 mg cholesterol, 1240 mg sodium, 8 g carbohydrate, 3 g sugars, 2 g fiber, 31 g protein.

egg cups with dilled crab

Serves: *24 portions*

Prep: less than 30 minutes | Bake: 10-15 minutes

1	1 pound can crabmeat (imitation crabmeat may be used)		1	cup sour cream
8	ounces cream cheese, cut into ½-inch cubes		1	cup whole milk
	chopped fresh dill			fresh dill sprigs, chopped
18	eggs			fresh salad greens, lightly dressed with oil and vinegar

Preheat oven to 450 degrees. Divide crabmeat and cream cheese evenly among 24 standard-size greased muffin cups. Sprinkle fresh dill into each cup. In a large bowl, whisk together eggs, sour cream, and milk. Pour egg mixture into muffin cups, filling each three-fourths full. Top each with a sprig of dill.

Bake for 10 to 15 minutes or until eggs puff and brown. Cool slightly and loosen with a knife before inverting muffin tins to remove. Serve each egg cup on a bed of lightly dressed salad greens.

NUTRITION INFORMATION: 135 calories, 9 g fat, 5 g saturated fat, 186 mg cholesterol, 99 mg sodium, 4 g carbohydrate, 1 g sugars, 0 g fiber, 9 g protein.

Chef Tip: Keep your herbs wrapped in a damp paper towel in your crisper for longer shelf life. You can also cut the stems and keep them in water; now you have a beautiful culinary center piece.

ham and cheese crêpes

Serves: *6 portions*
Prep: 45 minutes | Cook: 30 minutes

CHEESE SAUCE

¼	cup flour	1¼	cups shredded sharp Cheddar cheese, or cheese of your choice
2	cups low-fat milk		

BATTER

1	cup flour	½	cup water
2	eggs	½	teaspoon salt
½	cup milk	2	tablespoons butter, melted

FILLING

6	ounces deli ham slices	1	cup grated cheese, such as sharp Cheddar or Gruyère
12	blanched asparagus spears		

Preheat oven to 375 degrees. Place flour in a medium-size heavy saucepan. Gradually whisk in milk until blended. Cook over medium heat, stirring constantly, for 8 minutes or until thickened. Remove from heat and stir in cheese until melted. Pour about one-third of cheese sauce into a 13x9x2-inch pan.

To prepare batter, whisk together flour and eggs in a large mixing bowl. Gradually add milk and water and stir to combine. Add salt and melted butter and beat until smooth. Heat a lightly greased griddle, skillet, or crêpe pan over medium-high heat. Pour or scoop batter onto griddle, using about ¼ cup for each crêpe. Tilt the pan in a circular motion, or use a crêpe rake, so the batter coats the surface evenly. Cook for about 2 minutes or until the bottom is lightly browned. Loosen with a fork and turn to cook on the other side. Repeat with remaining batter for a total of 12 crêpes.

While warm, top each crêpe with a slice of deli ham and an asparagus spear, and sprinkle with cheese. Roll each crêpe like a wrap and arrange in pan. Cover with remaining cheese sauce. Bake for 20 to 30 minutes or until the sauce bubbles.

NUTRITION INFORMATION: 391 calories, 20 g fat, 12 g saturated fat, 140 mg cholesterol, 935 mg sodium, 28 g carbohydrate, 7 g sugars, 2 g fiber, 25 g protein.

eggs with smoked salmon

Serves: *4-6 portions*
Prep: *less than 30 minutes*
Cook: *15 minutes*

4 tablespoons unsalted butter

4 green onions, chopped with white and green parts separated

8 eggs, beaten

salt and black pepper to taste

3 ounces smoked salmon, crumbled

3 ounces cream cheese, softened and cubed

Melt butter in a nonstick skillet. Add white part of chopped green onions to butter and sauté about 3 minutes. Season beaten eggs with salt and pepper and add to skillet. Cook and stir scrambled eggs for 7 to 8 minutes or until almost firm. Remove from heat and add salmon and cream cheese and stir until mixed. Garnish eggs with green part of chopped green onion.

NUTRITION INFORMATION: 371 calories, 30 g fat, 15 g saturated fat, 496 mg cholesterol, 416 mg sodium, 3 g carbohydrate, 2 g sugars, 1 g fiber, 22 g protein.

no crust spinach quiche

Serves: *4-8 portions*

Prep: less than 30 minutes | Bake: 30 minutes

1	10 ounce package frozen chopped spinach, thawed and squeezed dry	¼	cup chopped onions
8	ounces Swiss cheese, grated	1	tablespoon butter
4	slices day-old French bread, crusts removed, torn in small pieces	1¼	teaspoons nutmeg
6	eggs, lightly beaten		salt and black pepper to taste

Preheat oven to 350 degrees. Mix spinach, cheese, bread, and eggs together. Sauté onions in butter, then add to spinach mixture. Season mixture with nutmeg and salt and pepper. Transfer to a greased pie plate. Bake for 30 minutes or until a knife inserted in the center comes out clean.

NUTRITION INFORMATION: 458 calories, 27 g fat, 15 g saturated fat, 377 mg cholesterol, 471 mg sodium, 24 g carbohydrate, 3 g sugars, 3 g fiber, 31 g protein.

tuscan egg casserole

Serves: *8 portions*

Prep: less than 30 minutes | Cook: 30 minutes

1	pound Canino's Mild Italian Sausage, casings removed	8	eggs
½	cup chopped shallots	1	cup half-and-half
2	cloves garlic, minced	1	cup heavy cream
½	cup oil-packed sun-dried tomatoes, drained and chopped	½	teaspoon salt
3	tablespoons chopped fresh parsley	2	cups grated four-cheese Italian blend or mozzarella cheese, divided
		3	tablespoons chopped fresh parsley

Preheat oven to 375 degrees. Sauté sausage in a nonstick skillet, breaking up sausage into small pieces, over medium heat for 10 minutes or until brown and cooked through. Add shallots and garlic and sauté 3 minutes. Add sun-dried tomatoes and 3 tablespoons parsley and sauté for 1 minute longer. Spread sausage mixture in a greased 13x9x2-inch glass baking dish. (Optional: casserole can be prepared a day in advance, covered, and refrigerated at this stage.)

Whisk together eggs, half-and-half, cream, salt, and 1½ cups cheese in a large bowl. Pour egg mixture over sausage mixture. Sprinkle remaining ½ cup cheese and 3 tablespoons parsley on top. Bake for 30 minutes or until casserole is golden brown and a knife inserted in the center comes out clean. Let stand 5 minutes before serving.

NUTRITION INFORMATION: 437 calories, 35 g fat, 18 g saturated fat, 300 mg cholesterol, 779 mg sodium, 8 g carbohydrate, 1 g sugars, 1 g fiber, 21 g protein.

classique
desserts

bavarian apple torte

Serves: *8 portions*

Prep: less than 30 minutes | Bake: 55 minutes

CRUST

½ cup unsalted butter; softened

⅓ cup sugar

¼ teaspoon vanilla extract

1 cup flour

FILLING

8 ounces cream cheese; softened

½ teaspoon vanilla extract

¼ cup sugar

1 egg

TOPPING

4 cups peeled and sliced Granny Smith apples (about 4 apples)

⅓ cup sugar

½ teaspoon cinnamon

¼ cup slivered almonds

Preheat oven to 350 degrees. Cream butter with sugar. Mix in vanilla and flour. Press dough into the bottom and 1 inch up the sides of a 9-inch springform pan. (Line bottom of pan with parchment paper if bottom will eventually be removed.)

For filling, mix cream cheese, vanilla, sugar, and egg; mixture will resemble pudding. Pour filling over crust.

To prepare topping, mix apple slices with sugar and cinnamon. Arrange slices over filling. Sprinkle with almonds. Bake for 10 minutes. Reduce heat to 300 degrees and bake for 45 minutes longer. Cool before removing side of pan.

NUTRITION INFORMATION: 402 calories, 24 g fat, 14 g saturated fat, 88 mg cholesterol, 95 mg sodium, 44 g carbohydrate, 29 g sugars, 2 g fiber, 6 g protein.

Wine Pairing: The sweetness of this torte calls for a late harvest Riesling. Germany, the Pacific Northwest, and Colorado make some excellent wines.

fresh peach crisp

Serves: *8-10 portions*

Prep: less than 30 minutes | Bake: 60 minutes

4	pounds ripe peaches, peeled and sliced	2	teaspoons cinnamon
½	teaspoon salt	1½	cups sugar
1½	cups flour	½	cup oats
		1	cup unsalted butter

Preheat oven to 350 degrees. Place peach slices in a greased 13x9x2-inch baking dish. Sprinkle with salt. Mix together flour, cinnamon, sugar, and oats. Add butter and mix with hands until crumbly. Sprinkle over peaches and pat down. Bake 50 to 60 minutes. Serve plain or with vanilla ice cream.

When peeling peaches, place whole peaches in boiling water for a few seconds to loosen skins.

When peaches are not in season, substitute Granny Smith apples as a nice alternative.

NUTRITION INFORMATION: 529 calories, 24 g fat, 15 g saturated fat, 60 mg cholesterol, 149 mg sodium, 78 g carbohydrate, 54 g sugars, 4 g fiber, 5 g protein.

Chef Tip: Peaches are at their best in the summer and the ones that are overripe are perfect for this recipe.

Wine Pairing: Sautenes from France which is a blend of late harvest Semillon and Sauvignon Blanc. The honeyed character of the wine is great with the peach flavors.

toffee blondies

Serves: *12 brownies*

Prep: less than 30 minutes | Bake: less than 30 minutes

½	cup unsalted butter, softened	1⅓	cups all-purpose flour
⅓	cup sugar	¼	teaspoon salt
½	cup light brown sugar	½	teaspoon baking soda
1	egg	1	8 ounce bag toffee bits
½	teaspoon pure vanilla extract	½	cup white chocolate chips

Preheat oven to 375 degrees. Beat butter and both sugars until fluffy. Beat in egg and vanilla. Add flour, salt, and baking soda and mix until combined. Stir in toffee and white chocolate chips. Transfer to a greased and floured 9-inch square glass pan. Bake for 18 to 23 minutes or until light brown; be careful to not overcook.

NUTRITION INFORMATION: 332 calories, 18 g fat, 9 g saturated fat, 47 mg cholesterol, 221 mg sodium, 42 g carbohydrate, 32 g sugars, 0 g fiber, 3 g protein.

Beer Pairing: Nut Brown ales are a perfect after-dinner supplement to this toffee dish.

Wine Pairing: A late harvest red wine with some sweetness. Banyuls from the Southern part of France goes quite well with these desserts.

award winning cherry pie

Serves: *8 portions*

Prep: 30 minutes | Bake: 60 minutes

PIE CRUST

2½	cups flour		1	cup unsalted butter, chilled
1	teaspoon salt		½	cup water
1	teaspoon sugar			

FILLING

2	14½ ounce cans water-pack pitted tart cherries		1	cup sugar
2½	tablespoons quick-cooking tapioca		2	tablespoons unsalted butter, cut into 4 pieces
¼	teaspoon almond extract		¼	cup sugar
1	teaspoon lemon juice			

Combine flour, salt, and sugar in a food processor. Cut butter into tablespoon-size pieces and add to dry ingredients. Pulse until mixture resembles coarse meal. With processor running, add water in a slow stream and pulse until dough comes together; do not over mix. (If mixture is too crumbly add extra water, 1 tablespoon at a time, to desired consistency. If mixture is too sticky or wet, lightly coat ball of dough with flour before wrapping and refrigerating.) Divide dough into 2 equal portions. Flatten each into a disk and wrap with plastic wrap. Chill for at least 1 hour.

Preheat oven to 400 degrees. To prepare filling, drain cherries, reserving liquid. Measure ⅓ cup of reserved liquid into a mixing bowl. Add tapioca, almond extract, and lemon juice to liquid and stir. Stir in 1 cup sugar. Add drained cherries to the liquid and gently stir. Let filling stand while rolling out crust.

To assemble, roll out each crust large enough to drape over a deep-dish pie plate with extra hanging over the edge. Fit one rolled crust into pie plate and score with a fork. Add filling and dot with unsalted butter. Add top crust and seal edges together. Make decorative cuts in top crust and sprinkle with ¼ cup sugar. Bake for 45 to 60 minutes or until light golden brown. To prevent edges from overbrowning, wrap edge of pie crust in foil or use a pie crust guard 30 minutes into baking time.

NUTRITION INFORMATION: 542 calories, 26 g fat, 16 g saturated fat, 68 mg cholesterol, 303 mg sodium, 74 g carbohydrate, 40 g sugars, 2 g fiber, 5 g protein.

Beer Pairing: The cherry aroma of a Belgian Lambic sets off a flavor explosion with this dish.

lemon delight

Serves: *12 portions*

Prep: 45 minutes | Bake: 30 minutes

PECAN CRUST

2 cup flour

1 cup chopped pecans

1 cup unsalted butter, softened

CREAM CHEESE LAYER

8 ounces cream cheese, softened

1 cup powdered sugar

1 cup whipped cream

LEMON CURD LAYER

3 large lemons

¾ cup sugar

2 teaspoons cornstarch

2 eggs

2 egg yolks

4 tablespoons unsalted butter, cut into ½-inch cubes

2 tablespoons fruity olive oil, such as lemon or orange olive oil

TOPPING

1½ cups heavy cream

1 lemon, cut into thin slices

fresh mint leaves for garnish

Preheat oven to 350 degrees. Combine all crust ingredients in a bowl and beat with a hand mixer until blended. Press crust into a greased 13x9x2-inch pan. Bake for 20 to 30 minutes or until light brown; cool.

For cream cheese layer, blend together cream cheese and powdered sugar with a hand mixer. Fold in whipped cream. Spread mixture over crust. Refrigerate while preparing next layer to let cream cheese layer set.

For lemon curd, grate enough zest from lemons to measure 1 tablespoon, then squeeze ¾ cup juice from lemons. Whisk together lemon zest and juice, sugar, cornstarch, eggs, and egg yolks in a medium saucepan. Bring to a boil over medium heat, whisking constantly for 2 minutes. Remove from heat and whisk in butter and oil until smooth. Cool to at least room temperature. Spread lemon curd over cream cheese layer. Refrigerate for at least 2 hours.

To make topping, whip cream to soft peaks. Spread a thin layer over lemon curd, or top individual servings with a dollop of whipped cream. Cut into individual squares. Garnish each serving with a thin lemon slice twist and fresh mint.

NUTRITION INFORMATION: 649 calories, 51 g fat, 27 g saturated fat, 195 mg cholesterol, 87 mg sodium, 43 g carbohydrate, 23 g sugars, 2 g fiber, 7 g protein.

summer berry lemon tarts

Serves: *4 portions*

Prep: 45 minutes | Bake: 10-12 minutes

CRUST

1	cup graham cracker crumbs	4	tablespoons unsalted butter, melted
1½	tablespoons sugar		

FILLING

2	tablespoons light brown sugar	4	ounces cream cheese, softened
¼	cup sour cream		zest of 1 lemon
¼	teaspoon vanilla extract	2	tablespoons freshly squeezed lemon juice

TOPPING

1⅓	cups blueberries (6 ounces), or other seasonal berries	1⅓	cups raspberries (6 ounces), or other seasonal berries
			powdered sugar for dusting

Preheat oven to 350 degrees with a baking sheet on center rack. Stir together all crust ingredients in a bowl with a fork until combined well. Press mixture with fingers or the back of a spoon evenly and firmly onto the bottom and ¾-inch up the sides of four 4-ounce ramekin dishes. Place ramekins on preheated baking sheet and bake for 10 to 12 minutes or until crust is slightly dark. Cool 25 minutes on a rack; leave crusts in ramekins.

While crusts cool, prepare filling. Whisk together brown sugar, sour cream, and vanilla in a small bowl until sugar is dissolved. Beat cream cheese in a medium bowl with an electric mixer until smooth. Beat in sour cream mixture and lemon zest and juice until completely combined. Divide filling among ramekins, spreading evenly.

Top with blueberries and raspberries or other seasonal berries. Just prior to serving, dust with powdered sugar.

NUTRITION INFORMATION: 415 calories, 26 g fat, 16 g saturated fat, 71 mg cholesterol, 220 mg sodium, 42 g carbohydrate, 25 g sugars, 5 g fiber, 5 g protein.

Beer Pairing: An unfiltered Witbier will end your meal with a refreshing finish.

ultimate carrot cake

Serves: *12 servings*

Prep: more than 2 minutes | Bake: 40-50 minutes

PECAN FILLING

1¾	cups sugar
¼	cup flour
½	teaspoon salt
1½	cups heavy cream

¾	cup unsalted butter
2	teaspoons vanilla extract
1½	cups chopped pecans

BATTER

2	cups flour
½	teaspoon baking soda
½	teaspoon baking powder
1½	teaspoons cinnamon
½	teaspoon allspice
½	teaspoon salt

4	eggs
1	cup brown sugar
1	cup sugar
1¼	cups canola oil
4	cups grated carrots
1	cup chopped pecans

CREAM CHEESE FROSTING

1	cup unsalted butter, softened
1	cup cream cheese, softened
1	pound powdered sugar
1	teaspoon vanilla extract

1½	cups shredded coconut, toasted, optional

Cake Assembly: If desired, toast (in oven); 1½ cups of shredded coconut and apply to cake sides after frosting.

For filling, combine sugar, flour, and salt in a heavy saucepan. Gradually stir in cream. Add butter and cook over low heat, stirring frequently, until butter is melted. Simmer filling for 1 hour, 30 minutes or until golden brown in color, stirring occasionally. Cool to lukewarm, then stir in vanilla and pecans. Cool completely, preferably overnight in refrigerator. If needed, heat slightly during cake assembly to make spreading easier.

To make batter, preheat oven to 350 degrees. Sift together flour, baking soda, baking powder, cinnamon, allspice, and salt. Beat eggs slightly in a large bowl. Add both sugars and mix well. Slowly add oil while continuing to mix until well blended. Slowly add sifted ingredients and mix well. Add carrots and pecans and mix. Pour batter into 3 greased and floured 8-inch cake pans, filling each about two-thirds full. Bang pans on counter to remove air bubbles. Bake for 40 to 50 minutes or until a toothpick inserted in the center comes out clean. Cool 10 minutes, then remove cake from pans and continue to cool on wire rack.

For frosting, cream butter and cream cheese together until blended. Mix in sugar and vanilla. Frosting may be refrigerated, but bring to room temperature before spreading on the cake.

To assemble, spread filling between cake layers. Spread frosting on the top and sides of the cake. Pat toasted coconut on the sides of the cake.

NUTRITION INFORMATION: 1306 calories, 87 g fat, 32 g saturated fat, 203 mg cholesterol, 390 mg sodium, 129 g carbohydrate, 104 g sugars, 4 g fiber, 10 g protein.

Wine Pairing: A lighter style sweeter wine would be ideal with this cake. Muscat would be just lightly sweet with citrus and honeyed flavors or late harvest Gewürztraminer.

Brought to you by:

**The Seasoned Chef
Cooking School**

*DID YOU KNOW...At this altitude,
1-2 tablespoons of additional flour or
sugar can ruin a recipe, so be sure to
measure properly. Consider these tips
when adjusting low-altitude recipes
for baking here in Denver.*

Measure ingredients accurately. Use
dry measuring cups for ingredients
such as flour, sugar, cornmeal, etc.
Use liquid measuring cups for water,
milk, etc.

At Denver's mile-high elevation,
leavening agents (baking powder,
baking soda) work more easily (due
to less air pressure), causing batters
to over-rise. Reducing baking powder
and/or baking soda by about 25%
is helpful.

Beat egg whites only to soft peaks to
keep them from deflating.

Our mile-high elevation also means
drier air, so adding 2-4 tablespoons
additional liquid is helpful.

Sugar helps to tenderize baked
goods, but too much sugar causes
the structure to be too soft, thus
collapsing before it has baked long
enough. Reduce the sugar by 2-3
tablespoons per cup.

Increasing oven temperatures by
about 25 degrees helps batters
set faster, preventing the dreaded
"sink hole" in the middle. Be sure to
check your oven to make sure the
temperature is accurate.

Because all recipes are different, it
is important to experiment with only
one or two adjustments at a time to
discover what will work best.

www.theseasonedchef.com

citrus angel food cake
Serves: *8-10 portions*
Prep: 1 hour, 30 minutes | Bake: 20-30 minutes

BATTER
10	egg whites, at room temperature	⅛	teaspoon salt
1¼	teaspoons cream of tartar		zest of 1 orange
1½	cups sugar		zest of 1 lemon
1	cup cake flour, sifted		zest of 1 lime

GLAZE AND TOPPING
¼	cup fresh lime juice	finely grated lemon zest
1¼	cups powdered sugar	fresh berries and real whipped cream

Preheat oven to 350 degrees. In the bowl of a standing mixer fitted with a whisk attachment, whip egg whites on medium-low speed for 30 seconds or until frothy. Add cream of tartar and beat on medium-high for about 15 seconds longer. With machine running, add sugar in a slow, steady stream. Whip until whites are thick, satiny, and stiff, but still moist. Reduce to low speed and carefully mix in flour and salt. Mix in zests. Gently spread batter into an ungreased angel food cake pan or divide evenly among individual angel food cake pans. Tap pan on counter to eliminate any air bubbles.

Bake 20 minutes or until a wooden skewer inserted in the center comes out clean. Turn pan upside-down on counter and cool completely in pan. When cool, run a knife around inside edge of pan and gently remove cake. Place on a cooling rack or pedestal.

For glaze, combine lime juice and powdered sugar and blend until smooth and free of lumps. Drizzle glaze over cake and sprinkle with lemon zest. Serve with fresh berries and real whipped cream.

NUTRITION INFORMATION: 305 calories, 0 g fat, 0 g saturated fat, 0 mg cholesterol, 107 mg sodium, 71 g carbohydrate, 57 g sugars, 0 g fiber, 6 g protein.

Chef Tip: Why cream of tartar? It helps in keeping the whites stiff.

Wine Pairing: Muscat with its citrus and orange blossom flavors would delight the palate. Moscato D'Asti from Italy would add a little sparkle.

decadent peanut butter chocolate cake

Serves: *12 portions*

Prep: 1 hour | Bake: 20-25 minutes

FILLING

2¼ cups heavy cream

½ cup brown sugar

12 ounces semi-sweet chocolate chips

½ cup natural peanut butter

BATTER

2¾ cups flour

2 teaspoons baking powder

1 teaspoon baking soda

½ teaspoon salt

10 tablespoons unsalted butter, softened

½ cup natural peanut butter

1 pound brown sugar

4 eggs

1 teaspoon vanilla extract

1 cup buttermilk

FROSTING

12 ounces low-fat cream cheese, softened

1¼ cups powdered sugar

6 tablespoons unsalted butter, softened

1 teaspoon vanilla extract

¾ cup heavy cream

¾ cup powdered sugar

2 Butterfinger candy bars, coarsely chopped

½ cup glazed honey peanuts

In a saucepan, bring cream and brown sugar to a simmer, stirring to dissolve sugar. Remove from heat and add chocolate chips. Let stand for a minute before whisking until smooth. Whisk in peanut butter. Chill filling, uncovered, overnight.

Preheat oven to 375 degrees. For batter, sift together flour, baking powder, baking soda, and salt. In a separate bowl, beat butter and peanut butter. Beat in brown sugar and eggs, one at a time. Add vanilla. Beat in dry ingredients in 4 additions, alternating with buttermilk. Divide batter among 3 greased and floured 8½-inch cake pans. Bake for 20 to 25 minutes or until a toothpick inserted in the center comes out clean. Cool cakes for about 5 minutes before removing from pans.

For frosting, beat cream cheese, 1¼ cups powdered sugar, butter, and vanilla. In another bowl whisk cream and ¾ cup powdered sugar to firm peaks. Fold in cream cheese mixture. Chill 1 hour or until firm but spreadable.

To assemble, divide filling among and spread over two cake layers. Stack layers, placing third layer, bottom-side up, on top. Spread frosting over top and sides of cake. Sprinkle and press chopped candy bars and peanuts over top of cake.

NUTRITION INFORMATION: 1145 calories, 67 g fat, 35 g saturated fat, 209 mg cholesterol, 552 mg sodium, 122 g carbohydrate, 88 g sugars, 5 g fiber, 19 g protein.

english trifle

Serves: *12 portions*

Prep: 45 minutes | Bake: 1 hour, 30 minutes

POUND CAKE BATTER

1	cup unsalted butter, softened		½	teaspoon salt
1¾	cups sugar		1	cup buttermilk
3	eggs		3	tablespoons finely grated lemon zest
3	cups flour		¼	cup fresh lemon juice
½	teaspoon baking soda			

CUSTARD

2	cups whole milk		1¼	cups sugar
8	egg yolks		1	teaspoon vanilla extract

ASSEMBLY

1   cup cream or sweet sherry, Grand Marnier™, or apricot brandy; or substitute orange juice or your favorite liquor

2   10 ounce jars raspberry preserves

4   pints raspberries, ¾ pint reserved for garnish

3   pints strawberries

1   cup heavy cream

1   teaspoon vanilla extract

2   tablespoons powdered sugar

½   cup sliced toasted almonds

Preheat oven to 325 degrees. Cream butter and sugar until fluffy. Beat in eggs, one at a time. Combine flour, baking soda, and salt. Add dry ingredients to creamed mixture, a little at a time, alternating with buttermilk, and beating after each addition. Add lemon zest and lemon juice. Beat until well blended. Pour batter into a greased and floured 10-inch Bundt pan. Bake about 1 hour, 15 minutes or until a wooden pick inserted in the center comes out clean. Cool in pan for about 10 minutes. Invert cake onto a cooling rack. When completely cooled, cover until ready to use.

For custard, heat milk in the top of a double boiler over medium-low heat until a film forms on top. Beat egg yolks with sugar and vanilla in a double boiler until it forms a ribbon. Very slowly pour hot milk into egg mixture, beating constantly. Place the mixture in a heavy saucepan and stir over low heat for 10 to 15 minutes or until the custard coats the back of a spoon; do not allow mixture to boil. Strain custard through a fine sieve. Cool custard in a bowl set in ice water, stirring occasionally.

To assemble, cut pound cake into 2x1-inch strips, or cut to desired size. Prick cake strips with a fork and sprinkle with sherry. Spread each piece of cake with jam on all sides and place in a trifle bowl or large glass bowl, filling the bottom and the sides of the bowl with raspberry cake. Place half the raspberries and half the strawberries on top of the cake. Fill with cooled custard. Place remaining berries on top of custard and chill overnight.

To serve, whip cream until soft peaks form. Add vanilla and powder sugar and whip until stiff peaks form. Spread over fruit and custard. Decorate the top with reserved berries and toasted almonds.

You can use fresh or frozen berries. Trifles were made to use leftover pieces of cake so you may substitute almost any type of heavy cake, angel food cake, or ladyfingers. Other berries may be used and you can add a banana or two, if desired. This is best if it is left overnight to allow flavors to blend.

NUTRITION INFORMATION: 882 calories, 31 g fat, 17 g saturated fat, 262 mg cholesterol, 223 mg sodium, 136 g carbohydrate, 99 g sugars, 8 g fiber, 11 g protein.

almond raspberry bars

Makes: *35 portions*

Prep: less than 30 minutes | Bake: 1 hour

CRUST
2	cups flour		1	cup unsalted butter, chilled
½	cup powdered sugar			

FILLING
2	cups raspberry preserves		¼	cup Chambord liquor

TOPPING
½	cup flour		4	tablespoons unsalted butter
¼	cup sugar		⅔	cup sliced almonds
7	ounces almond paste			

ICING
1	cup powdered sugar		1	teaspoon vanilla extract
3	tablespoons milk			

Preheat oven to 350 degrees. Combine all crust ingredients in a food processor and quickly pulse until crumbly. Pat crust into a greased 13x9x2-inch glass pan. Bake for 20 minutes or until light golden brown; remove for oven.

For filling, mix preserves and liquor together and spread on top of crust.

To prepare topping, combine flour, sugar, almond paste, and butter in a food processor and quickly pulse until crumbly. Sprinkle over filling and top with sliced almonds. Bake at 350 for about 40 minutes or until golden brown; filling will still be jiggly, but will set up as it cools. Cool in the pan on a wire rack.

Stir together all icing ingredients until smooth. Drizzle icing over bars while still in pan. Cool completely in refrigerator before cutting into bars with a sharp knife.

NUTRITION INFORMATION: 204 calories, 9 g fat, 4 g saturated fat, 17 mg cholesterol, 2 mg sodium, 29 g carbohydrate, 20 g sugars, 1 g fiber, 2 g protein.

trail mix cookies

Makes: *50-60 cookies*

Prep: less than 30 minutes | Bake: 10-12 minutes

2	cups flour		1½	teaspoons vanilla extract
1½	teaspoons baking soda		4	cups quick cooking oats
1	teaspoon salt		⅔	cup chopped pecans
1⅓	cups butter, softened		⅔	cup chocolate chips
1⅓	cups brown sugar		⅔	cup M&M's candies
1⅓	cups sugar		⅔	cup raisins
2	eggs			

Preheat oven to 350 degrees. Combine flour, baking soda, and salt in a small bowl. In a very large bowl, cream butter and both sugars for about 1 minute. Beat in eggs and vanilla on medium-high speed for about 1 minute. Add dry ingredients, a little at a time. Mix in oats until well blended. Stir in pecans, chocolate chips, M&M's, and raisins, one at a time, mixing well between each addition. Drop dough using a tablespoon onto a greased baking sheet. Bake for 10 to 12 minutes or until golden brown. Remove and let cool.

NUTRITION INFORMATION: 176 calories, 8 g fat, 4 g saturated fat, 22 mg cholesterol, 126 mg sodium, 25 g carbohydrate, 16 g sugars, 1 g fiber, 2 g protein.

ginger spice cookies

Makes: *40 cookies*

Prep: less than 30 minutes | Bake: 8-10 minutes

1	cup sugar	½	teaspoon salt
¾	cup butter, softened	1½	teaspoons ground ginger
1	egg	1	teaspoon ground cinnamon
3	tablespoons molasses	½	teaspoon ground cloves
2	cups flour	½	teaspoon ground nutmeg
1	teaspoon baking soda		sugar for rolling

GLAZE

1½	cups powdered sugar	1½	teaspoons lemon juice
1½	tablespoons water		

Preheat oven to 350 degrees. In a bowl, cream 1 cup sugar with butter for 3 minutes or until light and fluffy. Mix in egg and molasses. In a separate medium bowl, stir together flour, baking soda, salt, ginger, cinnamon, cloves, and nutmeg. Add dry ingredients to creamed mixture and blend well. Fill a shallow bowl with sugar. Break off walnut-size pieces of dough and roll into balls. Roll balls in sugar and arrange on greased baking sheets. Bake 10 minutes or until golden brown. Transfer cookies to racks to cool.

Meanwhile, make glaze. Combine powdered sugar with water and stir until smooth. Stir in lemon juice. Drizzle glaze over cookies, or dip half of cookie tip in glaze.

NUTRITION INFORMATION: 97 calories, 4 g fat, 2 g saturated fat, 14 mg cholesterol, 87 mg sodium, 16 g carbohydrate, 10 g sugars, 0 g fiber, 1 g protein.

Beer Pairing: Ginger and Amber ales are a perfect match!

Wine Pairing: This spicy and sweet flavorful dessert should have a sweet and flavorful counterpart. The Pedro Jimenez grape from Jerez in Spain would be quite fun.

chocolate peanut butter bars

Makes: *6 dozen bars*

Prep: less than 30 minutes

1	cup butter, softened	1	pound powdered sugar
1½	cups creamy peanut butter	4	cups semi-sweet chocolate chips, melted
1⅔	cups graham cracker crumbs	⅓	cup chopped peanuts

In a large bowl, beat butter, peanut butter, cracker crumbs, and powdered sugar with a mixer until well combined. Spread and press mixture into a 17x11-inch baking sheet. Spread melted chocolate over the top and sprinkle with chopped peanuts. Refrigerate about 30 minutes or until chocolate cools a little. Cut into 2x1-inch bars. Cool completely before serving. Keep refrigerated.

NUTRITION INFORMATION: 137 calories, 8 g fat, 4 g saturated fat, 7 mg cholesterol, 55 mg sodium, 15 g carbohydrate, 13 g sugars, 1 g fiber, 2 g protein.

mint chocolate brownies

Serves: *24 portions*

Prep: less than 30 minutes | Bake: 20-25 minutes

BATTER

1	cup sugar
½	cup unsalted butter
4	eggs, beaten
1	cup flour

½	teaspoon salt
1	16 ounce can chocolate syrup
1	teaspoon vanilla extract
½	cup chopped walnuts

MINT FROSTING

2	cups powdered sugar
½	cup unsalted butter
2	tablespoons milk

½	teaspoon peppermint extract
1-2	drops of green food coloring, optional

GLAZE

1	cup chocolate chips
6	tablespoons unsalted butter

fresh mint leaves for garnish, optional

Preheat oven to 350 degrees. Combine all batter ingredients in order given in a mixing bowl. Pour batter into a greased 13x9x2-inch pan. Bake 20 to 25 minutes; cool.

Combine all frosting ingredients and beat with a mixer until smooth. Spread mixture over cooled brownies; cool.

For glaze, melt chocolate chips and butter and stir until smooth. Pour glaze over frosting. Cover and refrigerate until ready to serve. To serve, cut into squares and garnish with fresh mint leaves.

NUTRITION INFORMATION: 307 calories, 16 g fat, 9 g saturated fat, 63 mg cholesterol, 74 mg sodium, 40 g carbohydrate, 33 g sugars, 2 g fiber, 3 g protein.

Beer Pairing: The coolness of the mint and the richness of the brownies cry out for an Imperial Stout for the perfect end to a meal.

whole wheat peanut butter chocolate chip cookies

Makes: *about 20 cookies*

Prep: less than 30 minutes | Bake: 8-10 minutes

½	cup unsalted butter, softened
1	egg
½	cup brown sugar
½	cup sugar
1	teaspoon vanilla extract
½	cup natural crunchy peanut butter

¾	teaspoon baking soda
¼	teaspoon salt
1¼	cups whole wheat flour
¾	cup high quality chocolate chips
½	cup sugar for rolling

Preheat oven to 400 degrees. Beat butter and egg in a bowl with an electric mixer on medium speed. Add brown sugar, ½ cup sugar, vanilla, and peanut butter and continue mixing until all ingredients are incorporated. Mix in baking soda and salt. Slowly add flour on low speed and mix until dough is just moist. Mix chocolate chips into batter using your hands or a large wooden spoon. Form dough into 1- to 1½-inch diameter balls and roll in sugar. Place balls on a baking sheet. Bake for 8-10 minutes.

This recipe can easily be doubled or tripled.

NUTRITION INFORMATION: 200 calories, 10 g fat, 4 g saturated fat, 23 mg cholesterol, 107 mg sodium, 26 g carbohydrate, 19 g sugars, 2 g fiber, 3 g protein.

meringue clouds with strawberries in zinfandel sauce

Serves: *6 individual portions*

Prep: 1 hour | Bake: 2 hours and then must sit overnight

STRAWBERRIES IN ZINFANDEL SAUCE

1 cup white Zinfandel wine	1 cup sugar
2½ cups water	2-3 pints strawberries, quartered

MERINGUE

1½ cups sugar	4 egg whites, room temperature
1 tablespoon cornstarch	½ teaspoon cream of tartar

WHIPPED CREAM

2 cups heavy cream	1 tablespoon sugar
1¼ teaspoons vanilla extract	

Combine wine, water, and sugar in a saucepan. Bring to a boil and simmer for 45 minutes or until consistency reaches a thin syrup. Remove from heat and chill. When chilled, add strawberries and refrigerate overnight.

Preheat oven to 200 degrees. Draw six 3½- to 4-inch circles on a sheet of parchment paper. Crinkle parchment into a ball, then smooth it out to line a baking sheet, making sure pencil marks are face down so they do not transfer to meringues. Whisk sugar and cornstarch in a bowl; set aside. Beat egg whites and cream of tartar with a mixer on medium speed until soft peaks form. On low speed, add sugar mixture, 1 heaping tablespoon at a time. Increase to medium-high and beat for 5 minutes or to the consistency of marshmallow cream. Meringues can be shaped by spooning mixture into circle with a spatula or by piping through a pastry bag with a large star tip (tip number 827). If piping meringue, fill in circle and then add a second outer layer so the middle can be filled. Bake in center of oven for 1 hour, 45 minutes. Turn oven off and leave meringues in oven overnight. Do not worry if meringues crack as they will be filled with whipped cream and strawberries and sauce.

For whipped cream, whip cream into soft peaks in a large bowl. Whip in sugar and vanilla extract.

To assemble, refrigerate meringues for 30 minutes to 2 hours to soften. Assemble with whipped cream and strawberries just prior to serving.

Just prior to serving, place meringues on individual serving dishes. Spoon desired amount of whipped cream onto meringue. Divide drained strawberries, reserving sauce, among meringues. Spoon sauce around meringue and serve!

A large 9-inch meringue can be made instead of individual meringues. Draw a 9-inch circle on parchment, crinkle parchment paper, and spoon mixture onto parchment. Bake at 200 degrees for 2 hours and leave in oven overnight. Assemble as above. Serves 8 portions.

NUTRITION INFORMATION: *670 calories, 30 g fat, 18 g saturated fat, 109 mg cholesterol, 72 mg sodium, 97 g carbohydrate, 91 g sugars, 2 g fiber, 5 g protein.*

Chef Tip: For the perfect whites, make sure the bowl is very clean, grease free, and yolk free. Otherwise whites will not rise. Using a copper bowl also helps.

Wine Pairing: A late harvest red such as a Zinfandel Port or a vintage character Port would be excellent.

pecan puffs

Serves: *24 portions*

Prep: less than 30 minutes | Bake: 45-50 minutes

1	cup unsalted butter, softened		2	cups flour
½	cup powdered sugar, plus extra for rolling		2	cups whole pecans, chopped
2	teaspoons vanilla extract			

Preheat oven to 300 degrees. Cream butter with an electric mixer. Add ½ cup powdered sugar, vanilla, and flour. Add chopped pecans and mix together with a spoon. Form dough into 1-inch balls. Bake for 45 to 50 minutes. Roll balls in powdered sugar while still hot from oven, then cool cookies on a rack.

NUTRITION INFORMATION: 178 calories, 14 g fat, 5 g saturated fat, 20 mg cholesterol, 1 mg sodium, 12 g carbohydrate, 3 g sugars, 1 g fiber, 2 g protein.

Wine Pairing: The pecans and the sweetness would be an excellent complement to a cream sherry which has lush flavors of fruit and a nuttiness.

fresh mint ice cream

Serves: *8 portions*

Prep: less than 30 minutes | Freeze: 30 minutes

2	cups skim milk		6	egg yolks
2	cups heavy cream		¾	cup sugar
2	packages fresh mint, or 12-14 stems fresh mint from garden, a few leaves reserved for garnish		1	teaspoon vanilla extract

Place milk and cream in a saucepan and bring to a low boil over medium-high heat. Remove from heat and immerse fresh mint; cover and steep for 30 minutes. Strain milk mixture and discard wilted mint. Return mixture to saucepan and bring to a simmer.

Meanwhile in a large mixing bowl, whisk together egg yolks and sugar. When milk mixture is at a simmer, slowly whisk into egg mixture. Stir in vanilla. Return to saucepan and heat slowly over medium heat, stirring for 5 minutes or until mixture coats the back of a wooden spoon; do not bring to a boil. Cool in refrigerator overnight. Freeze mixture in an ice cream maker per owner's manual.

NUTRITION INFORMATION: 340 calories, 25 g fat, 15 g saturated fat, 236 mg cholesterol, 54 mg sodium, 24 g carbohydrate, 22 g sugars, 0 g fiber, 5 g protein.

peppermint bark

Makes: *12 cellophane gift bags, 4 servings per bag*
Prep: less than 30 minutes | Cook: 30-45 minutes

2 pounds milk or dark chocolate	1½ cups crushed candy (about 12 candy canes or 60 peppermint candies)
2 pounds white chocolate	1 teaspoon peppermint extract

Melt milk or dark chocolate in the top of a double boiler. Place candy canes or peppermint candies in a plastic bag and crush into ¼-inch pieces with the smooth side of a meat tenderizer or a rolling pin; set aside. Pour melted chocolate into a 17x11-inch baking pan lined with parchment paper; cool in refrigerator.

Melt white chocolate in top of double boiler. Stir in crushed candy and peppermint extract. Remove from heat and pour mixture over cooled milk or dark chocolate. Cool to room temperature, then refrigerate until hardened, or overnight is best. Break into pieces with the smooth side of a meat tenderizer or a small hammer.

NUTRITION INFORMATION: 215 calories, 12 g fat, 7 g saturated fat, 11 mg cholesterol, 34 mg sodium, 25 g carbohydrate, 21 g sugars, 1 g fiber, 3 g protein.

candied orange peel

Serves: *about 20 (2- to 3-piece) portions*
Prep: 20 minutes | Cook: 30-40 minutes

4 oranges	sugar for rolling
3 cups sugar	chocolate for dipping
juice of ½ lemon	

Cut oranges into quarters. Peel the quarters, keeping each quarter's peel in one piece. Scrape off excess pith with a paring knife, leaving only the orange rind; a small amount of white pith is acceptable. Slice rind lengthwise into ¼-inch strips, or to desired thickness. Place strips in a large saucepan. Cover with water and bring to a boil. Boil for 5 minutes; drain. Repeat cooking process 3 times.

After third time, drain water and return peel to saucepan. Add 3 cups sugar and 3 cups water to saucepan and bring to a boil. Boil for 30 minutes, watching carefully so syrup does not evaporate. Add lemon juice and boil for 5 minutes longer. Serve immediately or store in a sealed glass jar covered with reserved syrup.

To serve, drain peel and let dry, then roll in sugar or dip in chocolate. Serve peel separate as a candy or with a chocolate dessert such as chocolate mousse or a dense chocolate cake.

Beer Pairing: Wheat beers are a wonderful accompanist to this flavor.

strawberry mousse

Serves: *6 portions*

Prep: less than 30 minutes | Freeze: 3-4 hours

2	cups fresh or frozen strawberries, tops removed if fresh	2	tablespoons Grand Marnier™ liqueur, optional
1	cup sugar	1	cup heavy cream
			whole fresh strawberries for garnish

Mash strawberries into small pieces. Stir in sugar. If using Grand Marnier™, marinate berries for 30 minutes in liqueur.

Whip cream until thick and fluffy. Fold berries lightly into whipped cream. Pour mousse into dish and freeze for 3 to 4 hours. To serve, scoop into individual serving dishes and garnish with whole strawberries.

NUTRITION INFORMATION: 282 calories, 15 g fat, 9 g saturated fat, 54 mg cholesterol, 16 mg sodium, 38 g carbohydrate, 36 g sugars, 1 g fiber, 1 g protein.

Beer Pairing: Try this mousse with a snifter or Barleywine for an elegant repose.

palisade peaches and cream

Makes: *1 quart, 6 generous portions*

Prep: less than 30 minutes

3	cups peeled chopped peaches	¾	cup sugar
½	cup sugar	2¼	cups heavy cream
	juice of ½ lemon	¾	cup milk
2	eggs	½	teaspoon vanilla extract

Combine peaches, ½ cup sugar, and lemon juice. Refrigerate for 2 to 4 hours. Drain juice from peaches and set juice aside. Return peaches to refrigerator.

In a separate bowl, whisk eggs until fluffy. Slowly add ¾ cup sugar and whisk until sugar is dissolved. Add cream, milk, reserved peach juice, and vanilla. Heat mixture on stove to 165 degrees, being careful not to boil. Refrigerator mixture overnight. Transfer to an ice cream maker and process according to owner's manual. As ice cream stiffens, add peaches. Complete cycle. Transfer ice cream to a freezer-safe container and freeze until ready to serve.

Best with the ripest summer Palisades peaches harvested in August.

NUTRITION INFORMATION: 545 calories, 36 g fat, 22 g saturated fat, 196 mg cholesterol, 70 mg sodium, 54 g carbohydrate, 50 g sugars, 1 g fiber, 6 g protein.

Chef Tip: When you see a recipe for peaches, any stone fruit will do. What are stone fruit? Plums, nectarines, pluots, apricots, peaches.

classique
restaurants

gnocchi soufflé with fontina cheese and truffles

Serves 6

7	ounces whole milk			nutmeg to taste
3	ounces unsalted butter		1½	cups heavy cream
4¼	ounces all-purpose flour, sifted		6	ounces fontina cheese, grated
2	ounces freshly grated Parmesan cheese		3	ounces arugula
3	eggs		1	ounce white truffle oil
	salt to taste			truffle slices and micro greens

Bring milk and butter to a boil. Reduce heat and maintain at a simmer. Add flour and stir until a dough forms, pulling away from the sides of the pan. Add Parmesan cheese; stir to combine and season. Remove from the heat and transfer to a medium bowl. Add eggs one at a time, stirring between each addition. Season dough with salt and nutmeg. Transfer to a shallow pan and refrigerate to cool.

Bring a saucepan of salted water to a boil. With floured hands roll dough into 1-inch balls and score with a fork. Carefully place the dough balls in the boiling water. Simmer until the gnocchi rise to the top of the pan. Remove from the heat, strain, and chill in an ice bath.

Preheat oven to 375 degrees. Butter 6 ovenproof bowls and cover the bottom of each with cream. Strain the gnocchi from the ice bath and spoon 7 into each dish. Cover with fontina cheese. Place bowls on a sheet pan and bake until golden brown, about 15 minutes. Remove from the heat and set aside, keeping warm. To serve, garnish with arugula dressed with truffle oil, truffle slices, and micro greens.

Legendary Dining at Hotel Colorado

Baron's restaurant at Hotel Colorado is fashioned after the hotel's original "Palm Garden" dining room. Hotel Colorado features a centerpiece waterfall cascading over rocky mountain granite just as it was in the late 1800s. Similarly, natural light floods through a large glass ceiling warming dozens of plants, giving guests the illusion of dining outside. No longer are fresh trout caught by guests in the interior pool of sparkling water. Nevertheless, as in the 19th century, dining in this setting provides an abundant oasis in contrast to the roughness of the mountain surroundings.

Executive Chef Ron Jackson

historic hotel colorado's beef and ale pudding

Serves 6-8

BEEF AND ALE FILLING

¼	cup all-purpose flour
½	teaspoon salt
⅛	teaspoon freshly ground black pepper
2	pounds beef sirloin, trimmed of fat and cut into 1½-inch pieces
2	tablespoons olive oil
1	large onion, sliced ¼-inch thick

2	cloves garlic, minced
6	ounces (about 3) Portobello mushrooms, sliced ½-inch thick
1	cup dark ale
3	cups beef broth
1	teaspoon dried sage

YORKSHIRE PUDDING CRUST

2	eggs
1	teaspoon salt
1	cup all-purpose flour

1	cup milk
2	egg whites

Preheat oven to 350 degrees. In a mixing bowl, combine flour, salt, and pepper. Add beef, a few pieces at a time, making sure that the meat is coated on all sides with the flour. In a 5-quart Dutch oven, heat olive oil. Add meat, a few pieces at a time, and brown on all sides, about 8 to 10 minutes. When all the meat is browned, add onions and garlic and sauté for 2 minutes. Add mushrooms and continue to sauté for 5 minutes, until the onions are translucent and the mushrooms begin to give off some of their liquid. Add ale, stirring to loosen any browned bits that are stuck to the bottom of the pan. Add broth and sage and bring to a boil. Transfer to oven and bake 45 to 60 minutes or until the meat is tender.

To prepare batter for crust, place eggs in a blender or food processor and pulse on and off 3 times. Add salt, flour, and milk and blend for 45 seconds. Refrigerate the batter for 45 minutes. When ready to bake, beat egg whites until stiff and fold into the batter.

Increase oven temperature to 425 degrees. Cover the hot stew with crust batter. Bake for 15 minutes, then reduce the heat to 400 degrees and bake for 10 to 15 minutes longer. The crust will rise and be a golden brown color.

Tradition of Service

At Hotel Colorado's opening in June 10, 1893, no expense was spared in creating a grand resort for the elite, a playground for society's wealthy. To create the cosmopolitan atmosphere that the founders envisioned, they imported the entire staff from locations around the world. Londoners staffed the original front desk. Sixty chambermaids and servers were brought in from Boston. The Grand Dining room was set with fine crystal and imported china.

As in the tradition of the past, Hotel Colorado's service and award-winning chef provide guests with the finest in fresh culinary selections and romantic ambiance.

526 Pine Street

Glenwood Springs, CO 81601

800.544.3998

970.945.6511

fax 970.945.5437

www.hotelcolorado.com

Food with Integrity

The first Chipotle opened its doors near the intersection of Evans Avenue and Gilpin Street in Denver on July 13, 1993. About 15 years and more than 800 restaurants later, this national restaurant chain's *Food with Integrity* philosophy is changing the way the world thinks about, and eats fast food.

Food with Integrity was launched in 2000 when Chipotle began serving naturally raised pork carnitas in all of its restaurants after founder Steve Ells experienced what it was like to raise pigs the old fashioned way — outdoors or in deeply bedded pens, without the use of antibiotics or added hormones, and on a pure vegetarian diet. Raising pigs this way is more humane and more sustainable, and produces pork that just tastes better.

Today, all of the chicken Chipotle serves is naturally raised, as is most of its beef. In all, Chipotle serves more naturally raised meat than any other restaurant company in the world. Chipotle also offers cheese and sour cream made with milk from cows that are not treated with the synthetic growth hormone rBGH, and about 35 percent of the black and pinto beans it serves are organically grown.

Steve Ells
Founder, Chairman, and Co-CEO

grilled rack of pork

Serves 8

1	3-4-pound, 8-rib rack of Niman Ranch pork, Frenched	1	tablespoon chopped fresh thyme
	salt and pepper to taste	1	tablespoon chopped fresh marjoram
		1	tablespoon chopped fresh sage

Generously season pork with salt, then season with pepper and herbs. Bring pork to room temperature for about 1 to 2 hours. Make a charcoal fire, preferably with mesquite, heating to 350 to 375 degrees. When coals are white, grill pork, covered, until outside is nicely seared, the inside is slightly pink, and the internal temperature is 145 to 150 degrees. (Times may vary, so be sure to use a meat thermometer.) Be sure to avoid flair-ups, as this will impart a burnt/bitter flavor.

Remove pork from grill, tent with foil, and let rest for about 10 to 15 minutes at room temperature. Slice individual chops and serve with grilled vegetables and garlic roasted potatoes.

ancho chile marinade for meat

1	2 ounce package dried ancho chiles or dried pepper of choice	6	cloves garlic
1	teaspoon black pepper	½	red onion, quartered
2	teaspoons cumin powder	¼	cup vegetable oil
2	tablespoons chopped fresh oregano	4	cuts of meat of choice

Soak dried chiles in water overnight or until soft. Remove seeds. Add chiles and all ingredients except meat to a food processor. Purée until smooth. Spread mixture over meat and refrigerate at least 1 hour, or up to 24 hours.

Heat grill to about 400 degrees, or if cooking inside, heat small amount of oil in a skillet or grill pan over high heat. Salt meat to taste. Grill meat for about 4 minutes per side, depending upon thickness, or until done. Serve with rice, black beans, or choice of side dish. Garnish with fresh cilantro.

chipotle cornbread

Makes 1 loaf

1	cup yellow cornmeal	1	cup shredded Monterey Jack cheese
1	cup all-purpose flour	1	cup buttermilk
¼-½	cup sugar	3	eggs
2	teaspoons baking powder	6	tablespoons unsalted butter, melted and cooled
1	teaspoon baking soda	2	tablespoons minced chipotle chiles (canned or dried)
1	teaspoon salt		

Preheat oven to 375 degrees. Mix cornmeal, flour, sugar, baking powder, baking soda, and salt in a large bowl. Stir in cheese. Whisk together buttermilk, eggs, melted butter, and chipotle chiles in a medium bowl. Add liquid mixture to dry ingredients and stir until blended. Pour batter into a buttered 9x5x2-inch metal loaf pan. Bake bread 35 minutes or until knife inserted in center comes out clean. Cool in pan for about 15 minutes. Turn bread onto rack to cool completely. Slice and serve.

spicy guacamole

Makes about 1 cup

1	large ripe avocado, peeled and pitted	2	large cloves garlic, finely chopped
2	teaspoons fresh lime juice	2	large serrano chiles, seeded and chopped
½	cup chopped fresh cilantro	¼	teaspoon salt
¼	cup finely chopped onion		

Using a fork, mash avocado with lime juice in small bowl. Add cilantro, onions, garlic, chiles, and salt and stir to combine.

Choose Local

In 2008, Chipotle Mexican Grill became the first and only national restaurant company committed to buying local produce on a significant scale, yet another major initiative driving Chipotle's *Food with Integrity* vision. The local plan includes purchasing a growing percentage of produce for each of its more than 800 restaurants from local farms when it is seasonally available. In Colorado, Chipotle has partnered with Petrocco Farms, a fourth-generation family owned farm with more than 2,000 acres of land located between Brighton and Greeley, Colo., to provide produce items such as onions and green bell peppers. Petrocco Farms is locally and nationally renowned for its high-quality produce.

Chipotle recommends using produce from local farmers whenever it is available because the produce is fresher, better-tasting, reduces fuel consumption for shipping, supports rural economies, and helps to strengthen the overall food supply.

www.chipotle.com

SECOND HOME
KITCHEN AND BAR

A Second Home
Signature Dish

150 Clayton Lane
Denver, CO 80206

303.253.3000

www.secondhomedenver.com
www.sagerestaurantgroup.com

pork tenderloin, bourbon ancho sauce, jicama slaw

Serves 2

2	6 ounce pork tenderloins			pinch of salt
2	ounces brown sugar	6	ounces heavy cream
2	teaspoons ground cumin	12	spears asparagus
4	ounces corn kernels (fresh when in season, otherwise frozen)		olive oil
	pinch of cumin		salt and pepper to taste

BOURBON ANCHO SAUCE

2	red onions, finely chopped	4	cups chicken broth
2	ounces vegetable oil	1	cup apple juice
2	cups bourbon	2	tablespoons brown sugar
4	ancho chiles		

JICAMA SLAW

1	ounce jicama, julienned		juice of 2 limes
1	ounce radishes, julienned	2	teaspoons olive oil
2	teaspoons chopped cilantro		

Preheat oven to 375 degrees. Rub tenderloins in a mixture of brown sugar and cumin. Sear in a hot pan on all sides and cook to desired temperature.

Cook corn over low heat with about 1 ounce of water until very soft. Add a pinch of cumin and salt. Purée in a blender until smooth, adding heavy cream as needed; the consistency should be slightly thicker than pancake batter; set aside.

Toss asparagus in olive oil, salt and pepper. Roast for about 5 minutes; depending on size.

BOURBON ANCHO SAUCE: In a small pot, sweat red onions in hot oil. Add bourbon and cook down until it has completely evaporated. Add ancho chiles, chicken broth, apple juice, and brown sugar. Simmer until the mixture is reduced by half. Place in a blender and purée until smooth.

JICAMA SALAD: Combine jicama, radishes, cilantro, lime juice, and olive oil.

To serve, spread corn purée in the middle of each serving plate. Cut pork tenderloin in half. Place half on the purée and top with asparagus. Lean the other half over the asparagus and top with slaw. Drizzle sauce around the plate.

crab pad thai

1401 Curtis Street
Denver, CO 80202
303.825.6500

www.thecornerofficedenver.com
www.sagerestaurantgroup.com

PAD THAI SAUCE

1	1¼ ounce containing tamarind pulp, broken into pieces
1	cup fish sauce
1½	cups sugar

1	cup white vinegar
3	tablespoons paprika
1	cup water

PAD THAI

1	pound dried 3mm rice noodles
2	tablespoons oil
1	tablespoon minced garlic
1	tablespoon minced ginger
1	tablespoon finely chopped green onions
4	ounces whipped egg
½	cup shredded carrots

6	ounces Pad Thai Sauce
½	cup bean sprouts
¼	cup lump crabmeat
1	tablespoon butter
2	tablespoons crushed toasted peanuts
1	tablespoon minced cilantro
1	lime wedge

Combine all sauce ingredients in a pot and bring to a boil. Reduce heat and simmer 20 minutes. Remove from heat and process in a food processor. Strain and reserve sauce.

To prepare pad thai, soak rice noodles in hot water until softened. Sauté in hot oil the garlic, ginger, and green onions until the aroma is released. While stirring, gradually drizzle in egg and cook through. Add softened rice noodles, carrots, and sauce. Cook until all the sauce is evaporated. Toss in bean sprouts last minute. In a separate pan heat crab in butter. Top the finished pad thai with heated crab, peanuts, cilantro, and lime wedge.

Enstrom Candies' roots go back to 1929, when Chet and Vernie Enstrom, along with their partner, Harry Jones, opened the Jones-Enstrom Ice Cream Company in downtown Grand Junction. Chet also had a passion for candy making, especially Almond Toffee, and began brewing up small batches as gifts for family and friends.

In 1960, he and Vernie renovated their ice cream factory and opened Enstrom Candies to immediate success.

For three generations, the Enstrom family has crafted its Almond Toffee to the delight of connoisseurs the world over. Enstrom's Almond Toffee and a wide variety of other confections may be ordered by visiting one of their Colorado retail stores; by phone at 1-800-ENSTROM; or on the web.

www.enstrom.com

enstrom's oatmeal chocolate toffee cake

¾	cup boiling water	1¾	cups flour
1	cup oatmeal	1	teaspoon baking soda
1	cup lightly packed brown sugar	½	teaspoon salt
1	cup sugar	1	tablespoon cocoa
½	cup butter	2	cups finely chopped Enstrom's World Famous Almond Toffee
2	eggs		
1	teaspoon vanilla extract	¾	cup nuts

Preheat oven to 350 degrees. Pour boiling water over oatmeal and let stand at room temperature for 10 minutes. Add both sugars and butter and stir until melted. Add eggs and mix well. Stir in vanilla. Sift together flour, baking soda, salt, and cocoa; add to oatmeal mixture and beat well. Add half of the toffee crumbs. Pour batter into a greased and floured 13x9x2-inch pan. Sprinkle with the remaining toffee and nuts. Bake for 45 minutes.

enstrom's almond toffee pie

1	cup sugar	¼	cup milk
¼	cup cornstarch	2	ounces grated German sweet chocolate
¼	teaspoon salt	1	tablespoon butter
¼	cup milk	½	teaspoon vanilla extract
2	egg yolks	1	baked pie shell
1½	cups milk	4	ounces ground Enstrom's World Famous Almond Toffee
4½	tablespoons cocoa		

Combine sugar, cornstarch, and salt. Add ¼ cup milk, mixing well. Blend in egg yolks. Scald 1½ cups milk over hot water in the top of a double boiler. Add cornstarch mixture to scalded milk, stirring constantly. Beat well with a wire whip or rotary beater until smooth. Cook mixture over hot water, stirring frequently until clear and thickened.

Meanwhile, dissolve cocoa in ¼ cup milk. Add cocoa and grated chocolate to cornstarch mixture. Continue to cook, stirring until chocolate is melted and mixture is thickened. Remove mixture from heat. Add butter and vanilla, stirring until butter is melted. Refrigerate pudding mixture until thoroughly chilled.

Turn chilled mixture into a baked pie shell and sprinkle ground almond toffee over the top. Chill.

In a hurry? The pie filling can also be made using a large package of double chocolate pudding and pie mix filling.

colorado potato hash

2   Colorado russet or purple potatoes
2   Colorado red potatoes
2   Colorado Yukon gold potatoes
¼   cup olive oil
½   tablespoon chopped fresh garlic
1   tablespoon chopped fresh shallots
½   cup blue cheese (Maytag or Clemson), crumbled

½   cup heavy cream
    kosher salt to taste
    white ground pepper to taste
    Italian parsley, finely chopped, to taste
6   slices Applewood bacon, cooked and chopped

Dice unpeeled potatoes into medium-sized cubes and blanch half way in boiling water. Drain potatoes and rinse with cold running water until fully cooled. Toss potatoes with a small amount of oil to prevent sticking; refrigerate.

Heat a sauté pan and add olive oil. Add potatoes slowly to avoid any splatter of oil, and sauté for 4 to 5 minutes. Add garlic and shallots and sauté until golden brown. Add blue cheese and cook until melted. Add cream and cook until reduced by three-fourths. This mixture should be thick and hearty. Season as needed with salt and white pepper. Garnish with chopped parsley and bacon.

Colorado Proud, created by the Colorado Department of Agriculture in 1999, encourages consumers to buy locally grown, raised or processed food and agricultural products. There are more than 1,000 members in the program including growers, processors, restaurants, retailers and associations.

Colorado Department of Agriculture/Colorado Proud

700 Kipling Street, Suite 4000

Lakewood, CO 80215

Ph. 303-239-4114

Fax 303-239-4125

www.coloradoproud.org

Chef Jason K. Morse, CEC, Valley Country Club, Aurora, CO

boulder beer co. planet porter stew

Serves 4-6

From humble origins in a goat shed in 1979, Colorado's First Microbrewery has grown to produce almost 9 million bottles of beer annually. Boulder Beer has a tradition of innovation, reintroducing the Porter style to America in the '80's, and now crafting new and interesting styles of beer like Hazed & Infused Dry-Hopped Ale and Mojo IPA, as well as Colorado favorites Singletrack Copper Ale, Buffalo Gold and many more.

As well as being a full-production brewery, Boulder Beer also houses a comfortable pub from which this recipe was borrowed. Boulder Beer invites you to come stay for a meal under the Flatirons on an unforgettable patio, or take a fun public tour at 2 pm M – F.

Cheers!

2880 Wilderness Place
Boulder, CO 80301
303.444.8448

www.boulderbeer.com

	vegetable oil	32	ounces Boulder Beer Planet Porter
1	large red onion, finely chopped	32	ounces beef broth
8	cloves garlic, minced	4	carrots, sliced ¼-inch thick
½	tablespoon salt	2	cups chopped celery
½	tablespoon coarse black pepper	2	russet potatoes, peeled and diced into ½-inch cubes
½	tablespoon chopped fresh rosemary		
24	ounces Maverick Ranch™ Naturally Raised Buffalo Top Sirloin Steak, cut into 1-inch cubes	2	bay leaves

ROUX

4	tablespoons unsalted butter, softened	1	tablespoon corn flour
		¼	tablespoon flour

In a large cast iron skillet, heat 2-3 tablespoons vegetable oil over medium-high heat. Add onions and sweat until translucent. Add garlic, salt, pepper, and rosemary and cook another 5 minutes, stirring often so garlic doesn't burn. Transfer onion mixture to a heavy 5-quart stockpot.

Tossed cubed bison with a few tablespoons of vegetable oil and season with salt and pepper. Reheat the skillet. When pan is hot, add meat and brown on all sides. Work in batches if necessary so as not to crowd the pan. Allow the buildup of browned bits on the bottom of the pan. The more you can brown the meat, the richer the flavor your stew. Transfer cooked meat to the stockpot with the onions. Turn off the heat. Deglaze the skillet with half a bottle of the Planet Porter. Transfer beer from skillet along with remaining beer to the stockpot. Bring to a simmer and cook the meat in the beer for 15 minutes. Add beef broth, carrots, celery, potatoes, and bay leaves. Bring to a boil, then simmer until vegetables and potatoes are soft. Taste and season.

To prepare roux, mix all ingredients with a fork to make a smooth paste. Add the roux to the stew and simmer for another 30 minutes, then ya done.

jarret d'agneau (roasted lamb shank)

Serves 4

4	Colorado lamb shanks		1	teaspoon chopped fresh thyme
	salt and pepper to taste		1	teaspoon chopped fresh rosemary
8	white onions, chopped		½	white wine and ½ beef stock to cover the shanks, you may split the difference with water if need be
	olive oil for sautéing			
2	medium eggplants, cubed		6	cloves garlic, unpeeled
6	cloves garlic, chopped			zest of 1 orange (untreated, no chemical sprays)
8	ripe tomatoes, peeled, seeded, and crushed			

Preheat oven to 325 degrees. Season lamb shanks with salt and pepper, then sear in hot olive oil in a deep heavy pot until golden brown. When the shanks are evenly seared (expect a lot of smoke), remove the shanks and carefully discard the fat from the pan. In the same pan, slowly cook onions in olive oil until translucent. Remove onions and set aside. Add olive oil and sear eggplant. Add chopped garlic, cooked onions, tomatoes, thyme, and rosemary and stir to mix the vegetables. Nest the lamb shanks in the mixture. Add the wine/stock liquid to barely cover the shanks and bring to a boil. Add unpeeled garlic cloves and orange zest. Simmer in the oven until fork tender, about 3 hours; the meat should fall off the bone.

The garlic cloves cook in the skin and are a delicacy in the south; they become soft and lose their bite. You can spread a clove on bread or eat just as is (but not the skin).

To serve, ladle the lamb stew into a wide-rimmed, shallow soup bowl on its own or over polenta. Garnish with chopped fresh parsley and serve with crusty French bread.

ROBERT'S WINE TIP: A Rhône-type wine would be perfect with this dish.

When I moved to Denver, I was happy to note that like Provence, Colorado has a semi arid climate, compatible to a vigorous lamb industry. The flavor of lamb varies with the region in which it grazed. Colorado lamb is milder than in the south of France. At Le Central, we buy the lamb whole and butcher it in the familiar pieces; one of them being the shanks used in this recipe. We use the hind shanks, which are meatier than the fore shanks. It is a great winter dish.

Le Central is a Denver landmark, first opening its doors in 1981. Robert Tournier (originally from Toulon, France) has been the sole restaurateur, never wavering from his mission of casual, hearty, friendly, traditional country style French food. Even today, Le Central employs several native French staff, who love to share bits of their cuisine, culture and wine.

Today, Le Central has established itself as a registered cultural center, providing guests with not only just lunch and dinner, but also cooking classes, wine dinners, one on one time with French chef's and servers, school parties geared towards learning the French language and fine French foods to take and share at home.

The spirit of Le Central comes from my family and our hometown of Toulon. Our cooking is the result of love, resourcefulness, hard work and passion for the aroma, ingredients and their flavor. Please enjoy our interpretation and escape to a part of France.

Merci, Robert Tournier, Owner
112 E. 8th Avenue
Denver CO 80206
303.863.8094
www.lecentral.com
Robert Tournier, Restaurateur

rioja

1431 Larimer Street

Denver, CO 80202

303.820.2282

www.riojadenver.com

Chef Jennifer Jasinski

heirloom tomato green tomato gazpacho

Serves 8

2½	pounds green zebra tomatoes	⅓	cup extra virgin olive oil
1	large European cucumber, seeded	1	tablespoon sherry vinegar
½	pound yellow bell peppers	1	tablespoon tomato paste
¼	pound celery stalks	½	tablespoon salt
1	cup Italian parsley leaves	1	teaspoon fresh black pepper
2	poblano peppers, seeds and stems removed	4	cups vegetable stock or water

AVOCADO MOUSSE

1	ripe avocado, peeled and seeded		salt to taste
1	teaspoon lemon juice	1	cup heavy cream, whipped until stiff

PRESENTATION

1	yellow heirloom tomato, cut into wedges	1	green heirloom tomato, cut into wedges
1	red heirloom tomato, cut into wedges		

Coarsely chop zebra tomatoes, cucumber, bell peppers, celery, parsley, and poblano peppers together and place them in a plastic container. Add olive oil, sherry vinegar, tomato paste, salt, and pepper and marinate gazpacho overnight.

The next day, process the gazpacho in a food processor until smooth enough to be a soup-like consistency but still a bit chunky in texture. After soup is blended, stir in vegetable stock and season with salt and pepper as needed. Chill until served.

To prepare the mousse, in a food processor, add the avocado and blend with lemon juice and salt. Fold the puréed avocado into the whipped cream.

PRESENTATION: Ladle gazpacho into the center of 8 serving bowls. Arrange heirloom tomato wedges in a spiral on top of the gazpacho, then finish with a dollop of the mousse in the center. If you like, garnish with a piece of lahvosh cracker and serve.

bistecca

Serves 4

POTATOES

1	pound russet potatoes	¼	cup whole milk
3	tablespoons sweet butter		salt and pepper to taste

BASIL PESTO

2	cups packed fresh basil leaves	⅔	cup extra virgin olive oil
2	cloves garlic	½	cup freshly grated Parmesan cheese
¼	cup pine nuts, toasted		

STEAK

6	ounces baby arugula	4	4 ounce portions skirt steak
1	tablespoon extra virgin olive oil	2	ounces Gorgonzola cheese, crumbled, for garnish
½	tablespoon 15-year old balsamic di Modena vinegar		

909 17th Street

Denver, CO 80202

303.296.3525

www.panzanodenver.com

Executive Chef Elise Wiggins

Steam potatoes until done. Using a food mill, rice the potatoes. Add butter and milk. Season with salt and pepper. Combine thoroughly but do not overmix; set aside.

For the pesto, combine basil, garlic, and pine nuts in a food processor and pulse until coarsely chopped. Add ½ cup olive oil and process until fully incorporated and smooth. Fold in cheese. If not using the pesto immediately, cover with a thin film of remaining olive oil and plastic wrap pressed down on the surface.

Toss arugula with extra virgin olive oil, balsamic vinegar, and salt and pepper. Grill steak to desired temperature. Allow to rest, covered.

PRESENTATION: Spread pesto on the bottom of 4 dinner plates. Place one scoop of potatoes on each plate on top of pesto. Slice steak into bite-size pieces and place on top of potatoes. Top with arugula. Garnish with Gorgonzola. Enjoy.

rocky mountain ceviche

Serves 6

24	ounces Rocky Mountain Rainbow Trout, skinned, deboned, cut crosswise into ¼-inch strips		2	tablespoons vegetable oil
½	cup shallots, finely diced		1	tablespoon extra virgin olive oil
2	cups chanterelle mushroom, julienned		3	limes
¼	cup Italian parsley, finely chopped			salt and pepper, to taste
1	clove garlic, finely chopped		1	bunch watercress

Separate and julienne cut (if necessary) chanterelle and sauté lightly with vegetable oil until edges become soft, about 3 minutes. Set aside and chill. Combine all ingredients, except watercress, in bowl. Squeeze lime over all ingredients, toss lightly, and allow to cure for 30 minutes. Serve over bed of watercress.

34295 Highway 6 C-1-B

PO Box 2990

Edwards, CO 81632

970.926.4740

www.thefrenchpress.net

Executive Chef/Owner
Juan Cruz Anon

mongolian lamb marinade with mint-cilantro vinaigrette

Serves 8

LAMB

2	cups mushroom soy sauce		3	green onions, coarsely chopped
1	cup honey		1	cup soy sauce
2	cloves garlic, peeled and smashed			pinch of red chili flakes
1	cup mirin or sake		8	double Colorado lamb chops
1	small finger ginger, peeled and smashed			

MINT-CILANTRO VINAIGRETTE

2	egg yolks		2	tablespoons macadamia nuts
¼	cup Chinese mustard		½	cup mint leaf
¼	cup rice wine vinegar		¼	cup cilantro leaf
¼	cup ginger vinegar		1½	teaspoons honey
2	tablespoons pickled ginger			juice of 1-2 limes
2	tablespoons peanuts, toasted		¾	cup peanut oil

Mix together all lamb ingredients except lamb. Place lamb chops in mixture with the bones out of the liquid and marinate for 4 hours. Remove lamb and allow to drain for 5 minutes. Season the chops with salt and pepper and grill over medium heat to desired temperature; do not allow the flame to flare over chops. (An indoor cast iron grill plate works well, too.)

To make the vinaigrette, add egg yolks, mustard, both vinegars, ginger, peanuts, and macadamia nuts to a blender and purée until smooth. Add mint, cilantro, honey, and lime juice and emulsify with peanut oil. Color should be bright green and smooth. Adjust seasoning with salt and sugar as desired.

The Ritz-Carlton Hotel

Bachelor Gulch

0130 Daybreak Ridge

Avon, Colorado 81620

970.343.1555

www.wolfgangpuck.com

Executive Chef Mark Ferguson

wild mushroom soup

Serves 4

1	ounce porcini powder	2	bay leaves
2	cups hot water	1	cup cream
4	shallots, minced	8	egg yolks, beaten
1	cup extra virgin olive oil		salt and pepper to taste
1½	pounds fresh mushrooms, cubed	4	ounces Parmesan cheese
¼	cup dry white wine	¼	cup chopped chives
2	quarts chicken stock		

Mix porcini powder and water; set aside. Sauté shallots in olive oil until translucent. Add mushrooms and sauté until pan is dry, adding more olive oil if needed to completely cook the mushrooms. Pour in wine and cook until reduced by half. Add chicken stock and bay leaves and simmer until reduced by half. Once stock has reduced, add porcini mushroom stock and cream. Just before serving, whip in egg yolks. Season to taste with salt and pepper. Garnish with Parmesan cheese and chives.

Loews Denver Hotel
4150 E. Mississippi Avenue
Denver, CO 80246
303.639.1600

www.loewsdenverhotel.com

Executive Chef
Christian Stephens

tuna cruda (tuna ceviche)

Serves 4 appetizer portion

SAUCE

2	teaspoons sambal paste		juice of 1 orange
1	teaspoon sugar	3	tablespoons rice wine vinegar
2	drops fish oil	⅓	cup olive oil
1	teaspoon sesame oil	1	tablespoon chopped fresh parsley
3	tablespoons soy sauce	1	tablespoon chopped fresh cilantro
⅓	cup fresh lime juice		salt and pepper to taste

CEVICHE

16	ounces fresh sushi grade ahi tuna, diced (4 ounces per person)	4	ounces green onions, thinly cut
6	ounces red onions, diced	8	ounces avocado, diced
		4	ounces wasabi peas

Mix all sauce ingredients in a small bowl with a whisk. Chill until ready to serve.

For the ceviche, toss all ingredients in a small bowl.

When ready to serve, for every 4 ounces of tuna, add 3 tablespoons of sauce to ceviche. Drizzle sauce around plate for presentation.

1173 Delaware Street
Denver, CO 80204
303.605.2822

www.cubacubacafe.com

Chef Enrique Socarras

19192 Highway 8

Morrison, CO 80465

303.697.4771

www.thefort.com

Executive Chef Trevor Dierolf

the fort restaurant's posole with pork

Serves *12*

1 tablespoon vegetable oil or bacon fat

2 onions, chopped

2 pounds pork shoulder, cut into fist-size chunks

4 quarts chicken broth

1 bay leaf

1 sprig fresh oregano

½ cup fresh red chile purée, or 4-6 tablespoons mild or medium ground pure New Mexican red chile (Dixon is best)

2 cups wet or dry white posole corn, soaked overnight if dry

2 teaspoons salt

1 whole boneless, skinless chicken breast, cut into bite-size pieces, optional

1½ pounds shredded mild cheddar cheese (6 cups) for topping

In a large stockpot, heat oil and fry the onions for about 2 minutes or until transparent. Add pork and cook, turning occasionally, for about 4 minutes or until brown. Deglaze stockpot with a little of the broth, scraping the bottom to loosen all the browned bits and incorporate them into the broth. Add remaining broth, bay leaf, oregano, chile, posole corn, and salt and simmer, covered, for 5 to 6 hours, stirring regularly. Keep the solids under liquid by adding hot water when necessary. The dish is ready when the pork is tender and the posole has popped. It will look like wet popcorn. Add chicken, if using, and simmer for another 12 minutes or until the chicken is cooked. Serve hot in bowls and top with the shredded cheese.

523 E. 17th Street Ave.

Denver, CO 80202

303.830.1001

www.steubens.com

Executive Chef Brandon Biederman and Chef Matt Selby

steuben's deviled egg mix

12 hard-boiled eggs

2 teaspoons Dijon mustard

¼ teaspoon Tabasco sauce

½ teaspoon salt

⅛ teaspoon freshly ground black pepper

1 tablespoon grated onion

¼ teaspoon minced fresh parsley

¼ teaspoon minced fresh oregano

¼ teaspoon snipped fresh chives

¼ teaspoon fresh lemon juice

¼ cup Hellmann's mayonnaise

Cut hard-boiled eggs in half lengthwise, being careful to keep the whites from breaking; set egg white halves aside. Place egg yolks in a mixing bowl and mash with a fork until completely smooth. Add remaining ingredients and mix well with a spoon. Fill mixture into the egg white halves and enjoy!

sticky toffee pudding

Serves 5

½	cup dried figs, chopped	2	tablespoons butter, plus extra to grease crocks
½	cup dark rum	1	egg, beaten
½	teaspoon vanilla extract	½	cup butter
½	teaspoon baking soda	¾	cup heavy cream
1	cup flour	1¼	tablespoons water
⅔	cup sugar	¾	cup brown sugar
½	teaspoon baking powder	1	tablespoon dark rum
	pinch of salt		

1822 Blake St.
Denver, Colorado 80202
303.296.1970

www.vestagrill.com

Executive Chef Wade Kirwan
and Chef Matt Selby

Preheat oven to 350 degrees. Combine chopped figs, rum, vanilla, and baking soda in a saucepan and place over high heat. Bring to a boil and simmer for about 5 minutes. In a mixing bowl, sift together flour, sugar, baking powder, and salt; set aside.

In a mixer, whisk fig mixture with 2 tablespoons butter until butter has melted. Whisk in dry ingredients. Add beaten egg and whisk to combine into a dough. Grease side and bottom of 5 oven-proof individual serving-size crocks with butter. Distribute the pudding dough equally among crocks and place crocks on a baking sheet. Bake for 20 to 25 minutes or until a toothpick comes cleanly out.

While puddings are in the oven, prepare the toffee sauce by placing butter, heavy cream, water, and brown sugar in a saucepan over high heat. Whisk mixture until sugar has dissolved and butter has melted. Whisk in rum and remove from heat. Remove pudding from oven and spoon toffee sauce over each. Increase oven to 450 degrees, and place the puddings back in to cook for 6 to 8 minutes longer or until the toffee is bubbling. Serve hot with vanilla whipped cream.

kobe beef tartare with harissa relish

Serves *4*

HARISSA RELISH

2   red bell peppers, diced very thin

⅓   cup pine nuts, coarsely chopped

1   small jar piquillo pepper, diced very thin

3   preserved lemons, diced very thin

5   shallots, chopped very thin

3   lemons, peeled, cut into segments, and diced

3   Roma tomatoes peeled and small diced

½   bunch Italian parsley, coarsely chopped

½   teaspoon chile flakes

½   teaspoon cayenne pepper

½   teaspoon paprika

½   teaspoon Tabasco sauce

2   cups extra virgin olive oil

    salt and pepper to taste

BEEF TARTARE

1   1 pound American Kobe beef filet

6   breakfast radish, cleaned and sliced thin on a mandolin, set aside in cold water

4   quail eggs

1   ounce micro cilantro

Make the harissa relish 2 hours prior to serving the dish. In a large mixing bowl, combine all ingredients for the relish. Season to taste with salt and pepper and set aside in the fridge.

For tartare, cut the beef filet in small dice or pass it through a meat grinder. Mix the harissa relish with the beef, reserving ¼ cup of the harissa for the presentation. Season with salt and pepper. (You don't have to use all the oil from the relish; you don't want it too oily.)

PRESENTATION: Place a ring mold in the middle of a plate and fill with beef tartare. Arrange sliced radish on top of the tartare like a fan. Cut off the top of the quail egg shell and separate the yolk from the white. Place the yolk back into the shell and place it on top of the tartare. Remove the ring mold. Drizzle the reserved harissa around the plate. Garnish with micro cilantro.

colorado peach and cucumber salsa

4   cucumbers, diced ¼-inch

6   Roma tomatoes, diced ¼-inch

½   red onion, diced ¼-inch

2   tablespoons chopped cilantro

6   Colorado peaches, diced ¼-inch

1   yellow bell pepper, diced ¼-inch

1   14 ounce can black beans, drained

1   tablespoon minced fresh ginger

1   tablespoon minced fresh garlic

1   tablespoon garlic oil

4   tablespoons sugar

3   tablespoons white wine

¼   cup sweet chili sauce

½   cup chili oil

Combine cucumbers, tomatoes, onion, cilantro, peaches, pepper, and beans and set aside. Mix the remaining ingredients together and place in a stock pot then reduce by half. Add hot liquid to dry ingredients and mix well, then transfer to a shallow container to chill. Serve chilled over lamb or grilled fish.

colorado striped bass with
olathe sweet corn and tomato seed-chive vinaigrette

Serves 4

MEL'S
BAR AND GRILL

8970 S. Holly Street
Greenwood Village, CO 80111
303.779.8223

www.melsbarandgrill.com

Chef/Owner Chad Clevenger

¼ pound Applewood smoked bacon, diced into ¼-inch pieces

3 Colorado heirloom tomatoes, divided

2 cloves garlic, minced

1 medium shallot, finely chopped

2 tablespoons champagne vinegar

¼ cup extra virgin olive oil

¼ cup thinly sliced chives

kosher salt to taste

4 ears Olathe sweet corn, shucked and cleaned

½ cup unsalted butter

salt and pepper to taste

¼ cup corn oil

2 12 ounce Colorado striped bass filets, each cut into 2 pieces, cleaned, pin bones removed, and skin lightly scored

1 cup wild arugula, cleaned

2 tablespoons avocado oil

kosher salt and pepper to taste

Sauté bacon over medium heat until crispy, about 10 minutes. Transfer to a strainer to drain off excess fat, then set aside bacon.

For the vinaigrette, cut 1 heirloom tomato in half and squeeze the seeds and juice into a small bowl, yielding about 2 ounces of juice. Add garlic, shallots, and vinegar. Whisk in olive oil. Add chives and season with kosher salt. Make compressed tomatoes by cutting 2 heirloom tomatoes in half and create balls using a melon baller. Set compressed tomatoes aside.

Cut kernels off ears of corn and place in a bowl. Cover with a moist towel until ready to cook. In a sauté pan over medium heat, add butter and corn and cook till al dente. Add bacon and season with salt and pepper.

In a sauté pan over medium heat, add corn oil. Season fish with salt and pepper on both sides. When the oil is hot, place the fish, skin-side down, in the pan. Cook for 4 minutes or until crisp golden brown, then flip over and cook for another 2 minutes to finish.

PRESENTATION: Place one fourth of corn mix onto 4 plates. Place fish on top of corn and sauce each plate with a tablespoon of vinaigrette. Toss arugula and compressed tomatoes with salt and pepper and avocado oil. Divide arugula evenly on top of fish and serve.

RESTAURANT
KEVIN TAYLOR

1106 Fourteenth Street
Denver, CO 80202
303.820.2600

www.ktrg.com

Chef Kevin Taylor

goat cheese with sweet 100 tomato relish on brioche

Makes 24 pieces

1	tablespoon diced garlic		juice of ½ lemon
2	tablespoons diced shallots		salt and pepper to taste
¼	cup diced onions	1	loaf brioche (soft, white bread)
48	sweet 100 tomatoes (baby tomatoes)	½	cup butter
½	cup balsamic vinegar	12	ounces goat cheese, crumbled
3	tablespoons honey		

Sauté garlic, shallots, and onions for 2 minutes or until tender. Add tomatoes, vinegar, honey, and lemon juice and cook until syrupy. Season with salt and pepper. Set aside to chill or serve at room temperature.

Cut bread into 2-inch square cubes. Sauté bread in butter until golden brown on both sides.

Top bread with tomato relish and finish with crumbles of goat cheese.

THE KITCHEN

1039 Pearl Street
Boulder, CO 80302
303.544.5973

www.thekitchencafe.com

Chef/Owner Hugo Matheson

mushroom and chèvre frittata

Serves 6-8

3	tablespoons olive oil	½	pint heavy cream or half-and-half
2	cloves garlic, sliced	4	ounces crumbled chèvre cheese
1	pound mixed mushrooms (cremini, shiitake, oyster, or any you like)	8	fresh mint leaves, finely chopped
			salt and pepper
3	sprigs fresh thyme	1	teaspoon unsalted butter
8	eggs		

Preheat oven to 350 degrees. Place an ovenproof 10-inch nonstick frying pan over medium heat. Add olive oil and garlic and cook for 1 minute or until garlic is light brown. Add mushrooms and thyme and sauté for about 10 minutes on high heat (you are cooking a lot of the water out of the mushrooms, which will increase their flavor).

In a mixing bowl, beat together eggs, cream or half-and-half, chèvre, mint, and a pinch of salt and pepper. Add mushroom mixture and beat all ingredients together. Taste and adjust seasoning.

Return frying pan to medium heat and add butter. Let it sizzle slightly, then add egg mixture. Cook until the bottom is slightly set, then stir. Repeat this process a couple of times; this helps distribute heat throughout the mixture. Place in oven and cook for 10 minutes or until a knife inserted into the middle comes out clean. Remove from oven and let rest for 10 minutes. Turn out onto a plate or serve straight from the pan.

escargot bourgogne

Serves 2

6	small red bliss potatoes		2	tablespoons Pernod
1	ounce butter, melted			salt and pepper
	salt and pepper to taste		½	carrot, julienned
18	canned Bourgogne snails		½	stalk celery, peeled and julienned
½	cup butter			a few parsley leaves
½	bunch Italian flat leaf parsley, leaves only (stems removed)			olive oil
2	cloves garlic, peeled			lemon juice

Preheat oven to 375 degrees. Hollow out each potato to form a nice cup. Toss potatoes in melted butter and season with salt and pepper. Place potatoes on a baking sheet. Bake until tender.

Meanwhile, in a food processor with the S blade, combine butter, parsley, and garlic and make a smooth purée. Add Pernod and season with a bit of salt and pepper, set aside or freeze for later use.

Combine carrots and celery and add a few leaves of parsley. The lemon juice and olive oil are to dress the tiny salad when you are ready to plate, so do not dress it until you are ready to serve. The proper amount per serving is 2 tablespoons of the salad.

PRESENTATION: Place a small sauté pan over high heat. When hot, add 4 tablespoons of the compound butter and the snails. Warm them together. Place 3 snails in each potato. Arrange 3 potatoes on each plate in a cluster and drizzle some of the excess butter on and around. Dress the carrot salad and place 2 tablespoons of salad on top of the cluster of potatoes. Serve immediately.

BISTRO
VENDÔME
RENDEZVOUS DES AMIS

1420 Larimer
Denver, CO 80202
303.825.3232

www.bistrovendome.com

Executive Chef/Owner
Jennifer Jasinski and Chef de
Cuisine Matt Anderson

ELWAY'S

2500 East First Avenue

Denver, CO 80206

303.399.5353

www.elways.com

Executive Chef Tyler Wiard

chile-grilled prime beef tenderloin with spicy anasazi beans and lobster avocado salsa

Serves *8*

BEEF

8	8 ounce prime beef tenderloins		2	tablespoons dry New Mexican chile powder
2	ounces canola oil			black pepper to taste

BEANS

2	ounces canola oil		½	tablespoon ground coriander
1	large yellow onion, diced		1	tablespoon Mexican oregano
2	ounces fresh garlic, minced			salt and black pepper
2	tablespoons dry ancho chile powder		2	cups dry anasazi beans
1	tablespoon ground cumin		2	quarts chicken broth

SALSA

1	1 pound Maine lobster		1	serrano chile, minced
2	avocados, ripe and ¼-inch dice			juice of 1 lime
4	green onions, julienned			

Marinate steaks in a large mixing bowl with 2 ounces canola oil, New Mexican chile powder, and black pepper. Mix together and leave out at least 1 hour before grilling.

In a 1-gallon saucepot over medium heat, add 2 ounces canola oil and yellow onions. Sweat onions for 15 to 20 minutes. Add garlic, ancho powder, cumin, coriander, oregano, and salt and pepper. Cook for 3 to 4 minutes, then add beans. Stir and cook for another 3 to 4 minutes. Add chicken broth and bring to a boil. Reduce heat and simmer 1½ hours or until beans are tender; keep warm.

To make salsa, fill a 1-gallon stockpot with water and bring to a boil. Cook lobster in boiling water for 15 minutes, then shock in an ice bath. Take lobster meat out of shell and chop into ¼-inch dice. Set aside and keep cold. In a medium mixing bowl, add avocado, green onions, serrano chiles, lime juice, and lobster meat. Season with salt and pepper and set aside.

Preheat a grill. Season steaks with salt before grilling and grill to desired temperature.

PRESENTATION: Place equal amounts of anasazi beans on 8 plates. Arrange grilled steaks on top. Place equal amounts of salsa on top of steaks and serve.

chocolate soup with spiced whipped cream

Serves 4

3	cups strong coffee	8	ounces bittersweet chocolate
1	cinnamon stick	2	ounces butter
1	cup sugar	1	cup heavy cream
2	tablespoons cornstarch, dissolved in 2 ounces dark rum		

SPICED WHIPPED CREAM

1	cup heavy cream	⅛	teaspoon ground cloves
⅛	teaspoon ground cinnamon	⅛	teaspoon ground nutmeg

Bring coffee, cinnamon stick, and sugar to a simmer. Thicken slightly by whisking in cornstarch/rum mixture. Bring to a boil and simmer. Melt chocolate and butter in a metal bowl placed over the simmering coffee/sugar/rum "broth". When melted, remove both the coffee and chocolate from the heat. Discard cinnamon stick. Whisk coffee into the melted chocolate. Whisk in heavy cream. Chill. If too thick, adjust with cream or milk.

For the spiced whipped cream, combine all ingredients and whip until firm.

PRESENTATION: Although this recipe is listed as a soup, it is really a dessert, and is very rich. Serve chilled. Place 4 ounces of 'soup' in a shallow bowl garnished with biscotti and Spiced Whipped Cream.

2575 West Main Street

Littleton, CO 80120

303.703.6787

www.opusdine.com

Chef Michael Long

buffalo bbq brisket

Serves 6-8

2	pounds or more whole grass-fed buffalo brisket	2	cups BBQ sauce (any kind, your favorite)
4	cups chopped onions	2	liters of cola (no diet) generic is fine

Combine all ingredients in a crock pot. You won't need all of the cola but the meat needs to be completely submerged by the cola. Slow cook 8 to 10 hours until brisket is fork tender. When the meat is done, slice against the grain then shred. Keep the shredded meat moist by using the cooking stock until ready to serve. Serve on Kaiser buns as a sandwich or on mashed potatoes. Serve with fresh BBQ sauce on top.

SE Corner of Parker & Ponderosa

Parker, CO

720.427.2664

www.coloradobuffalogrill.com

MESA VERDE
—COLORADO—

Metate Room
Far View Lodge

Mesa Verde

National Park

Mancos, CO 81328

800.449.2288

602.331.5210

www.visitmesaverde.com

Chef Brian Puett

apricot and cranberry stuffed elk chops

Serves 4

¼	cup dried cranberries	1	teaspoon minced fresh rosemary, plus extra for garnish
4	fresh apricots; 3 finely chopped, 1 cut into 12 wedges and reserved for garnish	8	3 ounce elk chops, frenched
1	teaspoon minced garlic		salt and pepper to taste

PORT WINE REDUCTION SAUCE

1	tablespoon clarified butter	½	cup port wine
1	cup Bing cherries, pitted	½	cup water
½	cup finely chopped red onions		salt and pepper to taste
1	tablespoon minced garlic		

Preheat a broiler or grill. Reconstitute dried cranberries by soaking in warm water. Drain and pat dry. Combine cranberries with chopped apricots, garlic, and 1 teaspoon rosemary and mix well. Let stuffing stand for 20 minutes.

Meanwhile, prepare reduction sauce. In a saucepan, combine butter, cherries, red onions, and garlic. Sauté on medium heat until onions are translucent. Add port to deglaze pan. Add water and reduce to low heat. Simmer for about 15 minutes or to desired consistency. Season with salt and pepper to taste.

Slice a small pocket into each elk chop. Pack stuffing into each pocket and seal with a toothpick. Season with salt and pepper. Grill chops for about 4 minutes on each side.

PRESENTATION: Plate the elk chops, crisscrossing the bones over mashed potatoes. Ladle port reduction around chops. Garnish with reserved apricot slices and fresh rosemary.

526 Pine Street

Glenwood Springs, CO 81601

800.544.3998

970.945.6511

fax 970.945.5437

www.hotelcolorado.com

Executive Chef Ron Jackson

the hotel colorado palisade peach cobbler

8	whole Palisade peaches	1½	cups self-rising flour
2	cups sugar	1½	cups milk
½	cup water		ground cinnamon
8	tablespoons butter		

Preheat oven to 350 degrees. Combine the peaches, 1 cup sugar, and ½ cup water in a saucepan and mix well. Bring to a boil and simmer for 10 minutes stirring occasionally. Remove from the heat. Strain the peaches and reserve the syrup. Allow peaches to cool a little, then peel and slice. Set aside.

Put the butter in a 3-quart baking dish and place in oven to melt. Mix remaining 1 cup sugar, flour, and milk slowly to prevent clumping. Pour mixture over melted butter. Do not stir. Spoon fruit on top, gently pouring the reserved syrup. Sprinkle the top with ground cinnamon. Batter will rise to top during baking. Bake for 30 to 45 minutes. To serve, scoop onto a plate and serve with your choice of whipped cream or vanilla ice cream.

JOHN FIELDER'S
COLORADO

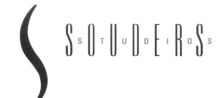
S·O·U·D·E·R·S
S·T·U·D·I·O·S

The VINEYARD
Wine Shop

ENJOYED SINCE 1979
BOULDER BEER

JOHNSON & WALES
UNIVERSITY

SECOND HOME
KITCHEN AND BAR

GARFIELD
ESTATES
Vineyard & Winery

HOTEL COLORADO

CHIPOTLE
MEXICAN GRILL

CANINO'S
SAUSAGE COMPANY INC.
SINCE 1925

MAVERICK
Ranch

beeyond the hive

COLORADO
PROUD
Better for you. Better for Colorado.

WORLD FAMOUS
Enstrom's
ALMOND TOFFEE

SUNFLOWER
FARMERS MARKET

WDA
WESTERN DAIRY
ASSOCIATION

ROCKY MOUNTAIN
BUFFALO
Association

AMERICAN
LAMB
FRESH HOMEGROWN FLAVOR

Le
Central

MARCZYK
FINE FOODS

DENVER COLORADO

TONY'S
MARKET
BON APPETIT

COLORADO'S
Best
BEEF
COMPANY

NOA
National Onion Association

Botanical
Interests
Seed Packets

50th Anniversary
NATIONAL
REPERTORY
ORCHESTRA
Carl Topilow·Music Director
Nurturing the Future of Music

COLORADO POTATOES
QUALITY AT ITS PEAK

Colorado Beef Council

The Seasoned Chef
Cooking School

ROTH DISTRIBUTING
DISTINCTIVE APPLIANCES

the
Tea Spot

Village Roaster
coffee, tea & spice

Crate&Barrel

PEPPERCORN
30

colorado *classique*
sponsors

PROFESSIONAL SERVICES

John Fielder's Colorado
Souders Studios
The Vineyard Wine Shop
Boulder Beer Company
Johnson & Wales University

INGREDIENT SPONSORS

Canino's Sausage
Maverick Ranch

RELEASE PARTY DONORS

The Vineyard Wine Shop
Boulder Beer Company
Second Home Kitchen & Bar
Garfield Estates

SIDE BAR SPONSORS

American Lamb Board
BeeYond the Hive
Botanical Interests
Boulder Beer Company
Colorado Beef Council
Colorado Potato Administrative Committee
Colorado's Best Beef Company
Garfield Estates
Marzcyk Fine Foods and Wines
National Onion Association
National Repertory Orchestra
Peppercorn
Rocky Mountain Buffalo Association
Roth Distributing
Sunflower Farmers Market
The Seasoned Chef
The Tea Spot
The Vineyard Wine Shop
Tony's Original Dry Creek Market
The Village Roaster
Western Dairy Association

COCKTAILS CLASSIQUE EVENT DONOR

Boulder Beer Company
In Good Taste
John Fielder's Colorado
Johnny and Anya Jazz Duo
The Perfect Petal
Reed Photo Art Gallery
All Seasons Rent All
Garfield Estates

PREMIERE RESTAURANTS

Hotel Colorado
Chipotle

FEATURED RESTAURANTS

Colorado Proud
Boulder Beer Company
Enstrom
Le Central

CONTRIBUTING RESTAURANTS

Bistro Vendome
Broadmoor Hotel
Colorado Buffalo Grill
Cuba Cuba Café
Elway's Cherry Creek
Mel's Bar and Grill
Mesa Verde's Metate Room
Opus Restaurant
Panzano
Restaurant Kevin Taylor
Rioja
Second Home Kitchen & Bar
Spago's Bachelor Gulch
Steuben's
The Corner Office
The French Press
The Kitchen
The Fort
The Tuscany
Vesta Dipping Grill

AMERICAN LAMB BOARD
www.americanlamb.com

BEEYOND THE HIVE
Fort Collins * Rocky Ford * Salida, Colorado
970.405.0709
www.beeyondthehive.com

BISTRO VENDÔME
1420 Larimer
Denver, CO 80202
303.825.3232
www.bistrovendome.com

BOTANICAL INTERESTS ONLINE, INC.
660 Compton Street
Broomfield, Colorado 80020
www.botanicalinterests.com

BOULDER BEER
2880 Wilderness Place
Boulder, CO 80301
303.444.8448
www.boulderbeer.com

CANINO'S SAUSAGE COMPANY, INC.
4414 Jason Street
Denver, CO 80211
800.538.0148
303.455.4339
303.455.2180 (f)
www.caninosausage.com

CHIPOTLE MEXICAN GRILL
www.chipotle.com

COLORADO BEEF COUNCIL
789 Sherman Street, Suite 105
Denver, CO 80203
303.830.7892
303.830.7896 (f)
www.cobeef.com

COLORADO'S BEST BEEF COMPANY
4791 Jay Road
Boulder, CO 80301-4341
303.449.8632
303.449.8629 (f)
www.naturalbeef.com

COLORADO BUFFALO GRILL, INC.
SE Corner of Parker
& Ponderosa
Parker, CO
720.427.2664
www.coloradobuffalogrill.com

COLORADO POTATO ADMINISTRATIVE
COMMITTEE
Monte Vista, CO 81144
www.coloradopotato.org

COLORADO DEPARTMENT OF AGRICULTURE/
COLORADO PROUD
700 Kipling Street, Suite 4000
Lakewood, CO 80215
303.239.4114
303.239.4125 (f)
www.coloradoproud.org

THE CORNER OFFICE
1401 Curtis Street
Denver, CO 80202
303.825.6500
www.thecornerofficedenver.com

CRATE & BARREL
101 Clayton Ln
Denver, CO 80206
303.331.9300
www.crateandbarrel.com

CUBA CUBA CAFÉ AND BAR
1173 Delaware Street
Denver, CO 80204
303.605.2822
www.cubacubacafe.com

ELWAYS CHERRY CREEK
2500 East First Avenue
Denver, CO 80206
303.399.5353
www.elways.com

ENSTROM'S ALMOND TOFFEE
www.enstrom.com

JOHN FIELDER'S COLORADO
Denver's Santa Fe Art District
833 Santa Fe Drive
Denver, CO 80204
303.744.7979
www.johnfielder.com

THE FORT
19192 Highway 8
Morrison, CO 80465
303.697.4771
www.thefort.com

THE FRENCH PRESS
34295 Highway 6 C-1-B
PO Box 2990
Edwards, Colorado 81632
970.926.4740
thefrenchpress.net

GARFIELD ESTATES VINEYARD & WINERY
3572 G Road
Palisade, CO 81526
970.464.0941
www.garfieldestates.com

HOTEL COLORADO
526 Pine Street
Glenwood Springs, CO 81601
800.544.3998
970.945.6511
970.945.5437 (f)
www.hotelcolorado.com

JOHNSON & WALES UNIVERSITY
7150 Montview Boulevard
Denver, CO 80220
303.256.9300
www.jwu.edu

THE KITCHEN
1039 Pearl Street
Boulder, CO 80302
303.544.5973
www.thekitchencafe.com

LE CENTRAL
112 E. 8th Avenue
Denver, CO 80206
303.863.8094
www.lecentral.com

MARCZYK FINE FOODS
770 E. 17th Avenue
Denver, CO 80203
303.894.9499
303.894.9491 (f)
www.marczykfinefoods.com

MAVERICK RANCH NATURAL & ORGANIC
MEATS
5360 N. Franklin Street
Denver, CO 80216
303.294.0146
www.maverickranch.com

MEL'S BAR AND GRILL
5970 S. Holly Street
Greenwood Village, CO 80111
303.779.8223
www.melsbarandgrill.com

FAR VIEW LODGE
Mesa Verde National Park
Mancos, CO 81328
800.449.2288
602.331.5210
www.visitmesaverde.com

NATIONAL ONION ASSOCIATION
822 7th Street, Suite 510
Greeley, CO 80631
970.353.5895
970.353.5897 (f)
www.onions-usa.org

NATIONAL REPERTORY ORCHESTRA
P.O. Box 6336
Breckenridge, CO 80424
970.453.5825
www.nromusic.com

OPUS RESTAURANT
2575 West Main Street
Littleton, CO 80120
303.703.6787
www.opusdine.com

PANZANO
909 17th Street
Denver, CO 80202
303.296.3525
www.panzano-denver.com

PENROSE ROOM
The Broadmoor
1 Lake Avenue
Colorado Springs, CO 80906
719.634.7711
www.broadmoor.com

PEPPERCORN
1235 Pearl Street
Boulder, CO 80302
303.449.5847
800.447.6905
303.440.6188 (f)
www.peppercorn.com

RESTAURANT KEVIN TAYLOR
1106 Fourteenth Street
Denver, CO 80202
303.820.2600
www.ktrg.net

RIOJA
1431 Larimer Street
Denver, CO 80202
303.820.2282
www.riojadenver.com

ROCKY MOUNTAIN BUFFALO ASSOCIATION
www.buffaloranchers.com

ROTH DISTRIBUTING (FOR SUB-ZERO & WOLF)
17801 E. 40th Ave.
Aurora, CO 80011
303.373.9090
303.373.2006 (f)
www.rothdistributing.com

THE SEASONED CHEF COOKING SCHOOL
999 Jasmine Street
Denver, CO 80220
303.377.3222
www.theseasonedchef.com

SECOND HOME KITCHEN AND BAR
150 Clayton Lane
Denver, CO 80206
303.253.3000
www.secondhomedenver.com

SOUDERS STUDIOS
1301 Ulysses Street
Golden, CO 80401
303.384.3128
800.990.3330
www.soudersstudios.com

SPAGO
The Ritz-Carlton, Bachelor Gulch
0130 Daybreak Ridge
Avon, Colorado 81620
970.343.1555
www.wolfgangpuck.com

STEUBEN'S
523 E. 17th Ave.
Denver CO, 80203
303.830.1001
www.steubens.com

SUNFLOWER FARMERS MARKET
The company has 20 stores located in
Colorado, Arizona, New Mexico, Nevada,
Utah, and Texas.
www.sfmarkets.com

THE TEA SPOT
4699 Nautilus Court, South
Suite 403
Boulder, CO 80301
303.444.8324
303.530.4707 (f)
www.theteaspot.com

TUSCANY
Loews Denver Hotel
4150 E. Mississippi Avenue
Denver, CO 80246
303.639.1600
www.loewsdenverhotel.com

VESTA DIPPING GRILL
1822 Blake St.
Denver CO, 80202
303.296.1970
303.296.4005 (f)
www.vestagrill.com

THE VINEYARD WINE SHOP
261 Fillmore St.
Denver, CO 80206
In Cherry Creek North
303.355.8324
303.355.1413 (f)
www.vineyardwineshop.com

TONY'S ORIGINAL DRY CREEK MARKET
4991 E. Dry Creek Road
Centennial, CO 80122
303.770.7024
303.290.8433 (f)
Between S. Colorado Blvd. and Holly
www.tonysmarket.com

VILLAGE ROASTER
9255 W Alameda Ave
Lakewood, CO 80226
303.238.8718
800.237.3822
303.233.4370 (f)
www.villageroaster.com

WESTERN DAIRY ASSOCIATION
12000 North Washington, Suite 175
Thornton, Colorado 80241
303.451.7711
303.452.5484 (f)
www.WesternDairyAssociation.org
www.3ADay.org

thank you to our wonderful underwriting donors
for your support of the cookbook

BERGEN PEAK - $1,000 - $2,499

Mr. and Mrs. Edward J. Anderson

Patricia A. Bainter, in Honor of Robert Wagner and Oscar and Sara Bainter

Julie Belden, In Memory of Patricia F. Belden

Ms. Kristen Busang, In Honor of Paul and Jacqueline Busang

Mrs. Catherine Walz Rundle

Becky and Brian Schaub

FRONT RANGE - $500 - $999

EnCana Oil & Gas Inc.

Jennifer Pomeroy Fronk and Rudi Fronk

Michelle K. Hanley

Mrs. Linda Osborn

Mary and Dan Peterson

Lee Wyma, In Honor of Courtney Keatinge

PIONEERS $300 - $499

Mr. and Mrs. George and Margie Browning

Mrs. Joyce Ann Burgett

Steve and Elaine Callas Williams, In Memory of George and Irene Callas

Neil and Stephanie Duncan, In Honor of Emma and Ethan

Ms. Kendy Cusick-Rindone and Mr. Greg Rindone

Mr. and Mrs. Will and Jennifer Greer, In Honor of Dylan and Tori Greer

Ms. Gillette K. Hansen, In Honor of Katharine Baird Hansen

Diane M. Hanson, In Memory of M. Evlyn Hanson

Kristin, Alyssa, and Robert Hartman, In Memory of Ginny Hartman

Nadia Helena Hartman, In Honor of David Watts and Julia & Steve Hartman

Kelly Werner Hedlund

Beverlee B. Henry

Arlene and Barry Hirschfeld

Cathy Hollis

Mr. and Mrs. William Kent, In Honor of Taylor & Grant Kent

Michael and Meredith Love, In Honor of William, Savannah and Ainsley

Mrs. Susan H. Moore

Eric P. and Brigette R. Ruffel

Aline Sandomire

Mr. and Mrs. Morey and Susan Schneider

Dick and Sonnie Talley

Mrs. Janyce Wald, In Honor of Leigh McMahon and the Seafood Tasting Committee

Mrs. Nancy Seacrest Wright

TRAILBLAZERS $25 - $299

Anonymous
Loring H. Amass
John and Margaret Ansted
Mrs. Wendy Baker
Vanessa Baptiste, In Honor of Pat Buensing
Ooh La La Events LLC
Marsha Pirie Berger
Fred and Stephany Bollin, In Memory of Don Duncan
Kristen and Martin Boublik
Lisle Bradley
Belinda K. Brehmer
Betty Brownson
Mr. & Mrs. William Buchholz
Jordan Bullock
Jan A. Carpenter, In Memory of Judith S. Davidson
Sarah Cornwell
Ramona Corvin-Brown
Linda Dean
Judith K. DeBord, In Memory of Mary Kathryn Steele
Ms. Susan Gabrielle DeVita,
    In Honor of Robert Smith Gaddy
Mr. and Mrs. Peter Durante, III
Mr. and Mrs. Christopher Elliott
Ms. Holly S. Emick, In Honor of Mrs. Freda K. Feeney
Mr. and Mrs. Ralph W. Emlong
Ms. Stephanie Farnsworth
Mrs. Courtney Ferer
Mr. Todd and Mrs. Lindsay Filsinger,
    In Honor of Tatum, Treva and Talya
Peg Frazier, In Honor of my JLD breakfast group,
    Cath, Laura, Gayle, Judy, and Janis
Mrs. Julie French
Mrs. Ginny Fuller
Eva Vasilas Fry, In Honor of
    Greg, Sophia and George Fry
Leah and Gaillard Garbe, In Honor of Margaret Garbe
Stephanie Gelfeld, In Honor of Anne Forsey
Mrs. Barb Adams Goettelman
Jean Miller Gordon, In Memory of Jean Johnson Smith
Marylin Gottesfeld
Judy Tienyan Wong Greco, In Honor of
    Dennis J. Greco
Mrs. Jennifer Bicknell Greer,
    In Honor of Colorado Classique Dessert Committee
Mrs. Jennifer Bicknell Greer,
    In Memory of Mrs. Betty J. Hawerlander
Mrs. Jennifer Bicknell Greer, In Memory of Mrs. Ethel Baum
Mr. & Mrs. Stephen Gregg
Lee Hagenstad, In Honor of Fun Club
Mrs. Kelly Happ
Sharon Hartman, In Honor of my family
Mrs. Joni Hilvitz
Mrs. Sarah Hite
Tamara Hoffbuhr Seelman
Laura Hopkins
Mr. and Mrs. Dave Hunter
Ms. Rebecca Jamieson
Winnie Johnson
Ms. Christy A. Jordan,
    In Honor of the JLD Community Program

Mrs. Heidi Keogh
Ms. Deborah J. King
Midge Fraser Kral, In Honor of Marguarite Currie Fraser
Janet Kritzer
Mary Lester in Memory of Joyce Metz
Jennifer and David Leuthold, In Honor of Ruby and Vivian
Mr. and Mrs. Juan Llaneza
Gloria A. Martin
Mr. and Mrs. Tom McKenna
Cissie Megyesy In Honor of Judy Megyesy
Ms. Jennifer Mehnert
Mrs. George Milton, In Memory of George Milton
Mr. and Mrs. Anthony and Nichole Montoya
Mrs. Jennifer Myers
Mrs. Tracy Newberry
Lyn Osborne, In Memory of C. Maxine Gebhard,
Mr. and Mrs. Chris Parise
Ms. Kimberly Ann Penney
Ms. Pam Piro
Lea Ann Reitzig, In Memory of Luzetta Miller
Dana Rinderknecht
Kathleen Blair Roberts, In Honor of Julie and Trish
Ms. Tina Rodocker in Honor of Meg Littlepage
Mr. and Mrs. Dean Rollins
Samuel and Carolyn Rowland,
    In Memory of Mitchel Tisdell
Mr. and Mrs. Michael Ruck
Amber Ryan
Mrs. Susan Schaub
Mr. & Mrs. Troy and Shannon Schell
Sukie Schroeder
Ms. Carolyn D. Smith In Honor of
    the Junior League of Denver Foundation
Ronda Barlow Smith, In Memory of Mrs. Ruth H. Smith
Mrs. Andrea Snyder
Carol Spensley, In Honor of
    my wonderful mother, Helen W. Schildhammer
Mr and Mrs Chris and Amy Stein
Autumn Lyn Stevenson
Ms. Jaclyn W. Thayer
Mrs. Christine S. Viney
Constance B. Watts and family
John & Lisa Watts, In Honor of George, Thomas & James
Nicole Warot
Ms. Barbara J. Webb
Michelle & Mitch Weinraub
Molly Ostarch Weiss, In Honor of Brian Weiss
Cynthia Wieleba
Mrs. Dudley Williams
Mrs. Graham B. Williams,
    In Memory of Mrs. Quinn D. Thomas
Margaret Wysocki
Tricia Youssi

Sherry Abbott	Carmen Carpenter	Katie Fox	Erin Hirstine
Laura Adams	Peggy Carpenter	Patrick Fox	Crystal Hodge
Tim Adams	Donna Carr	Caroline Fugler	Pat Hoeft
Leigh Adkins	Marilynn Carroll	Katherine Fulford	Cathy Hollis
Todd Adkins	Catherine Chaussart	Sandra Gaffin	Sarah Louise Holtze
Diane Ahonen	Cindy Christianson	Jan Gallegos	Hope Marie Hooper
Wendy Allen	Kate Cihon	Alexandria Woolcott Garbacz	Roger Hooper
Debbie Allison	Natasha Clare	Leah Garbe	Aleathia M. Hoster
Barb Anderson	Anna Clark	Katrina Garcia	M. Carolyn Hunter
Jenni Aronson	Suzanne Clark	Lynn Glassman	Stephanie Jackson
Sarah Aurich	Marilyn Cogswell	Anastasia Lantz Glennie	Sarah Arnold Jacobs
Patricia Bainter	Jennifer Corelli	Jean Gordon	Becky Jansen
Natalie Baker	Whitney Cortner	Joyce Gravlee	Sara Jansen
Sally Barker	Ramona Corvin-Brown	Debbie Gray	BJ Jeffers
Jean H Barr	Elizabeth Crites	Cynthia Greathouse	Preston Jenkins
Jessica Bennett	Pamela Curry	Jennifer Bicknell Greer	Susan Jenkins
Jane L. Bergman	Wendy Cyr	William J Greer	Jane Johnson
Natalie Bicknell	Martha G. Davis	Don Griffin	Leslie Johnson
Carroll Biddle	Kathy DeFranco	Arlene Gustafson/Hagen	Melanie Johnson
Jerry Biri	Barbara Deline	Karen Gutierrez	Janis Judd
Marilyn Biri	Melissa Demos	Catherine Guzelian	Laura Kachel
Chris A. Blakeslee	Linda Diekvoss	Marcia W. Hafemeister	Marcy Kaufman
Sue Blakeslee	Maureen Dillie	Lee Hagenstad	Audrey Keller
Marci Block	Corry Doty	Barb Halsell	Leigh-Anne Kent
Stephany Bollin	Fay Dreher	Connie Hambrook	Erika Kessenger
Courtney Borus	Jessica Duffy	Anne Hammer	Kim Kessenger
Sandy Borus	Barbara Duncan	Fran Handman	Krystal Khuu
Stacy Brase	Stephanie Duncan	Diane Hanson	Cara C. Kimsey
Belinda Brehmer	Bonnie Edelman	Kelly Happ	Debby King
Lara Brown	Carrie Erickson	Kimberly Harrington	Sabina King
Lisa Bown	Andrea Evashevski	Maryanne H Harry	Keli Kinsella
Linda Brune	Amy Falcone	Kristin Hartman	Merrie Margolin Kippur
Tony Bruton	Deven Farris	Nadia Helena Hartman	Amy Kissinger
Jane Bullock	Ann Fawcett	Marianne Hayes	Sally Kneser
Jordan Bullock	Lindsay Filsinger	Susan Henderson	Jennifer Knollenberg
Adele Burnham	Heather Finlayson	Erin Hendrick	Beverly Kohnert
Kristen Busang	Paula Finlayson	Millie Hendrix	Lynda Kolb
Sally Cadol	Ellen Fisher	Jo Henson	Lisa Korsen
Karmen Cadwell	Lisa Fisher	Ann Herring	Lindsay Korstange
Christi Cage	Cheryl L. Fitzgibbon	Murray Herring	Karen Kosten
Jennifer Cambpell	Darlene Fjeldsted	Kate Hibberd	Jenny Kostka
Leah R. Camper	Susan Flanagan	Eleanor Hill	Joanne Kostka

Katie Kostka
Julie LaFontano
Brenda Lambert
Vicki Lang
Becky Langer
Judy Lariscy
Lois Laitinen
Susie Law
Ginger A. Lemberger
Terry LeMieux
Lorel Lenaers
Nicole Lenaers
Paige Lentz
Mary Lester
Emily Levorsen
Jim Levorsen
Janet Lewis
Erin Llaneza
Marian Lokey
Linda Loope
Melissa Lopez
Ford Lux
April Luxner
Nancy Macdonald
Lori Magazine
Janet Manning
Meg Mara
Kathleen Markey
Anne Marquis
Laura Giordano Martin
Angie Mathias
Ruth McAllister
Tammy McDonald
Blair Lindberg McGroarty
Amy McKenzie
Wanda McKnight
Martha McMahon
Lauren McMonagle
Judy Medley
Cissie Megyesy
Jennifer Mehnert
Betty Mellberg
Kenneth Mellberg
Katie Mickelson
Nichole Montoya
Ann Moore
Gina Moore

Katie Moore
Katie Moore
Elizabeth Morton
Dick Moss
Susan Moss
Colleen Moylan
Robyn Muramoto
Pat Murphy
Kelly Nelson
Kelly Witherbee Nelson
Mimi Nelson
Angella Nims
Michele Noblitt
Edrie O'Brien
Keira O'Connor
Lisa K. Olson
Kathy Oman
Helene Orsulak
James Orsulak
Flo Pancir
Suzanne Payne
Stephanie Percival
Christa Peterson
Darcy Peterson
Kristie Peterson
Lauren Peterson
Susan Peterson
Elizabeth Peyton
Ann Pierson
Jennifer Pingrey
Pam Piro
Heather Pollock
Rita Pollock
Stephanie Preston
Edy Purcell
Lynne Quoy
Elizabeth Jane Reagan
Katie Reagan
Mary A. Reagan
Colby Reed
Hannah Reinhart
Jen Rettig
Lindsey Rice
Brenda D. Rickert
Mette Riis
Nancy Riley
Dana Rinderknecht

Kathye Ripley
Jan Robbins
Lara Robinson
Brigette R. Ruffel
Eric Ruffel
Julie Rumfelt
Catherine Rundle
Amy Rygmyr
Heather Sanders
Clark D Schaefer
Becky H. Schaub
Christine Schaub
Sydney Schaub
Leslie Schenker
Cristin Schott
Nancy Schotters
Linda Scott
Kelly Brush Seaton
Becky Seely
Mary Seely
Marty Carey Segelke
Brittany Sever
Mary Sherman
Becky Shew
Linsay Shirley
Marjie Skalet
Andrea Snyder
Carol Spensley
Kathy Spohn
Sandi Sprinkle
Darin Squires
Kathy Squires
Katie Stapleton
Marha Starick
Beth Starkey
Amy Stern
Ashley Stevens
Michele Stewart
Charmaine Stolz
Monica Strachan
Lindsey Summers
Elizabeth Suter
Mindy Switzer
Elizabeth Sylvan
Janina Tabaka
Marilyn Shield Taylor
Grace Teeple

Kathy Terry
Caryl Thomason
Heather Thomason
Heather Tierney
Tammy Tobey
Page Tredennick
Lucile B. Trueblood
Rachael Ulizio
Karen Valdez
Dan Vanek
Sara Vanek
Suzie Vanek
Angie Vasilas
Eva Vasilas-Fry
Lelia Vaughan
Victoria L. Vernon
Jane Vertuca
Louise Volpe
Elaine Walter
Tom Waltz
Barbara J. Webb
Pam Weber
Pamela Place Weber
Reene Weinstein
Molly Ostarch Weiss
Teddi Weist-Kent
Megan Wesley
Evelyn Whitaker
Kori White
Landon C. White
Kristen Wieder
Jeanne Wilde
Stacia Wilkins
Dudley Williams
Katy Word
Margaret Wysocki
Meg Yarka
Posey Young
Tricia Weber Youssi
Julia Zawalski

colorado *classique*
testers

Corinne Lamb Ablin *
Laura Adams
Wendy Allen *
Barb Anderson *
Jenni Aronson
Jessica Bennett
Marianne Bergen *
Ann Berlin
Natalie Bicknell
Jennifer Bigger
Patti Black
Marci Block *
Stephany Bollin *
Courtney Borus
Kelli Browning
Maureen Buchholz
Rosemary Buehler *
Adele Burnham
Sally Cadol *
Marilynn Carroll *
Shelley Cassady
Kate Cihon *
Amy Cooper
Julianne Cooper *
Aimee Corazzari *
Kristy Cressman *
Ashley Dammerman
Kathy Daniel
Amy W Davis
Glenna C. Day *
Linda Dean *
Barbara Deline *
Erin Dougan
Dorothy Easton
Katie Fairchild
Nikki Feltz
Lindsay Filsinger *
Heather Finlayson *
Cheryl L. Fitzgibbon *
Kellie Flowers
Katherine U. Fulford *
Leah Garbe *
Katrina Garcia *
Abby Goodman *
Beth Graham *
Joyce Gravlee *

Debbie Gray *
Nancy Greenley *
Jennifer Bicknell Greer *
Rosalind Grenfell *
Marla Groves *
Stephanie Guldy
Catherine Guzelian *
Lee Hagenstad *
Barb Halsell *
Connie Hambrook *
Anne Hammer *
Kimberly Harrington *
Maryanne Harry
Marianne Hayes
Susan Henderson *
Erin Hendrick *
Karen Henry
Crystal Hodge *
Krystal Hoeft
Jodie Hohensee *
Cathy Carlos Hollis *
Hope Marie Hooper *
Aleathia Hoster *
Carolyn Hunter
Stephanie Jackson *
Sara Jansen
Melanie Johnson
Janis Judd *
Laura Kachel
Courteney Keatinge *
Maureen Keefner *
Sheryl Kelts*
Martha Kennedy
Leigh-Anne Kent *
Erika Kessenger *
Kim Kessenger
Sabina King
Amy Kissinger *
Barbara Knight *
Jennifer Knollenberg *
Lindsay Korstange *
Kimberly Kukuchka
Julie LaFontano *
Brenda Lambert *
Vicki Lang *
Becky Langer

Susie Law *
Ginger Lemberger
Nicole Lenaers
Mary Lester
Erin Llaneza
Janet Manning *
Meg Mara *
Angie Mathias *
Amy McKenzie
Corinne McKenzie *
Leigh McMahon *
Cissie Megyesy *
Jen Mehnert
Betty Mellberg
Ken Mellberg
Katie Mickelson *
Leslie Miller
Nichole Montoya *
Gina Moore *
Katie Moore *
Kelly Witherbee Nelson *
Mimi Nelson *
Angella Nims
Edrie O'Brien
Jennifer Ouimette
Kathy Oman *
Kristie Peterson *
Mary Peterson
Jennifer Pingrey *
Pam Piro *
Heather Pollock *
Laura Quam
Maria Ratchford *
Colby Reed
Hannah Reinhart *
Jennifer Rettig *
Meagan Riordan
Debra Rodarte
Tina Rodocker
Brigette R. Ruffel *
Julie Rumfeldt *
Amy Rygmyr
Ana Sandomire *
Carrie Schmeltekopf
Nancy Schotters *
Becky Seely *

Brittany Sever *
Mary Sherman
Karon Sherwood *
Nicole Sidebottom
Lynne Moore Siegel *
Destin Sims
Andrea Snyder
Stephanie Sommers
Alberte Spencer *
Christine Spencer *
Lori Stacy
Alex Stansbury
Laura Stenovec *
Ashley Stevens
Monica Strachan
Brooke Straughan *
Vinita Sturgeon *
Betsy Sturges
Elizabeth Suter
Elizabeth Sylvan *
Nancy Tankersley *
Lana Tasker
Kerry A. Tate
Francine Terrell *
Kathy Terry *
Jaclyn Thayer
Tracey Thompson
Tammy Tobey
Page Tredennick *
Sara Vanek
Eva Vasilas-Fry
Melissa Vaughan
Christine Viney *
Pam Weber *
Pattie Welch *
Megan Wesley
Kori White
Kristen Wieder
Tracey Davis Wifall
Stacia Wilkins
Katy Word
Margaret Wysocki *
Tricia Weber Youssi *

* Tester who tested at 80% or more
of tasting sessions

classification index

ENTERTAINING

recipe index

landscape index

For information about the
Junior League of Denver's
collection of Cookbooks and
to purchase, please visit
www.jld.org.

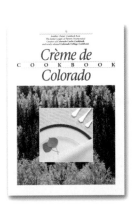

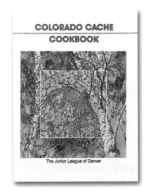